CITIZEN
LANE

Also by Mark Lane

BOOKS

Rush to Judgment
A Citizen's Dissent
Arcadia
Chicago Eyewitness
Conversations with Americans
Executive Action (with Donald Freed)
Murder in Memphis (with Dick Gregory)
The Strongest Poison
Plausible Denial
Last Word

SCREENPLAYS

Executive Action (with Donald Freed)
Arcadia
Slay the Dreamer
Plausible Denial

PLAYS

The Winds of Doctrine
The Trial of James Earl Ray

DOCUMENTARIES

A Rush to Judgment
Two Men in Dallas

CITIZEN LANE

DEFENDING OUR RIGHTS
IN THE COURTS, THE CAPITOL, AND THE STREETS

MARK LANE

FOREWORD BY MARTIN SHEEN

Lawrence Hill Books

Chicago

Published by Chicago Review Press, Incorporated
814 North Franklin Street
Chicago, Illinois 60610
ISBN 978-1-61374-001-9

A Note on the Title

I had created a rather convoluted title for this book. While I was not enthusiastic about the title, my publishers were even less so. When I told them
that Pauley Perrette, a talented actor and producer and star of the smash
television hit *NCIS*, was producing and directing a documentary about my
life that she named *Citizen Lane*, they were very excited and asked if we
could use the same title for this book. I related that to Pauley and said that I
would credit her with the title. Her answer was, "Yes. Because I want to see
how you explain that you stole my title with my permission and my love."

Thank you, Pauley.
ML

Library of Congress Cataloging-in-Publication Data
Is available from the Library of Congress.

Interior design: PerfecType, Nashville, TN

Lane, Mark, 1927–
  Citizen Lane : defending our rights in the courts, the capitol, and the streets
/ Mark Lane. — 1st ed.
     p. cm.
  Includes index.
  Summary: "The autobiography of Mark Lane, who has been inspiring social
consciousness, influencing history makers, and inciting controversy for more
than six decades. Icons of the American political and social landscape appear
throughout his narrative as cohorts and companions and as opponents"—Pro-
vided by publisher.
  ISBN 978-1-61374-001-9 (hardback)
  1. Lane, Mark, 1927– 2. Lawyers—United States—Biography. I. Title.
  KF373.L35A3 2011
  340.092—dc23
  [B]
                                        2011042566

Printed in the United States of America
5 4 3 2 1

This book is dedicated to the First Amendment to the Constitution of the United States, to those who wrote and ratified it, and to those who have pledged their sacred honor to support it. It is only one sentence, but it remains the most important statement in the life of our country. It is unique in world history, and it tells us, when it is not traduced, who we are and always whom we aspire to be.

|||||

"Congress shall make no law respecting an establishment of religion, or prohibiting the free exercise thereof, or abridging the freedom of speech, or of the press, or the right of the people to peaceably assemble, and to petition the government for a redress of grievances." (Ratified on December 15, 1791)

|||||

It is not a pledge of loyalty or allegiance. It is far more important, for it speaks of our resolve to be free women and men and it establishes and ensures the rights of each individual. It should be known, word for word, throughout this land, and if anything need be recited by schoolchildren or adults it ought to be that one glorious promise from those who founded this great experiment we call a democracy.

Contents
||||||||||||||||||||||||||||||

Foreword
||||||||||||||||||||||||||||

Martin Sheen

On more than one occasion Mark Lane has risked his life for the American people and for truth: for whites, blacks, and Latinos in East Harlem where he chose to open a storefront office and practice law; for American Indians at Wounded Knee; for African Americans in Mississippi where he became the only public official arrested as a Freedom Rider. *Citizen Lane*, his life story, is riveting, a page-turner that demonstrates how one man can make a difference.

His ability to wrest the truth from the desperate grasp of our own intelligence agencies make his book impossible to put down. His first book, *Rush to Judgment*, inspired my own thoughts of activism and thus changed my life.

His work with veterans of the war in Vietnam and with vulnerable children falsely imprisoned in brutal asylums by the state of New York, and his successful struggle to free an innocent man on death row in Florida, imprisoned for two decades before Mark undertook his cause, are examples for every individual of the power of passionate commitment. He teaches that each of us has the capacity to make this place a better place because we have passed through.

Written with humor and a touch of sophisticated satire, *Citizen Lane* is at once lighthearted, joyous, and suspenseful. Not just a great read, Lane's autobiography is an essential example in a jaded world of the reach of one fearless individual. It pulls you along Mark Lane's remarkable life: outrageous, historic, funny, and inspiring.

No person can look at the life of Mark Lane and say that America does not have unlimited compassion or that greatness is beyond our reach. Mark Lane's life, written over the years with deeds, not words, has been an inspiration for many of us, and he is a reason that I am an activist for the powerless.

For all its tales of struggles and suffering, defeats and victories, *Citizen Lane* is a magnificent story of hope. If you read one book this year, even this decade, this is the one.

Introduction: My Life

|||||||||||||||||||||||||||||||||||||||||||||||||||||||

It was 1927. It was a very good year. Now we fly across the Atlantic in a few hours. That year Charles Lindbergh was the first to make that flight alone. It took him more than a few hours to reach Paris. Babe Ruth set the record for home runs in one season, sixty, and the pundits of the day assured us that Ruth's remarkable feat would never be equaled. A new car sold for $495, a gallon of gas to make it run for twelve cents. The Dow Jones average was 175.

Television was invented, and its first successful demonstration took place in New York. The first telephone call from London to San Francisco was made. The age of technology, based upon our understanding at that time, was upon us. Modern times, 1927. CBS, the Columbia Broadcasting System, was born in New York City. And on February 24, so was I.

As I move forward past my sixth decade as a lawyer, I sometimes cast a backward glance. It has been a long time. I have been at the bar for approximately one-quarter of the history of our nation's judicial system. Dr. King observed that longevity has its place; I believe that it is the most satisfying and certainly the liveliest revenge.

Now, more than three-quarters of a century later, I have lived in New York for more than a couple of decades, Washington, DC, for twenty-seven years, and many other American cities, including Memphis, San Francisco and Venice, California, and Mountain Home, Idaho, as well as in Denmark, Paris, and London. Now I try to put it all together.

CITIZEN LANE

Prologue: Our Time

||||||||||||||||||||||||||||||||||||||||||||||||||||||

In retrospect it is generally believed that we were a good generation. Tom Brokaw said "The Greatest Generation" several times, and others, not of our time, agreed. But at the time nobody articulated such an idea; nobody even thought in those terms. Generally, we played by the existing rules just because they seemed fair and we were expected to, and we thought others would act the same way, and they usually did.

We went to school every day. Mom took care of the children, shopped, cooked, and cleaned the house and our clothes and linens. Washing our clothing was not an easy task. There were two tubs in the basement, one with a washboard. Mom spent many hours there. Then she carried the wet wash to our small backyard where she hung the garments on a line, using wooden clothespins.

Our home in Brooklyn, New York, during the 1930s was typically heated by a coal furnace, also in the basement. Since it needed to be fed throughout the day and required special scrutiny and ash shaking and ash removal early in the morning, those tasks were carried out by Mom until the children were old enough to take over.

Dad went to work each day. Like Cal Ripken he never missed a day; like Cal he never thought it warranted being mentioned; and unlike Cal, in Dad's case, it never was. Our parents voted, were moderately religious, and sent their three children to school and for religious instruction. Two became teachers (a college history professor and a high school mathematics teacher) and one a lawyer. None of us was ever convicted of a crime or even arrested for any infraction except in a good cause. I was arrested a few times for marching in Dr. King's army for justice.

Narcotics were not a temptation. We did not drink to excess, except on a very rare occasion. We never sought escape perhaps because we were all quite certain that we lived in a wonderful place. We never sang songs at commercial sporting events proclaiming that we lived in God's only blessed territory, and we never waved or even flew the flag. We were all quite happy to be Americans. If we didn't brag about it, it was because some things went without saying and also because it was a matter of taste.

We discussed sports, the Brooklyn Dodgers primarily and with passion, but patriotism, as was the case with religion and how much or little money Dad made, never came up. We accepted the good fortune of being born in a free and democratic nation. My brother, Lory, two years older than me to the day—my father was an accountant—entered the US Army at Fort Dix, New Jersey. He served and fought with Patton's army. When I was eighteen it was my turn. And now for the first of many confessions—I cheated during my army physical examination. When I was a child I had been stricken with scarlet fever. The disease, misdiagnosed at first but by a doctor who did make house calls, apparently had an impact upon my eyesight. I knew I could not pass the eye examination for unlimited duty. Wearing glasses, I approached the chart and memorized enough of the lines to pass the test. Thus I, too, entered the US Army at Fort Dix during World War II at the age of eighteen, following both my brother and my father, Harry, who decades earlier had served during the First World War. Our generation had not made patriotic speeches about God and country, yet when the time came to defend our nation, we answered without doubt or hesitation.

We also accepted without much question the honesty of our leaders and their good intentions, and we felt secure in believing in the integrity of government. These were the times that created our generation. They seemed to us, before the war, the best and most tranquil of times, and for those reasons they were also, in retrospect, the most potentially troubling. We were a nation with serious problems that remained invisible to most of us but were too well known to poor whites in Appalachia, sharecroppers in the South, and above all by Latinos, American Indians, the natives who owned the land we conquered, and Africans whose ancestors were kidnapped from their homes and pressed into slavery here. Shamefully the list goes on. Some women, including those who were white and of a privileged class, also recognized with concern the limitations placed against their aspirations.

Everything changed on December 7, 1941, while we surrounded a radio listening to a sports event and learned that the outcome of the game was suddenly of no relevance. It was in the crucible of a world war that our nation and our generation were tested. If Americans then were different from those who preceded or followed them, it likely was due less to essential character and more to shared experiences. We were united in fighting a just war. We had little choice; we had been attacked.

The evils that had plagued us since our inception—racism, discrimination, and segregation—were being considered, not confronted except perhaps tangentially; certainly they were not resolved. Blacks, Latinos, Japanese Americans, and white GIs, among others, fought the same enemy. Often the units were separated and segregated, and people of color often faced greater danger and hardship and, always, humiliation. Yet it seemed that a modest start had been made.

In relative terms there were not many women in the armed forces. Yet the war changed the lives of women dramatically. With millions of men in the military and the urgent need for the production of weapons of war including tanks, airplanes, jeeps, rifles, automatic rifles, and machine guns and the tens of millions of rounds to feed them, women filled the factories and turned them into arsenals. Their enormous contribution was popularly celebrated. Rosie the Riveter still reverberates.

When the war came to a close the women, for a substantial period of time, fared no better than the members of minorities who had courageously helped win the war. In spite of efforts of a conservative society to return to the unfair normalcy of the past, the inexorable passage of time and events was eventually to prevail.

When the war ended, former GIs were proud of their contribution, and a nation was grateful for their service. I doubt that during the war there was a GI anywhere who did not fantasize about wearing the golden eagle—we sardonically called it the ruptured duck—in the lapel of a dark suit jacket that would replace the uniform. The little pin was given to all who had achieved an honorable discharge; I wore mine with pride for a long time. We never wore flag pins in our lapels, just our country's uniform in time of war and that little eagle when it ended.

The government demonstrated its gratitude in other, more substantive ways as well. There was the 52-20 Club, available to each of us. For one year, each unemployed former service member received twenty dollars per week. The idea was that adjustment to a new and very different life would be made easier if some basic financial needs were met by the government.

Above all there was the GI Bill of Rights that provided an opportunity for former military personnel to achieve a college education. This revolutionary concept was likely the single most important factor in determining who we were and what we might be, for it removed limitations upon our dreams. It was the foundation for our time, as we became the first generation of Americans, and thus far the last, to have almost unlimited access to higher education.

And there were functioning and funded Veterans Administration hospitals to care for those in need of medical care whether or not the problem was service related and whether it was a physical or mental disorder. We had loved our country and offered our lives to protect it, and our nation had fully responded. No generation of American soldiers since has been treated as fairly or appropriately. If our generation was different from others, in large measure these are the factors that shaped it, and, although rather obvious, they have apparently gone unnoticed by ruling politicians. We remain the only industrial country without a universal health plan for our people, and higher education is denied to millions of our country's qualified young men and women.

As the war ended, blacks and other minorities, having made at least equal sacrifices, were asking why equal opportunities were not available to them. Many of us, having worked for the first time along with Americans of different colors and national heritages, had gained a new appreciation of the difference between how things were and how they ought to be and, above all, how they could be. From these demands for equality led by blacks willing to march and die for freedom in an America at peace, as they had been willing to do for an America at war, and joined by some members of the newly educated majority, a civil rights movement was born.

Our generation had come home with a vision enhanced by our shared experiences demonstrating that we had not forgotten the lessons learned during the national crisis. For some those lessons have remained with us to this day as a continuing inspiration.

Brooklyn Days

1

‖‖‖‖‖‖‖‖‖‖‖‖‖‖‖‖‖‖‖‖‖‖‖‖‖‖‖‖‖‖‖‖‖‖‖‖‖‖‖

I was born in the Bronx and grew up in Brooklyn. My father, Harry A. Lane of Buffalo, New York, studied to be a chemist, but the ingestion of some fumes in a laboratory damaged his lungs. Instead he became a certified public accountant. My mother, Elizabeth Lane, one of nine sisters raised in Rochester, New York, had been an administrative assistant to Gus Edwards, a vaudeville impresario. We—that is, my brother, Lawrence, known in the early years to all as Lory, and my sister, Ann Judith, called Sissy—suffered no shortage of uncles, aunts, and cousins. The appellation Sissy has not survived, although Ann has, to become a historian, an author, and a professor at the University of Virginia. The name Lory has almost disappeared; all of his friends and even his wife addressed him as Larry, yet the name lives on when Ann and I speak of him.

Lory had a long career as a New York City high school teacher and a leader of the teacher's union, and, in his retirement, he continued to both teach and travel, as did his wife, Patricia. Lory died just a few days before I wrote these words. During the early years I probably knew him better than did anyone else. Certainly I spent more time with him. We shared a twin-bedded room, and in almost every picture taken at the time, there he is, with his arm around my shoulder. He was my protector and buddy as we grew up. Later in life he became my role model. I never knew him to make an unkind remark about anyone. While he opposed the policies of the second Bush administration, he would make no personal statement against their author.

When the principal of the school where he taught began to circulate Polish jokes, one of the horrors of the 1950s, Lory, unable to dissuade him through logic, initiated and circulated at school a number of principal jokes. *How many high school principals does it take to screw in a lightbulb?*

Lory possessed a well-developed sense of humor and, being a mathematician, a most precise approach to specifics. I last saw him in a hospital bed too weak to speak. I held his hand, and he whispered, "I love you," as he did a moment later to Ann. Pat, his wife, patted his sweating forehead and said, "You look better, Larry." He tried several times to say something, but he lacked the energy. Finally, he looked at all of us and then smiled and turned to Pat and said, "Better than whom?" Those were his last words.

He was truly a teacher and a wise, kind, and generous man. I might have followed the path he took, but I became a trial lawyer.

Dad was known as "the honest accountant." Many years later my father told me that when the US government sought to convict Al Capone, it had secretly flown two accountants to Chicago to review his books. The agents said they required the services of certified public accountants who were without reproach or blemish. Apparently two came to mind. My father was one of them. Capone was convicted of income tax evasion.

My siblings and I walked to school, first Public School 193 and later James Madison High School, from our modest home, all located in the Flatbush neighborhood of the borough of Brooklyn. Our lives seemed unremarkable. We were active in various sports, almost all played in the street where there was little traffic, including hockey on roller skates, touch football, and stickball, a baseball game played with a rubber ball and a broomstick. I joined with Lory and his friends in most sports encounters; they were a couple of years older and more skilled. I tried to make up for that gap with perseverance.

The declaration of war in 1941, when we were still quite young—my sister was nine, I was fourteen, and my brother sixteen—brought an end to the innocence of our childhood. Until then there was schoolwork, sports, and, above all, the Brooklyn Dodgers. My parents were not political activists; they supported President Roosevelt—Eleanor Roosevelt was my mother's only candidate for first lady of the world—they spoke at home of their sympathy for the Loyalists in faraway Spain and their opposition to the fascist Franco regime, and they treated the very few Negroes—that was then the proper word—with whom we came into contact fairly. The subject of race relations did not come up often. However, I remember my mother telling my dad how disappointed she was in one of her friends who had just hired a black maid for some part-time work. The neighbor had not set the hourly rate in advance, later saying to my mother that she had done that on purpose. I was just a child, but an inquisitive one. What was wrong with that? I asked. My mother explained that the maid, a woman without power, I think my mother said "influence," would be forced to accept whatever she was offered once the job was done.

The episodes of daily life then had little resemblance to the world of today. We were not attached to the ubiquitous television sets, smart phones, and tablets of the present. We did sit around the kitchen table Sunday evenings to listen to the radio: Jack Benny and Fred Allen. Fibber McGee and Molly never quite made it in our house. Mr. Keene, Tracer of Lost Persons, and the drama set in Grand Central Station, "the crossroads of the world," and the Shadow were also favorites.

Mother—later in life we called her Betty—played the baby grand piano in our parlor and led us in singing songs of the not-so-recent past. "Smoke Gets in Your Eyes" was her favorite. She was also partial to "School Days." She told us that had been a favorite song when she worked for Gus Edwards, and he had been associated with the song.

We never considered the lack of crime or visible criminals to be a blessing. We accepted that as part of the normal environment just as we expected good drinking water to come from the faucet. I cannot recall ever hearing of a criminal act in our neighborhood; of course, no one bought bottled water. Our trusty 1936 Plymouth, purchased when the government paid a bonus to veterans of World War I, was parked, unlocked, windows open unless rain was expected, in the driveway alongside our semidetached rented home. We did not lock our doors at night. During the summer the windows, including those on the ground floor, were open with just removable screens in place so that nature might provide in the summer months the only air-conditioning then available.

The Elm Theater was AIR COOLED, as the icicle-shaped banners flowing from the marquee proclaimed. We spent hours there every Saturday afternoon. It was cool, and we were able to see two feature films, an episode of a continuing action serial often set in the West, sometimes *The Lone Ranger*, newsreels, and animated cartoons. The newsreels were important; they made it possible for Americans to see their leaders and others both speak and move. We had heard them on the radio and could see their still photographs in the newspapers, but only in the theater could we really observe them.

To assuage the pain of our beloved Brooklyn Dodgers losing yet again, a southern gentleman came to town. Red Barber, who surely set the mark by which any sports broadcaster may be measured even now, half a century later, brought with him a knowledge of the game, a pleasant drawl, and folksy expressions with which we had not been previously acquainted and which we assumed, perhaps incorrectly, were staples that were in common usage in the southern regions. Soon on Bedford Avenue, Kings Highway, Flatbush Avenue, and in the mom-and-pop-run soda fountains, and likely the bars as well, arguments were being described as *rhubarbs* and confrontations were defined as *tearing up the pea patch*, all, of course, in the distinctive patois described elsewhere as Brooklynese. Red Barber became our sage; his descriptions elevated baseball's sweaty endeavors to the level of poetry.

More than forty years later I met Red Barber for the first time. By then the treasonous owners of the club had moved the team to Los Angeles, demonstrating that baseball was less a sport than a business and that team spirit and community support ranked far below greed on their charts. I had been invited to appear as a guest on a national television program originating in Florida. I checked into the hotel and was awaiting a ride to the station when a black stretch limousine pulled up. As I entered it I saw Red Barber seated in the back. He, too, was to appear on the program in support of a book his wife, who was then ill, had written. I was speechless for a moment, for here was the maximum hero of my youth. I was about to tell him that when he offered his hand to me, and in that delightful soft-spoken manner, so familiar to me, he said, "Mark Lane, you have been a heroic figure for me for many years. I am so very pleased to meet you." We became fast friends at once.

Later that evening I told Red ("Please call me that, everyone does") that Lory and I had attended a World Series game as kids. It was perhaps one of the best-known ones. We had camped out overnight on the street outside of Ebbets Field along with hundreds of others so that we might buy bleacher tickets. The regular season rate, fifty-five cents per ticket, had been doubled, but we were determined to splurge. I described the final and most memorable moment. With the Dodgers leading, the final Yankee batter had been struck out, but the catcher, Mickey Owen, "had dropped the ball," I said.

Red stiffened. "It was a fast breaking sharp curve off of his mitt. He did not 'drop' it, Mark. Frankly, I'm quite surprised that you, such a meticulous researcher and writer, would say that Owen 'dropped' the ball."

Of course, Red was correct. I apologized profusely, endlessly, abjectly. I am pleased to be able to report that our friendship was not permanently damaged and that it survived my almost unforgivable imprecision.

||||||

During 1945, as the war was raging in Europe and the Far East, I entered the US Army at Fort Dix, New Jersey. I was eighteen years old. My father had been inducted into the army at Fort Dix almost three decades earlier during World War I, which at the time was called merely the Great War. The older and wiser leaders confidently predicted, as the younger bodies fell about them, that this war was going to end all wars. Soon, out of a paucity of imagination, we began to name them by number and then, euphemistically, deny they were wars at all. They became conflicts or police actions, and we suffered only "light casualties." In my now more considerable experience in such matters, I have never met a single maimed soldier who considered himself to be "a light casualty" or even the family of a deceased one who employed such an evaluation. I have concluded that peace, not war, tends to end war.

As I endured basic training in Camp Blanding, Florida, during the steaming, blinding summer months, the heat waves were visibly omnipresent as they rose from the shining blacktopped roads on our long forced marches, made even less bearable by the effect of sleep deprivation, all part of the program. Blanding, which since 1943 served as a training center for those to be sent to fight in the Pacific or in Europe, was located near Starke, a small town we never visited, and Jacksonville, a major city where we would occasionally spend a rare Saturday or Sunday. Starke, however, invited my attention again almost a quarter of a century later, since it was an official killing ground where the state of Florida executed guilty and innocent prisoners. Serial killer Ted Bundy fell into the former category, and James Joseph Richardson was in the latter category and scheduled for execution when I met him in prison. His remarkable story, for reasons of chronological discipline to which I have not always succumbed, appears later in this work.

In the army I also experienced the serious side of anti-Semitism for the first time. Years before in Brooklyn, some of the older boys had taunted me with a ditty clearly intended to be derogatory. I had heard the words just two or three times decades ago, but I remember them still.

Matzos, matzos, two, four, five
That's what keeps the Jews alive
Matzos and gefilte fish
That surely is their favorite dish

At the time I was puzzled. As a child I never did much like either matzos or gefilte fish. And the arithmetic progression was perplexing, from two to four and to five, but I concluded that rhymes have their own universe of logic. Above all, of course, I was frightened and offended by the jeering tone that was directed at me and indicated I was both different and inferior because I was different. The impact of those words upon me might be determined, at least in part, by the fact that they have remained with me through my life.

But in the army anti-Semitism was not offered with a musical accompaniment. My companions were a mixture drawn from all around the country, with an inordinate number from the southern states. The remarks, not directed at me, since I was not suspected of being one of *them*, were mean-spirited, stereotypically based, and grounded in ignorance. When asked about my nationality, I always said American and added that my parents were born in New York State. My answers were true, but I felt they were designed to deceive and were motivated by unworthy cowardice.

When I was stationed in Austria, I was a private first class, almost as low as one can rate in the martial hierarchy. A master-sergeant, near the top of the noncommissioned officers rank, told me that he was not going to spend his leave in Paris since "there are so many fucking Jews there." I was silent. I have been to beautiful, wonderful, incredible Paris many times since then. The sergeant's bigotry cost him dearly.

While on the firing line at night to operate the Browning automatic rifle, I noticed that my assigned buddy for the exercise—who had previously observed how dumb "niggers and kikes" were—was enamored of the power of the weapon and the excitement of actually watching the path of the bullets. Each sixth round was a tracer that glowed brightly as it raced through the dark and heavy southern night. He told me that he was going to volunteer to carry the BAR in combat. When I asked what about the tracers fascinated him, he said that you could see where the bullets struck. I pointed out that the very nature of that phenomenon posed certain risks. He seemed bemused. I said that an enemy sniper could just as clearly see exactly where the bullets were coming from. He said "Fuck!" several times, decided to withdraw his request, and offered to buy me a beer. After a number of 3.2 PX beers, he concluded that I had just saved his life. He asked what he could do for me.

I said, "Don't call Negroes niggers and Jews kikes."

He said, "OK—why?"

I told him that I found the former offensive and that I was one of the latter.

In addition to anti-Semitism, I encountered the sting of official racism. In those days I had very short hair in compliance with army regulations. I spent a great deal of time under the summer sun at the urging of the basic training instructors, who would have it no other way. I always tanned well, and soon I was a dark, six-foot, short-haired guy in a uniform visiting Jacksonville on a two-day pass. Taxis refused to stop when I hailed them—a situation that persists to this day for men and women of color—and in mental repartee suffused in denial, I told myself that on my salary as a private I could hardly afford that ride anyway. But then I boarded a bus and was ordered to sit in the back. I despised segregation, and I could not condone it by stating that I was white, implying that, unlike my fellow citizens, I was entitled to a front seat view. Neither was I a heroic Rosa Parks. I took a seat in the back of the bus. The black passengers looked at me; some smiled, some nodded, and others seemed perplexed. All knew what the bus driver did not recognize.

Basic training was a never-ending challenge, primarily physically, but not without its share of psychological aspects as well. As a child I had spent part of one summer in camp. I did not enjoy the experience, and I was eager to return home. The first weeks at

Camp Blanding made Camp Wel-Met in the Adirondack Mountains of New York State seem to be, for the first time, a pleasant children's camp, which, of course, was what it was. We were always exhausted during training. We engaged in calisthenics. Marched to the firing line regularly to fire a variety of weapons. Marched back. Marched to the firing line to serve in the trenches just below the targets so that we could report the score as others fired. Crawled through obstacles with live machine gun fire just overhead, or so we were told and believed. Climbed over walls by pulling ourselves up by the use of ropes. And marched and marched and marched. Many of the GIs collapsed from heat exhaustion or heat stroke in temperatures above 100 degrees in the shade, but we were always in the sun. We learned how to disassemble and then assemble the M-1 rifle, an accurate and remarkably sturdy weapon that never jammed if adequately cared for, and then how to do it with our eyes closed. We also learned to obey orders with our eyes closed and never to question the decision of an authority even when the decision was flawed.

A couple of older men in our barracks, "older" then being a term for anyone who had passed his twentieth birthday, both from New Jersey, expressed their concern about the excessive punishments meted out for minor infractions, such as not having made the bed with crisp and precisely angled hospital corners. They approached me as the only other northerner present in an effort to mount a protest. I declined to join the gentle mutiny, stating that I had mastered the hospital corner art and that it was not difficult. While that was true, and that bit of military training remains with me and is employed daily decades later, as my wife will confirm, the basis for my refusal was fear of confronting authority. That characteristic seems to have faded in time.

We prepared as ground troops to fight in Europe. When that war ended we prepared to fight on the islands of the Pacific and the invasion of Japan. Not long before we were set to sail a decision was made to drop atomic bombs upon two Japanese cities. Even those of us whose lives may have been spared by that decision, the initial beneficiaries of the use of weapons of mass destruction against the enemy, celebrated in muted tones.

Tens of thousands of our lives may well have been saved, mine included, yet the enemy who died in much larger numbers in their homes, in their schools, on playgrounds, at workplaces, were civilians. They were children, women, elderly people; they were noncombatants, or so they thought until that sudden, blinding, terrifying moment that evaporated that portion of the world. We were relieved, but that emotion was mixed with awe and guilt.

Instead of fighting on a Pacific island beach, I was sent to Europe in the army of occupation. The highlight of my stay took place the day I arrived at Camp Phillip Morris near the port of Le Havre in France. All the US Army reception camps had been named after American cigarette brands. After some investigation I discovered that my brother was on his way home and was not far away. We were unable to meet, but we managed to sufficiently compromise the military communication system so that we could speak by telephone for the first time in years.

I was stationed in Bad Schallerbach, Austria, a small village known for its healing waters, about seventeen miles from where Hitler had lived and attended school in 1903 at the Realschule in Linz. It was also close to the Danube River. I had been assigned to the headquarters unit of a mechanized cavalry outfit, a pretty flashy group equipped with gold-colored scarves instead of neckties and high combat boots into which we tucked the cuffs of our trousers. I replaced a sergeant who was about to leave. He was happy to see me arrive, and we became good friends in the weeks we worked together. I took over his very nonmilitary quarters, and since he could not take Alice home, she lived with me. Alice was a medium-sized, very pregnant black-and-white dog.

A movement began soon after my European service began. It called for the return to the United States of all of its personnel. It was supported by political groups of various ideologies throughout Western Europe and was adopted by some members of the American military. To those who sought to enlist me, I said that our presence in

Europe must be needed or our government would not have sent us here. I was only eighteen years old.

The commander of our headquarters was obligated to fill a vacancy at S-1, the organization's intelligence unit. The captain apparently confused the name of the office with the qualifications required for the service in it. He examined the files of those under his command and discovered that I had scored highest on the Army General Classification Test, the AGCT being the military's version of an intelligence quotient test administered to all recruits. I was forthwith transferred to S-1 after my file revealed that I had not been involved with any subversive or controversial activities.

My subversive career began in a little intelligence office located in a small Austrian village a few days later. The captain summoned me. I was to visit a somewhat remote location near the Danube and interview a group of enlisted men and a noncommissioned officer regarding an argument that had blossomed into a fistfight with a number of Russian soldiers.

"Investigate thoroughly. Write an accurate report," the captain said. "I know you will do the right thing. That is an order. Dismissed."

I questioned the noncom and the GIs, an appellation for soldiers universally employed in spite of its sardonic implications, it being an abbreviation for *government issue*. They said that the Russians were entirely at fault, given the circumstances a politically sound assessment, although one lacking in credibility since the Americans had crossed the Danube, entered the Russian zone without permission, crashed a party given in honor of a Russian colonel, and engaged in a violent brawl over the question as to which of the two superpowers was more dedicated to peace. I asked for permission to interview the Russian personnel. After considerable fuss, the Soviets reluctantly and conditionally granted the request. They would provide the interpreter, and a Russian political officer was to be present to advise the soldiers. No notes were to be taken.

My captain was not pleased. He said I did not need to listen to the "godless enemy" and that he had already ordered me "to do the right thing." For a moment I considered my options and then decided to compromise. I drafted a report that tended to ignore the place of the encounter and focus on the ringing proclamations of innocence offered by the GIs. The captain was still not pleased; he began, he said, to doubt the accuracy of the AGCT. He directed me to write a report that placed the responsibility exclusively upon the Russians, adding that it was a court-martial offense to disobey a direct order. I complied. My modest attempt to tell some semblance of the truth yielded to the order "to do the right thing." Even that experience with governmental cover-up was later of some value in civilian life; I was able to understand, although not entirely sympathize with, the methodology adopted by the distinguished members of the Warren Commission as they allegedly investigated the death of President Kennedy.

A driver named C.W. was assigned to me. He outranked me by a couple of grades, which might indicate to those unaware of the full measure of martial logic that I should have been driving him about. The fact that I had not yet learned to drive was not a factor. The table of organization commanded that the person conducting such an inquiry, regardless of rank or lack of it, was to be the passenger, and that another person, drawn from the motor pool, was to be in full charge of the vehicle. On one trip I decided that I would acquire at least one skill that I could use in civilian life. I asked my driver if I could get behind the wheel. He was reluctant since the jeep had been signed out to him and because I did not know how to drive. Finally and tentatively he agreed.

The two-way road leading from Bad Schallerbach was rutted, narrow, one and one half lanes wide, and raised about five feet above the fields that it crossed. The motor pool had that day provided a jeep with a plywood top to shield us from the elements. It was a clear and pleasant day. As I bounced along at a decent clip I was beginning to relax and enjoy my newly acquired skill. Suddenly a large, lumbering truck appeared on the scene, headed directly for me. In that postwar period, immediately after the conclusion of hostilities, the nonmilitary European vehicles were either very small automobiles or outsize trucks, and there would be just inches to spare were we to pass each other. At that critical moment, a young girl pushed her bicycle up the ridge to our right directly into our path. I had few options. If I swerved to the left there would have been a head-on collision with a truck; if I continued forward I would have hit and likely killed the young girl. I turned the wheel sharply to the right, drove suddenly down the embankment behind her, and was about to strike a large tree when I attempted to drive up the embankment. It was at that point that the jeep rolled over a number of times. I emerged with nothing more than a deep cut on my chin. C.W. had been thrown out and lay prostrate in a ditch. I ran to him, fearing that he was dead. When he regained consciousness several minutes later his first words were, "You ain't fucking driving back!" He was uninjured but very frightened about his future since I had been an unauthorized driver who had wrecked the vehicle assigned to him. The plywood top had been so badly splintered that no piece large enough to be recognizable remained. We tipped the jeep over, and it started at once. On the way back he insisted that we tell the story as it had happened but state that he had been driving. That way, he reasoned, although he might be court-martialed for reckless driving leading to damage to government property or at least face company punishment and be forced to pay for the damaged top, he would escape responsibility for the more serious charge of allowing me to drive. I was troubled about having the blame for the accident shift to him but saw the wisdom of his plan. I insisted that I would reimburse him.

The officer in command of the motor pool was outraged. At that point the truck arrived with the bicyclist in the passenger seat. The driver was very emotional. A translator was located. The driver wanted to express his deepest gratitude to the soldier who had saved the girl's life. He kept looking at me. I looked away. There was talk about a medal for C.W. for his work in helping develop a better relationship with the people whose country we were occupying. He left for home before the matter was resolved; I never heard if he received that honor. I still bear a small scar on my chin, covered these many years by a black, and now a gray, beard. I later became a driving instructor in Brooklyn for young men and women, mostly women, as I earned enough money to send myself through college and still eat.

During my European tour I visited the Salzburg Festival and attended a Mozart opera there, began to learn to ski in the Alps, rode a horse for the first time in my life, became very ill from a near-fatal ear infection, spent a month in an army hospital, and learned to live communally with other teenagers from my country. I also met Germans and Austrians and was surprised to learn how much we had in common. I knew, of course, that had I arrived a little earlier we might have tried to kill each other.

||||||

Once back in New York after almost two years in the military, I decided to become a lawyer as quickly as I could and open a neighborhood office in some depressed area where legal services were both needed and not available. Those decisions shaped the rest of my life.

In little more than three and a half years, attending Long Island University and Brooklyn Law School during the summers and into the evenings, aided by the GI Bill of Rights and a New York State scholarship, I completed the required college and law school courses and began preparation for the difficult New York State bar examination.

Kenneth Harris and I taught two other law students in a bar review course that we created. Kenny was one of the very few black students in our class; he was the best scholar in the law school. He was so emaciated that he resembled a concentration camp victim who had been very recently liberated. One of his legs was much shorter than the other due to a childhood disease, and even with a built-up shoe he limped noticeably. He was the most antisocial person in school, and he gave the impression that he relished that distinction above all others. For the first several months it seemed that he had no friends at school and that he preferred that arrangement.

I watched him play Ping-Pong in the school's recreation room one afternoon. He won each game handily. He had heard, he later told me, that I was a fairly good player.

"Pick up the racket, Lane," he said in a rather brusque tone. "We'll see if you're any good."

I complied. I won one of the three games.

He threw down his paddle and said, "You drink beer, Lane?"

We went to a nearby bar, had a few drinks, and began a friendship that lasted through law school.

Years later I asked him why, during that segregated period at the close of the 1940s, he had formed a friendship with me. He said, "You were the only one who treated me equally. You tried to beat me by slamming the ball to the right, left, and then right again. I was quicker than you, had better reflexes and better eyesight. You used your one advantage."

We picked two of the slowest students in the school to study with. That was not through design; they were both friends of mine and sometimes even tolerated by Kenny. One in fact was so inexpert in grasping legal concepts that we marveled at his ability to squeak through to graduation. They were both good and sincere men who I thought might make a contribution to the profession if they could ever be admitted. When Kenny was asked why he wasted his talents with the inferior students he replied acidly, "They're so dumb that by the time Lane and I get through explaining to them what the law is, we both know it well enough to recite it in our sleep."

At that time approximately half of the students who took the New York State bar examination passed it. The test was given in two separate parts and could be taken repeatedly, over a period of months, until one passed or gave up. All four of us passed both parts on our first try. Kenny, I read years later, went on to become a judge.

I learned one thing at law school. A teacher of torts wrote the word *judgment* on the blackboard. He said, "There is only one *e* in *judgment*. Place a second one there, after the *g*, in answer to any question this semester, and you will fail torts. Spell it correctly, and you will pass this course. The one thing you will learn at law school is how to spell *judgment*, an attribute which has some application to our profession." I believe that I have never misspelled the word *judgment*. Thank you, Mr. Thorton. However, numerous reviewers of my first book, *Rush to Judgment*, may not validly make the same claim.

Passing the bar does not qualify you to become a lawyer in New York State. First you must appear before the official Committee on Character and Fitness and seek its approval. While in law school I spent little time at my studies; I devoted more time as the only national student leader of the National Lawyers Guild. There had been two elected national officers of the student division, but my colleague had resigned due, he said, to pressure from his parents. But after talking with him, I believed the resignation was prompted by the fear that association with the guild could adversely affect his career.

The guild had been created in 1937, during the New Deal era, and was an answer to the American Bar Association. At that time the ABA refused admission to black lawyers and opposed the concept of social security and other legislation as left-wing plots. Today, the ABA is a far different organization and has made significant contributions to the profession and to the nation. I organized students at numerous law schools around the principle that we were dedicated to see the law as an instrument for the protection of the people, rather than for their repression. Our goal was to safeguard the rights of workers, women, farmers, and minorities and to maintain and protect our civil rights and liberties in the face of persistent attacks upon them. This was during the first days of 1950. It was also during the first days of McCarthyism, which began that year and spread terror throughout our country until 1954.[1]

I was required to submit the names of two sponsors to the Committee on Character and Fitness. My parents had a nodding acquaintance with Maximilian Moss, the president of the board of education of the city of New York, whose views differed from mine, as would become clear in my later battle against spending

$50 million to build mandatory bomb shelters in schools. They knew him just well enough to say hello or, more likely, "Good Yontif" as they passed each other on the High Holy Days once a year. At their request he agreed to be my sponsor. He seemed to have no idea about my political views; after all, he was vouching for my character, and I had never been arrested, never used drugs, and never had a fistfight.

My mother also suggested that I ask Mr. Gibbs to be a sponsor. He was an elderly man who had been our next-door neighbor when we lived on East Twenty-Fourth Street. I knew that he had been a clerk somewhere, but I had not heard that he was a lawyer. Years before, I had often, as a courtesy, mowed his lawn, a very small plot, when I was taking care of ours. Mom said Mr. Gibbs would be so happy to be asked. He was indeed a lawyer, he said, and he agreed to be a sponsor.

At that time applicants for the bar were being rejected for their progressive beliefs, and when I appeared before a representative of the committee I was not sanguine about my prospects. He picked up my file, and I noted that "National Lawyers Guild" and the paragraph under that heading had been circled in red ink. He sighed and shook his head from side to side. Then something else caught his attention. He smiled and said, "How well do you know him? How did you meet him? Is he well?" I was about to conjure up an anecdote or two about the distinguished Mr. Moss when he said, "I haven't seen Mr. Gibbs in decades. There must be hundreds of lawyers in this town who remember him as the chief clerk in the court system and who are indebted to him for his kindness and for helping us along when we first were admitted. He is a legend."

I spoke about my neighbor, and the committee representative said, "Welcome to the bar. His recommendation is good enough for me."

And thus, improbably, began my improbable journey.

||||||

Between taking the bar, awaiting the results, and finally being processed through, I served as what now may be called a paralegal with Bernard Davis, a single practitioner. Bernie shared office space at Thirty-Fourth Street and Seventh Avenue with an attorney named Bella Abzug. Bella was a principled and forceful advocate, and when we met in the office for the first time she said, "Every man is a male chauvinist, with the possible exception of my husband, Martin, whom I have personally trained." I remember those words quite clearly now, a half century later. She was a precursor of the current women's movement and an indomitable fighter for civil rights.

For Bernie Davis I did research, served papers, met with clients, including officers of the one trade union local he represented, and made a rare, and always inadequate, court appearance. I saw the difficulties of life as a sole practitioner. There was no corporate pension or golden parachute at the end of the line, no medical coverage, and you could not be adequately prepared for either feast or famine. Of the two, feast is preferable, but it is accompanied by its own wicked issues.

One day, two different courts required Bernie to be present to represent different clients at the same time. He asked me to cover one matter, explain the circumstances to the judge, and ask for thirty minutes for him to arrive. I went to the courtroom and found no judge and no adversary. They were conversing in the judge's chambers. When I was invited in, they continued their conversation about the poker game they had enjoyed the night before in the local political club to which they both belonged. The club was responsible for bestowing the robe upon the judge, and the lawyer had been his political advocate. I asked the court for a few minutes for Davis to arrive. The judge, all of this being off the record, asked the lawyer for his opinion, and he promptly said that the case for the plaintiff in the civil suit, whom Bernie represented, should be summarily dismissed. The judge dismissed the case and then said to me, "You understand that the fact that I know the lawyer for the defendant has nothing to do with my ruling." I nodded and left.

I walked to the federal courthouse next door to see how justice was being dispensed there. I saw Carol Weiss King, a founder of the National Lawyers Guild, arguing on behalf of an impoverished immigrant. She was indignant and forceful. She stood there alone in that huge and impressive courtroom, a woman in her mid-fifties opposed by three assistant US attorneys who were supported by their federal police associates and clerks. Her hands were on her hips as she spoke to the judge in challenging tones: "Just who does this government think it is that it can violate the law with impunity, that it can traduce the rights of ordinary people, that it can tell us that the law doesn't count because these are extraordinary times. . . ."

I thought of my own recent timid appearance, and I vowed that it would not be repeated.

Working with the National Lawyers Guild

2

‖‖‖‖‖‖‖‖‖‖‖‖‖‖‖‖‖‖‖‖‖‖‖‖‖‖‖‖‖‖‖‖‖‖‖‖‖‖

During the early 1950s the National Lawyers Guild was under attack by regressive congressional committees and Herbert Brownell Jr., the US attorney general who had falsely accused the Lawyers Guild of being "the legal mouthpiece of the Communist Party" and who had tried to designate the group as a subversive organization. (Years later the Department of Justice withdrew its fabricated claim.)

My sense of appropriateness was offended by such egregious conduct. In response I agreed to become the full-time administrative assistant to the New York chapter of the guild. Among the leaders and members of the guild were the finest, most skilled, and most dedicated lawyers in the nation. They certainly needed no advice from a young man just out of law school. Yet one matter did concern me about the organization I had joined. Funds were raised through membership dues democratically scaled based upon years in practice and through an annual theater party where tickets to a Broadway show were purchased and then resold to wealthy members at inflated prices as contributions to the guild. No law student could afford to attend, and many younger lawyers were also excluded. Adequate funds were raised, but only a small minority of the members participated. I suggested a new approach.

I asked the board to rent a suitable hall, hire artists to perform, and set ticket prices starting at a moderate range. To each question—such as *Who will produce the show? Who will find the artists? Who will hire the artists?* and above all *Who will sell the tickets?*—I responded that I would. The only time I answered in the negative was when I was asked if I had ever done anything like that before.

An incredulous board authorized me to proceed, with the strong advice of one member, a lover of the opera, that I enter into an agreement with Richard Dyer-Bennet as the main attraction. Dyer-Bennet was billed as an English "minstrel," not a folksinger, and one who performed "in a white tie." So far as anyone knew he had no political ties. He was elite; some music lovers were partial to him, and he did have a beautiful tenor voice.

I rented Town Hall in midtown Manhattan and wondered how many of the 1,495 seats we might be able to fill. I called Dyer-Bennet, who told me his fee would be $1,500 for a short appearance. He asked in a melodious voice if we were some sort of a radical or subversive group. I told him that we believed in the Constitution and saw the law as a living instrument to protect the rights of the people. He had someone else conduct additional research and then deliver the message to me that he would not appear before such an organization. I never much blamed him; the McCarthy period made cowards of many.

I called iconic folksinger Pete Seeger, my own first choice. He had been barred from appearing on television programs and denied access to concert halls. Even when he was a member of the famed Weavers, the group met similar oppositions. I knew him to be a good man, a true patriot, and a multitalented composer and singer. He played the guitar and the recorder and was the acknowledged expert on the banjo. He asked if that was a Saturday. I said that it was. He said, "Well then, Mr. Lane, I'm afraid I'm going to ask for my higher Saturday night fee if the guild can afford it." It was $50. Later Pete called me to ask if he could bring along Blind Sonny Terry. He assured me that there would not be any additional charge for us.

"I'll just share my fee with him," Pete said. To those knowledge-able about the blues and folk music, Sonny remains a musical genius. Professor Irwin Corey, widely known as "*The* World's Foremost Authority"; Morris Carnovsky and Howard DaSilva, two wonderful black-listed actors; and several others also performed.

The next call was to Martha Schlamme, a remarkably talented folksinger who sang in many languages. When the Nazis were about to enter Austria, where Martha and her family lived, she and her mother had escaped through France to England, where they were interned as "enemy aliens" by the British government on the Isle of Man, along with other refugees from Austria, even though they were Jewish and had fled rather than suffer the fate of Martha's father, who had been sent to a concentration camp. Martha agreed to sing at Town Hall.

Every ticket was sold. Others, unable to find tickets for seats, pur-chased standing room. More than fifteen hundred lawyers, students, and their spouses or close friends stood together and joined hands as on the stage Pete, Martha, Sonny, Morris, Howard, and others led us, in that dark McCarthy moment, to rejoice in the future as we sang "We Shall Overcome."

Soon Martha, Pete, and I became good friends. Martha and I were married in 1953. We rented an apartment on the Upper West Side, so close to Harlem and East Harlem that I could walk to my office in East Harlem each day and back each night.

During the early days, Martha shared a couple of issues with me that confronted her. Her income was very limited, although those who heard her sing were almost universally enthralled. She had been invited to tour South Africa for a very substantial fee. Soon after she signed the contract, she was visited at our apartment in New York by a representative of Nelson Mandela's African National Congress. I was present when he very politely informed her that the ANC had decided to ask artists everywhere to boycott South Africa, since they, black South Africans, were the subject of apartheid and were iso-lated in their own country. Martha asked numerous questions, and the ANC representative left after she assured him that she would consider his suggestion.

She decided to cancel the agreement and notified her white sponsors in South Africa of her decision. The ANC was very pleased, thanked Martha, and told her she was the first artist to actually reject a signed contract. The South African sponsors immediately threatened to bring legal action against her, stating that they had expended funds for advertising and other costs related to her tour. They threatened to identify all of those who might employ her in the United States and urge them to boycott her. They demanded that she travel to South Africa.

When Martha asked for my advice, I began to research the laws of South Africa. I drafted a letter for her to her sponsors saying that she agreed to fulfill her obligations. We said in the letter that she sang songs of freedom and national liberation and would publicly condemn the practice of apartheid and call for its abolition; she knew that the present laws made such statements treason and that the punishment was death. She was informing the sponsors of her intentions, she wrote, knowing that they, now informed, faced the same penalties that she did and that bravely together they would confront this evil. Within a week the sponsors cancelled the contract. When I suggested that she had a cause of action against them for taking such precipitous action, she smiled and said she was satisfied that the matter was closed.

A little later Martha decided, after finally resolving conflicting emotions, to record an album of German folk songs. Her first language was German, and she had sung German and Austrian folk songs as a child. Although she and her family and numerous friends suffered from the Nazi holocaust, after a great deal of intense soul searching she was able to separate German culture from the Nazis and the millions of Germans who supported Hitler. She entered into an agreement with a well-known recording company to make the album when they generously told her that she could choose any artist to accompany her.

She chose Peter Seeger; he agreed, and they began to discuss songs for the album. The company declined, saying that "Seeger's political views would damage our company and our artists." Martha asked for my advice, and I suggested that she talk to Pete, since his "political views" were very much the same as ours. Pete said, "Martha, this company is too small to treat us that way." Within hours Pete arranged for Folkways to produce the album. I was a privileged spectator in the studio as Pete played the guitar, the recorder, and the banjo and Martha sang. When they needed one song more than the ones they had rehearsed, Martha hummed it for Pete, who arranged the accompaniment in minutes.

IIIIII

Our apartment on Central Park West near 107th Street was too far north by far to be fashionable and too close to Harlem to be even universally acceptable. It was a spacious place and perfectly located for us. One day the mail included a note from Dr. W. E. B. Du Bois and his wife, Shirley. Martha and I were invited to dinner at their home in Brooklyn. Dr. Du Bois was one of the most respected leaders and political activists of the twentieth century. He was a leading intellectual, a professor, a columnist, and a founder of the NAACP. He was the editor in chief of that organization's publication, *The Crisis*, for a quarter of a century.

Our excitement in contemplating the meeting was tempered by the thought that we were uncertain about how to address him. I had heard Dr. Du Bois speak several times and had briefly met him, and I had had conversations with Shirley. Martha had sung at meetings and rallies where he spoke, and he had said, "Martha, sometimes I think that the best reason for coming to these affairs is to hear your lovely voice." Shirley, Martha, and I were on a first-name basis; but what would we call this almost ninety-year-old intellectual giant of our century? We decided that likely it would be a crowded affair and the question might never arise.

I rang the bell, and Dr. Du Bois appeared, greeted us warmly, and ushered us into the large living room. It was dominated by a portrait of Frederick Douglass, one of the most significant figures in American history. I commented on the beauty of the painting. Dr. Du Bois said, "Yes, and a very good likeness. I heard him speak, you know."

Douglass's speech must have dated back to well before his death in 1895. We were traveling rapidly backward in time. I probably looked surprised if not astonished.

Dr. Du Bois put his hand on my arm and said, "Well, you were probably very young at the time."

We had a glass of sherry before dinner, and as it turned out we were the only guests. Shirley cooked, and later her husband cleared the dishes. We talked for hours about contemporary politics, the outspoken actor Paul Robeson, and the work still ahead. As we said good-bye, Shirley told us that Dr. Du Bois would be at his office at the Civil Rights Congress in Manhattan the next morning. He took the subway there each day.

Years later, I met a young black activist in the civil rights movement. She told me that Dr. Du Bois, by then long deceased, had been her hero. She explained, "No one can read or hear him and believe that I am inferior."

||||||

Martha and I were not often at home together. I was practicing law with court appearances almost every day. Martha traveled to give concerts. Our circle of friends might find us at home late in the evening, as did Pete Seeger one night.

The first time he stayed the night at our apartment remains with me half a century later in exquisite detail. The telephone call came from Pete rather late one evening. He asked how I was, I said I was fine and asked how he was, and he said he was fine. After a minute or two of small, or probably minuscule, talk, I asked where he was. He said that he had just given a concert in Manhattan and possibly was a

little too tired for the drive home to Beacon, New York. I invited him
to stay with us. He said he would be there in a minute, since he was
calling from a telephone booth just a few yards away.

Martha greeted him and asked if he would like something to
drink. Pete said that he knew that he could always get a good cup of
tea there. Martha had lived for years in London. Pete's nose seemed
to be a bit inflamed. He asked Martha if she had a potato in the
house, and she showed him where they were kept. They had been
around for a while and had begun to wither and sprout. Pete looked
them over and said, "Martha, just about ready for planting." At his
request I brought out a roll of adhesive tape. He cut the potato in
half, scooped out some of it, placed it over his nose, and secured it
with the tape, while saying, "Best natural poultice around."

When I asked him about his concert that evening he said it went
well, but he never thought of himself as a singer; he really wanted to
devote his time to studying the history of folk songs. Somehow we
were considering India. Pete described the beauty of the Taj Mahal
in exquisite detail. It was not a professorial or pedantic effort; it was
a moment of excitement in which I could not but be moved by his
appreciation and vast knowledge. "How often have you visited?" I
asked. He said he had not been to the palace but he had read a great
deal about it.

If there was a subject that he did not know about—the rights of
working folks to form a union, anything in any way related to music,
his opposition to senseless wars, the beauty of things men and women
had accomplished—I never discovered it. Finally, by the time he was
in his nineties, accolades had begun to arrive from people other than
those he had marched with, sung for and with, and led for most of
our lives. Of one thing I am certain. His current celebrity status will
not change the way he looks at the world or himself.

When called before the inquisitorial and infamous House Committee on Un-American Activities in 1955, he was ordered to name
his colleagues in the struggle. He was asked if he would name names
"to make a contribution to his country." Pete for a moment set aside

his characteristic modesty and answered that his whole life had been a contribution to his country. And so it has been.

Later, I produced a concert at Town Hall in Manhattan for Martha, who filled the hall with fifteen hundred delighted fans, mesmerized the audience, and earned rave reviews. I also produced two children's Christmas concerts for Pete at the little theater at Carnegie Hall. For a moment or two I thought that life as an impresario might be an option. But my brief apprenticeship at law had concluded, and with my certificate in hand proclaiming that I was a lawyer, I decided to find a store in East Harlem and hang up my shingle. I walked across Central Park to East Harlem and didn't leave for more than a decade. Martha was very supportive during those early years while she also pursued her career. One day, while performing on a stage in the Midwest, she suffered a stroke and went into a coma. I rushed to the hospital and held her hand. She opened her eyes, looked at me, tried to smile, and then died.

Storefront Lawyer

3

||||||||||||||||||||||||||||||||||||||||||||||||||||

F inding an empty store in the crowded, deteriorating community required many weeks of canvassing the area on foot and hundreds of conversations with owners of the small businesses that abounded. Unable to locate an available street-level store, I began to look upward. I saw what appeared from the street to be an empty apartment on the second floor of a four-story building on Madison Avenue between 110th and 111th streets in the heart of East Harlem. I found a young woman named Olga who seemed to have some relationship with the premises. She was a prostitute who worked out of the building, 1677 Madison Avenue, and also temporarily ran the business that utilized the third and fourth floors. The street-level store roasted and sold Puerto Rican coffee. The second floor was indeed vacant.

Olga told me that the building was owned by Romulo Rosario, a rather famous community semi-legend who envisioned himself as a Spanish Robin Hood. Actually Romulo was committed to stealing from the poor and the poorer and keeping the proceeds for himself, but the mantle of no ancient legend fits the modern man perfectly. A violent racketeer, Romulo operated a house of prostitution and a numbers ring and worked in a relatively minor capacity in the heroin trade that was then dominated by the Italian mob. His silent partner in the enterprises, it was rumored, was a judge. Accordingly, he felt with some degree of confidence that he was above the law.

Romulo was in La Tomba, I was informed—"the Tombs," the New York jail adjacent to the criminal court building in lower Manhattan. Early one morning in a bar in which Romulo had an interest—he collected protection money from the proprietor—he was insulted by another gentleman. He responded in kind. A fistfight broke out, and Romulo was trounced. The bruises were less traumatic to him than the affront to his majesty.

He returned to the bar within the hour carrying a fully loaded .45-caliber pistol, a military weapon that he had purchased illegally. He walked up to his former assailant, who had all but passed out at the bar from celebrating his recent victory, and emptied the handgun into his head and back. Romulo's knowledge of the New York penal law was deficient; he surrendered to the police and pleaded self-defense. Unfortunately a judge other than his friend was chosen to try the case, and Romulo was awaiting a death sentence when I met Olga.

She told me that Romulo was married to a "straight lady" and that she, Olga, was his mistress. She referred to Romulo's wife as her "wife-in-law." We liked each other at once. Perhaps it was a combination of her candor and my wide-eyed naivete. In any event, I prepared a long-term lease; Olga took it to Romulo, who signed it, stating that it was his last act and one he was doing to uplift and enhance the community that he had so faithfully served. He was executed on February 17, 1955, at Sing Sing.

|||||

A narrow, dark, vermin-infested hallway that had too often been mistaken by wandering drunks for a urinal led to my office. A flimsy expanding metal gate and an interior door were all that maintained the sanctity of my offices, a three-room suite with peeling painted surfaces and a decorative metal ceiling.

Today, my wife and some of my friends react favorably to old buildings with tin ceilings as we encounter them in their latest manifestations in restaurants or inns. The charm escapes me, for I remember the unique sound that results from rats constantly scattering across them. Yet, despite a few distractions, it was my office, my first office. The legend on the window proclaimed that I was both an ABOGADO and a NOTARIO PUBLICO, the latter, for reasons I couldn't fully comprehend, resulted in more respect from some members of the community. Later I was informed by Ramon Diaz, an East Harlem fixture, that at first nobody believed I was a lawyer, but the community was willing to suspend its disbelief regarding my claim to be a notary public.

For a while I was known as "the good Jew" by oppressed people whose only contact with people they thought were Jewish had been exploitative. Most of the landlords were not Jewish, neither were most of the pawnbrokers nor the storekeepers nor even a majority of their employers, yet all were presumed to be. I was displeased neither with the appellation nor with my unexpected role of combating anti-Semitism as I went about my daily work. I was, however, most satisfied when, as time passed, neither my religion nor my race figured in the evaluation of my adopted community. In time I was Don Marco to some and to all a lawyer with a listed home telephone number available to anyone in trouble.

During the first weeks in my office my only assets were a disreputable couch, which came with the place and which was too large to fit through the door, causing me to wonder if it was built in the room, and a typewriter, the essential engine that drove the office. We typed our pleadings on thin paper and had several alternating layers of carbon paper and onionskin paper for copies. A mistake required considerable time to correct, since each carbon copy had to be erased by hand. For those of you who have come of age more recently and wonder what the "cc" is at the bottom of letters, it is an homage to the old days of carbon copies.

One early morning I arrived at my office, having walked there from my apartment on the West Side of Manhattan across Central Park. Even in the dark hallway I could see the metal gate had been badly damaged. I approached cautiously as I did each day ever since a large rat resting on top of the gate had jumped onto my shoulder before fleeing down the stairs. This day the security gate had been ripped out and the wooden door to my office had been broken. I was disappointed to see that the couch was still there but shaken when I realized that the typewriter had been stolen.

That morning Ramon Diaz came into my life. He was a community organizer loosely associated with the East Harlem Protestant Parish but more intimately connected to the people of East Harlem, including youth gangs, churches, social clubs, and ordinary unaffiliated folks with more daily problems than solutions.

"Excuse me for not knocking," he said as he walked into my office. Pieces of the door were strewn about, and there was nothing standing to knock on. He introduced himself and then looked around. "Is anything missing?" he asked.

I mentioned the indispensable typewriter.

He shook his head sadly. "They probably don't know how much you are helping us here."

After he left, I repaired the door, fixed the gate, locked it behind me, and walked home discouraged.

The next morning I saw evidence of another unauthorized entry, although this time with minimum damage to the door and gate. On my desk was my typewriter. A note had been typed on it. "Sorry for it. We did int no about you. Thanx."

||||||

During 1955 the most publicized murder case of the period took place in the Bronx. The *Journal-American*, a Hearst afternoon daily newspaper published in New York, rightfully took credit for mesmerizing the population with the details. It later ignored the evidence, demonstrating that its version of the events was skewed by racism and its commercial commitment to boosting its circulation.

Frank Santana, a Puerto Rican teenager, shot and killed William Blankenship Jr., a white American teenager. If a member of a minority, black or Latino, killed another nonwhite American, the event was sometimes barely mentioned in the press and often not covered at all. White-on-white murders were reported with little more interest unless one of the parties was a celebrity. The media reserved their full-court press for when a member of a minority was accused of killing a white American. Those trends continued for a very long time and, in a diluted sense, still remain with us.

But to make this murder worthy of front-page coverage, day after day, including front-page editorials demanding the death penalty and guest editorials written by William Blankenship, the father of the deceased, additional ingredients were required. These sensationalist details and exaggerations were supplied on a daily basis. The murderer was a Puerto Rican "thug" who demanded to be called "Tarzan." He was "cold-blooded" and "heartless" and a "trouble-making hoodlum from Puerto Rico." Even his mother was referred to as "the hoodlum's mother." The campaign reached into the pages of the *New York Times*, which stated in a headline "Hoodlum, 17, Held in Slaying of Boy."

The deceased was "Billy, the model boy," who "had never been a member of any gang" and who was "an innocent victim just walking down the street," the press reported daily. Pictures of Billy, taken years earlier, were published regularly. Billy was "handsome" and "very blond." Frank "Tarzan" Santana, the gang member, "grinned cockily" when he was arrested. These versions of the facts were set in stone as newspapers and ordinary citizens quoted by them demanded that "Tarzan Santana must be executed." Those emotions were further stirred by the district attorney of the Bronx, Daniel V. Sullivan, who quickly had Frank "Tarzan" Santana indicted for first-degree murder. He vowed publicly and repeatedly that he would ask for and obtain the death penalty. He assured the public: "Santana will die in the electric chair."

I had been a lawyer for a very short time when Mrs. Santana came to my office and asked me to represent her son. Between fits of crying and sobbing, she said that she knew her son had killed another boy and that he must be punished. "But please don't let them kill him. He is a little boy, and he never has been in trouble before."

I could only promise her that I would do my best. I had little confidence that anyone could stop the process under way to execute him. If a jury had been selected at that time it would have been primed to vote guilty after the district attorney's opening statement or perhaps before it. With the assistance of another attorney with no more experience than I had, I became counsel in my first capital case. I could conjure up no winning strategy. I began by investigating the facts surrounding the killing.

I met Frank in a Bronx jail cell. He did not look much like Tarzan, and he did not grin or seem cocky. He was five feet four inches tall, and he weighed 120 pounds. He spoke with a stammer, and he was still in shock with fear. Before we discussed the facts regarding the circumstances of the shooting, I asked how he got his nickname. He said he was not called Tarzan. "I saw the movie, and I liked Taza," he said.

The film, then current, was *Taza, Son of Cochise.* Rock Hudson played the title role, and Jeff Chandler was his legendary father, Cochise. In the film, Taza promised his dying father that he would keep the tribe united and at peace. Frank was a member of a gang called the Navajos, and he had chosen Taza as his role model. We still had no defense, but I was beginning to learn the public relations campaign against my client had been entirely fabricated.

Billy, the victim, was six feet tall, a football player at his high school who had planned to enter the Air Force Academy. He was not the innocent young man who went for a walk on the street and was killed by a total stranger as was often reported. He was known as a bully in the gang he belonged to, the Redwings, and he was shot in a gang confrontation with the Navajos. There were, of course, two versions of what had transpired that evening. Each gang blamed the other. Neither version, however, bore any resemblance to the story the media had created and sold.

Whatever the provocation, Frank had fired the killing shot, and it was not in self-defense, as he freely confessed to the police when they arrested him and when he produced the weapon. Our only hope was that the jury might choose the verdict of murder in the second degree, which could not result in an execution. How then, given the atmosphere, could we proceed?

I obtained a list of the names of the members of the grand jury from which the indicting grand jury in this case was drawn. There were many names, and none of them appeared to be Latino. I found a linguistics expert who was prepared to testify that there were no Puerto Ricans on the grand jury list. I filed a motion challenging the indictment, stating that Puerto Ricans had been deliberately prohibited from grand jury service in the Bronx. We suspected that blacks too had been barred from serving on the grand jury, but that issue could not be resolved by merely reading the names. When we inquired into the process by which the grand jurors were chosen, it became clear that members of minorities had been systematically excluded. Known as the Special Jury System, this racist method of jury selection had been established by the New York State Legislature and deemed to be constitutionally sound by the US Supreme Court in 1948 in *Moore v. New York*. Four justices dissented, stating that two defendants had been convicted of murder "not by a jury of their peers, not by a jury chosen from a fair cross-section of the community, but by a jury drawn from a special group of individuals." Those jurors lived in expensive apartments or townhouses, and members of minorities were excluded. The special jury law only applied to large counties or subdivisions where blacks and Puerto Ricans resided. Justices Black, Douglas, Rutledge, and Murphy, who wrote the dissent, became my favorites, and their words encouraged me to become a defense lawyer. As a member of the New York State

Legislature in 1961, I introduced legislation to abolish the Special Jury System. Four years later New York State abolished it.

Since the district attorney had chosen to try the case in the press, we were forced to reciprocate. I held a press conference that had little effect. My meetings with the editors of the Spanish press in New York were far more fruitful. Together we created a campaign to challenge the discrimination against Puerto Ricans carried out by the Bronx authorities, including the district attorney.

The Spanish-language press demanded to know why their readers were not permitted to serve on grand juries. Important Latino organizations became curious at first and then involved. The district attorney had no answers in public and little more in court. The campaign reached into churches and community organizations and took on an active life of its own. Schoolchildren discussed the issue in class, some of their parents in bars, while ministers and priests and rabbis addressed it from the pulpit.

I received a telephone call from Sullivan, the district attorney who had before then refused to talk with me about the case when I had called, replying at that time, "You want the facts? Read the newspapers." He cordially invited me to visit him that afternoon in his spacious and well-appointed office. I was politely ushered into the office by Andrew McCarthy, a Bronx assistant district attorney.

Sullivan stood up as I entered, offered his hand, and after we shook hands invited me to sit. He began, "Mr. Lane, I've got a problem."

I listened intently.

"I am up for reelection, and here in the Bronx the Puerto Ricans always vote Democratic. You have poisoned them against me. Our captains say it's a revolt. They won't vote for me. If you agree that there is no discrimination by me against them, I will give you what you want."

In the midst of that offer, McCarthy tried to interrupt by directing the discussion to a more appropriate exchange. "Mr. Sullivan means in looking over the facts of the case he now believes that perhaps a lesser included crime—"

Sullivan waved him away and added, "No bullshit, Andy. Mr. Lane wants the facts," and then he continued with his proposal.

We then began to bargain; the facts in the case were not mentioned because Sullivan had made it clear that neither were they relevant nor would they be the subject of the discussion.

"What will Frank Santana get out of the deal?" I asked.

Sullivan was nothing if not direct. He bluntly said, "His life." He paused and then explained. "He takes a plea to murder-one, and I don't recommend the death penalty."

That was a step, but it was clear I was being asked to make an agreement and that Sullivan could later change his mind and state that no such arrangement had been made. I made my counter-proposal. "How about Frank enters a plea to murder-two, which was the crime that should have been charged in the first place?"

Sullivan finally agreed on the condition that I would say publicly that there was no discrimination in the Bronx practiced against Puerto Ricans by him and that he was a friend of the Puerto Ricans.

I responded, "If I made such statements, nobody would believe me."

Finally the matter was resolved. I would withdraw my motion challenging the indictment and state that I was not certain that it would have been granted. The petition campaign would end. I would ask my friends at *El Diario* and *La Prensa* not to mention his name again, although I could not speak for them. Actually, the political reality had convinced me that the motion would probably be denied because, if it were granted, hundreds of people in prison after indictment by the same or a similar grand jury would likely file motions, and the court was both aware of and likely opposed to such a result.

Sullivan then added one more condition. I could not reveal our agreement for forty-eight hours while he took care of other matters. Sullivan had put out one fire that threatened his career. He had others to confront. He could not publicly endorse a plea agreement he had already entered into without the blessing of William Blankenship, who had become a legend—a community leader and a media-blessed guru. Blankenship had vowed to leave the contaminated city to bury his son in the pure "clean dirt" in the country. He called for the execution of "Tarzan Santana" and made it clear that he would move out of New York unless his demand was met. The *Journal-American* initiated a campaign to convince him to stay and help "us" fight the menace. Editorials and letters to the editor begged Blankenship to remain.

Sullivan met with Blankenship and lied to him, saying, "Lane's motion will win, and Santana will go free." In fact, if we did prevail, another grand jury, more fairly selected, would have been impaneled and a new indictment would have been returned. Sullivan also said that the jury would probably acquit the defendant of murder-one in the belief that murder-two was a better charge. "When that happens, Santana walks," Sullivan advised the distressed father.

In murder-one cases the prosecution includes lesser counts, often murder-two, manslaughter-one, and manslaughter-two, giving the jury the power to select. Frank, who had freely confessed to the killing, would have been fortunate to escape the death penalty at trial; he was not about to be set free. Of course, Sullivan knew all that, but Blankenship did not. Blankenship was distraught but not yet convinced.

Sullivan added that while Santana would go free, "Lane will have a holiday blackening your son's name. He is an experienced trial lawyer and good at that." Nothing resembling the truth was contained in those warnings, including the statement about my experience. Sullivan then offered a solution. "If you ask for mercy, you know, have one of the press people you work with write up a statement, then we can send Santana to prison for life and both you and Billy will be even bigger heroes than now."

That approach appealed to Blankenship as a means of escaping from the quandary Sullivan had articulated. On June 8, 1955, he appeared in a courtroom crowded with the press and addressed the judge.

"I am here in the spirit of Christian forgiveness." He urged leniency for "young Frank Santana." "Tarzan" had been edited out of his repertoire. He added, "The defendant is the product of our social environment. All society should be made to share its proper part for guilt in this crime."

The *New York Times* quoted those words under a sub-headline that read "Blankenship, Victim's Father, Asks Mercy for Santana."[1]

He closed, wiping a tear from his eye, with his most compelling one-liner. "This is what my loving son Billy would have wanted me to do." There was a respectful silence in the court.

I looked at the smiling prosecutors, and I thought that Sullivan was satisfied. He was not; he was still concerned that voters might conclude that he had improperly allowed Frank to escape the electric chair. McCarthy rose to speak for the district attorney's office. It was a speech for the press assembled in the front rows and filling the jury box, meant to appear as if the district attorney's office were addressing the court after the business that concerned the judge had been concluded.

McCarthy launched into an unprecedented and scathing attack upon the dead boy. We were still in the dark ages of criminal trial procedure, and prosecutors were not constrained or even encouraged to share their findings with the defense. Sullivan's files were sealed and were never disclosed. We were never able to discover how much of McCarthy's rhetoric was accurate.

"He was not quite the innocent" he had been made out to be, McCarthy began. He was no "model boy." He continued, his voice rising in outrage, "Billy Blankenship was a bully; he was a troublemaker; he ran with a gang called the Redwings." The district attorney's office had determined, he roared, that on the night of the shooting, "Billy had been out spoiling for a fight." He added that it was Blankenship, while towering over Frank, who had initiated the quarrel. In conclusion, McCarthy said theatrically and almost in a regretful whisper, "Blankenship had contributed to his own tragedy."

||||||

Although my office was located in East Harlem, my law practice extended beyond that community. I represented many hundreds of tenants in the neighborhood facing eviction, loss of basic services such as heat and water, and the horror of living in rat- and roach-infested tenements. A case-by-case approach, while necessary, was not adequate. I set up sessions in school auditoriums to advise tenants of their rights and helped organize tenant councils and visits to city officials and agencies to remind them of their unfulfilled responsibilities. When all else failed, we organized rent strikes, paying the rent into a landlord and tenant court but withholding it from the landlords until they met their obligations under the law.

El Diario de Nueva York and *La Prensa* were the two widely read daily newspapers published in Spanish in New York City. *La Prensa* was a bit more staid, and *El Diario* slightly more innovative. Later they merged and became the largest Spanish daily in New York, *El Diario La Prensa.* Since I had been actively challenging the jury system, I was strongly supported in that effort by the Spanish press. Later I met with the publisher of *El Diario*, and we decided that I would establish a free legal clinic at the offices of the newspaper. There was such a great response that we were required to perform legal triage.

At one meeting with Mayor Wagner and the commissioners of relevant agencies, an official began to lecture the members of the audience about their role in creating the rat problem. Pedro Canino, a community leader, responded, "The pipes to our buildings leak, and the city and the landlords do nothing when we complain. The garbage cans are rusty and filled with holes, and no lids are provided. But above all, these rats that bite our children when they sleep are not Puerto Rican rats. They were here before we arrived. They greeted us. They are American rats. Mr. Mayor and Mr. Commissioner, they are your rats, and you should do something about them."

Most of our clients needed assistance in dealing with their landlords or companies that had sold them furniture or appliances on an installment plan at outrageous rates. Where letters seemed appropriate, we drafted them and sent them out each night. Where legal action was required, we referred them to their local legal aid offices.

We discovered that national grocery chains sold food at higher rates in the oppressed communities than elsewhere, and we sought to remedy that situation through the press. We assisted those who wanted to register to vote and those who wished to volunteer for jury duty. We made it clear that we would not accept payment for those services, although many of our clients tried to show their gratitude. The bar association expressed its concern; apparently it thought that free legal services comprised unfair competition for cases that commercial lawyers were entirely uninterested in.

One of the most effective tenant associations in the city was the Met Council, and its largest and most reliable affiliate was the Yorkville Save Our Homes Committee led by Jane Benedict. Yorkville bordered on the southern portion of East Harlem, and when Jane asked to work together we immediately agreed. Together we led a diverse coalition to save rent control in New York. We organized rallies throughout the city, distributed many thousands of leaflets, and led more than fifteen hundred people to the state capital in Albany, where they met with their representatives to demand an end to the efforts to weaken the rent control laws.

When I spoke at the Third Annual Met Council Convention in November 1961, I called for action to force the tenement repair bill out of the legislative committee. Those campaigns met with resistance from established city and state politicians, and successes on some issues were mixed with defeats on others. Now, many years later, New York City can boast that its rent control laws are still in effect and approximately one million apartments still provide protection for tenants.[2]

||||||

On August 15, 1957, seven boys ranging in age from fifteen to eighteen were indicted for first-degree murder in a gang-related confrontation. Each faced the mandatory death penalty if convicted. The victim was Michael Farmer, a fifteen-year-old boy who had been beaten and stabbed at a public swimming pool in the Highbridge

Park area of upper Manhattan. Michael had been a member of the Jesters, a gang involved in a turf war with the Egyptian Dragons for rights to the pool. The case was assigned to Judge Irwin D. Davidson of the Court of General Sessions in New York County. It was the most publicized and sensational crime of the year, and the judge decided to make it more memorable by appointing a dream team of notable lawyers and by later writing a book about the trial.[3]

He selected four lawyers for each defendant; the lead counsel in each case was well qualified. Among them was James D. C. Murray, the dean of the criminal defense lawyers' bar; five former assistant district attorneys; a prominent public official; the general counsel of a major New York trade union; and J. Michael Solomon. I was the only attorney chosen by the accused. Louis Alvarez had been charged by the state with being the leader of the Dragons and the person who had killed the victim with a knife. His parents asked me to represent their son. They had no funds, but those appointed by the court were not adequately compensated either. Each was paid five hundred dollars for the trial, since the maximum permitted by the law was two thousand for counsel for each defendant.

I had been practicing law for just six years and was in the company of men who had been attorneys for decades. Murray had tried hundreds of murder cases, some before I was born. There was little collegial spirit among counsel; each was appropriately concerned only with the fate of his client, and most were more than willing to have the prosecutors focus their lethal attention upon the others. I knew that I would learn a great deal during the trial; I was less sanguine about my ability to aid my client. I had strong feelings about some of the factual aspects presented by the case. It was clear that my young client had carried a knife to the battle, that he had been consumed by anger, and that in a moment of fury he killed Farmer. When interrogated at the police precinct, he was threatened and beaten and, not knowing that he was protected by the Fifth Amendment, he confessed to whatever crimes were suggested by the gendarmes.

Less than a decade later the US Supreme Court, in *United States v. Miranda*, would rule in the matter of Ernesto Miranda, who was arrested for the theft of eight dollars from an employee of a bank and, while in custody, signed a written confession in which he asserted that he had committed that crime and had also kidnapped and raped a young woman a few days before he entered the bank.[4] The court ruling (with four of the justices in opposition to the majority of five justices who favored the concept) established the Miranda Warning, requiring police to give criminal suspects in custody a brief statement as to their rights. Absent that warning, courts are required to preclude incriminating admissions at trial.

Miranda had been convicted, and that verdict was set aside by the Supreme Court, since he had not been advised of his right to remain silent once arrested. The case was tried a second time, without the incriminating admissions, and again Miranda was convicted. He spent eleven years in prison; four years after he was paroled he was stabbed to death in a fight in a bar. A prime suspect was arrested by the police; ironically he chose to exercise his Miranda right to remain silent, and he was, therefore, released and never prosecuted.

This brief historical retrospective was, of course, of no value to the young man in the dock. I would have to find another way to try to save his life. He had committed the crime and if convicted should not escape punishment. Yet, here again the state had overprosecuted, seeking the death penalty for a teenager who should have been confronted with a long prison sentence.

The Jesters were almost exclusively composed of white Irish American kids; the Egyptian Dragons were almost all either black or Latino. The confrontation that led to the killing was racially motivated. The enormous publicity surrounding the case was based upon a white boy being killed by nonwhites or Puerto Ricans, as was the case in the death of Billy Blankenship two years earlier.

I filed a motion to dismiss on the grounds "that in the selection of jurors there has been a deliberate and systematic exclusion of persons of Puerto Rican origin operating to the detriment of the defendant in that he is now deprived of his rights under the New York State Constitution and the Fourteenth Amendment to the Constitution of the United States." In his book about the trial Davidson wrote that he "had hoped that the racial issue would not arise. Here it was before the trial was a half-hour old."

I called witnesses to demonstrate the inequity of the selection process. The jury commissioner, who had made the decisions about who would be on the jury, was an important witness in proving my case that the selection was unfair. He testified that he found his qualified jurors by reading gossip columns in which white Americans moving in high society were mentioned. He employed reverse telephone books from which he chose luxury buildings where only wealthy white Americans resided. This guaranteed, he observed, that there would be intelligent jurors. That hearing was of little help for my client, but it proved to be quite rewarding for me in New Orleans some years later.[5]

Judge Davidson told his wife over the weekend that he was going to deny the motion and only regretted that "an entire week has gone by, consumed by a technicality." While the judge's decision was not surprising, his concept that the right to a fair trial was a "technicality" was. At least we had established a basis for an appeal if Louis was convicted of murder-one.

The prosecutor made his opening statement to the jury, followed by several opening statements made by attorneys for the various defendants. The jury seemed to be as restless and bored as I was, hearing the same basic points made over and over and then repeated once again. I decided to take a different approach. I asked for permission to make my opening not before, but *after* the People concluded their case. "I base this," I said, "on the theory that the District Attorney has been very vague in his opening statement, and has not yet informed us under which theory of law he is trying to prove his case."

Seventeen members of the Egyptian Dragons had been arrested; only the seven old enough to be put to death were tried. The others, too young to be executed by state law, were tossed back, for the state was eager only to execute defendants who were tried. A number of those not tried were more involved in overt acts than were some of the defendants who did little more than be present at a meeting that was planned as a peace council between the competing gangs.

I studied and learned from the techniques of all of my famous colleagues, but I was particularly impressed with the work of Mike Solomon, who brought a sense of humanity into the courtroom and, I thought, had successfully caused the jurors to see our clients as flawed human beings but not monsters. Mike became my mentor and dear friend. The state's witnesses offered evidence that clearly implicated Louis and one other teenager in the death of the victim. I was able to demonstrate through them, however, that Louis had been drinking and appeared to be intoxicated just before the confrontation, thus raising a question about his ability to have committed an act with deliberation and premeditation, two elements required for a verdict of murder in the first degree.

The strongest testimony that related to the state of mind of my client was offered by prosecution witness Detective John Weber, who had questioned him at the precinct soon after his arrest. I knew that if I could demonstrate that Weber was not credible, the jury would likely not return a verdict of murder-one.

Weber was silent for a moment before he denied that he was known as "Crazy Weber" and "Strong-Arm John" by his fellow officers. He was six foot three and weighed 240 pounds.

I approached him and said, "Didn't you feint with your left and hit Alvarez with your right and then kick him as he fell to the floor?"

Weber answered, "I don't know what it means, 'feint with your left.'" After a pause, Weber threw a punch toward the jury and said, "I think it means that."

I stood there staring at the witness and then said, "So you do know what a feint is."

Weber was clearly rattled; he replied, incomprehensibly, "I didn't say that." Then, as if in explanation, he added, "I don't do boxing. I wrestle—at the YMCA."

The judge, in his book, concluded, "The police looked so bad I was beginning to believe that perhaps the defense had a better chance than I had originally surmised."

I had done the best that I could, but I did not know if it was enough. When I returned to my seat, Mike Solomon said, "Good work. You just saved the kid's life."

The jury rejected the impassioned plea by the prosecutors for a verdict calling for the death penalty. Louis was sentenced to twenty years. My colleagues told him, as he hugged me, that with good behavior he could be home when he was still a young man.

Afterward, I had a drink or two with Mike Solomon at a bar near the courthouse. I thought of poor Michael Farmer, dead before his life really started, of Louis Alvarez and the others who would spend years in a prison that had no redemptive characteristics, of the hundreds of kids throughout the city, probably all over the country (although my moments of depression could not take me on such a long journey), who were members of gangs, many for defensive purposes or to fill needs their family life did not address and who might one day destroy their lives as well as the lives of their contemporaries in a senseless and brief encounter. I told Mike that I did not believe in placing a person in a cage.

He said, "And since I know you also don't believe in capital punishment, what solution do you believe in?"

I said, "I don't know."

And now, today, that useless answer remains the only one I have.

Wassaic

|||||||||||||||||||||||||||

4

It was a warm summer day in 1955. I was drafting a brief in my East Harlem office when a handsome, bright, and charming young man, Graciliano Acevedo, furtively entered. He was, he said, a fugitive from Wassaic. I did not know what *Wassaic* was. I later learned that he was referring to the state facility named the Wassaic State School for Mental Defectives (no state euphemisms based upon the word *challenged* in those days) in Wassaic, New York.[1]

It was a "school" without teachers, classes, students, or any form of instruction. It was operated by the State Department of Mental Hygiene and directed by a medical doctor. It provided no services to its "patients." In reality, it was a huge facility for warehousing children and adults, many of whom were not "retarded" by the state's own standards.

Graciliano said he and many others had been confined there as punishment, some sentenced to imprisonment for life. The inmates, he said, had been beaten, tortured, and starved. He had just escaped from the state facility, was wanted, and added that if he was forced to return he would kill himself.

When the authorities of the state learned that he had met with me, they ordered me to reveal his address and cooperate with their efforts to capture him so that he could be locked up again in the institution. They said that they would arrest me as an accomplice and refer the matter to the Bar Association of New York in an effort to disbar me if I did not assist them. They added that two units of the New York state police were at that moment on the way to my office. I had been a lawyer for just a few years, and the threat terrified me.

I knew, of course, I would not comply with that demand and I would look into the charges made by my young pro bono client before deciding how to proceed. I thought about what immediate action I might take. *Leave the office at once* was my first thought, followed shortly by an exit. That, of course, was a temporary measure at best.

Before I left I called an acquaintance, a respected psychiatrist. I explained the circumstances to him and what it was I wished for him to do. He agreed. I then contacted Graciliano, and together we drove to the psychiatrist's fashionable office on the Upper West Side. Doctor and patient met for a considerable period of time while I read old magazines, apparently required to be available in all medical waiting rooms since the adoption of the Hippocratic oath in the fifth century BCE.

When they emerged, the doctor thanked me for calling upon him, and then wrote a letter addressed to me stating that Graciliano was his patient and that he believed that returning him to the Wassaic institution would cause him serious harm and perhaps death. We left armed with a document that provided at least a modicum of protection for my client and for me. He was not going back, I assured him.

Within a few days Graciliano, with the help of Ramon Diaz and his associates, rounded up other former Wassaic inmates. They came from the Bronx, Brooklyn, Queens, and the Lower East Side, Harlem, and East Harlem in Manhattan. Like Graciliano, most were fugitives from the institution.

I called Fern Marja, an investigative reporter at the *New York Post*, and told her what I had learned. She called contacts, all of whom vouched for the integrity of Paul H. Hoch, the commissioner of the

New York State Department of Mental Hygiene, who immediately denied the allegations made by Graciliano, whom he referred to as a patient.

Hoch did not know why my client had been sent to Wassaic or how long his sentence was. Since I had looked into the matter, talking with Graciliano, his mother, and other witnesses, I did discover the facts. Graciliano had had a brief affair with a woman several years older than he was. His mother felt it was inappropriate and made a call to the local police precinct for advice. Officers raided their home and took Graciliano in handcuffs to the prison in Wassaic that was posing as a mental institution and school.

I prepared a meticulous questionnaire, designed to establish not just the facts of life at Wassaic but the details as well, such as the number of bars on the solitary confinement cells, the size of the rooms, the color of the walls, a description of the straps—size and color—used to restrain inmates, the names and descriptions of the guards who were most brutal, specific statements about their misconduct including dates and the names of victims, and, above all, the names of other witnesses to those events. Clearly, none of those to be questioned could have anticipated the specific questions, and the answers would be similar only if truth was the common denominator.

We gathered the fugitives—black, white, Puerto Rican—in a suite of rooms. The questionnaire was administered contemporaneously in isolation to each of them by lawyers and doctors. Fern Marja was present. We met to compare the results. Our worst fears were confirmed; Wassaic was worse than we could have imagined.

We were overwhelmed by the body of evidence suggesting that for years—in fact, decades—felonious acts, including torture, beatings, and long-term solitary confinement, had been regularly committed against those unable to protect themselves. Many children had been cruelly bound in restraining sheets. I knew that the state had committed unspeakable crimes, but I doubted my ability to be an effective agent of change. If it were not for the fact that the misconduct was still ongoing, I might have given in to despair and taken no action. I was a twenty-eight-year-old lawyer in a storefront office in East Harlem that I had but recently opened. But the continuing barbaric acts against the least of these was with me each day and required me to take up a battle against the state of New York, one that I thought I could never win. When I later discovered that an African American boy, just fifteen years old, had been murdered by a guard and the crime covered up by the state employees, I knew that I had no choice; whatever the result and cost, I made the only possible decision.

The state served a notice upon me, setting a date for the mandatory return of Graciliano. I called Dr. George Etling, director of the Wassaic State School, and told him what we had discovered about the facility for which he was responsible. I told him that Graciliano would never return, and I invited him to bring an action against me in a court of his choice where all of the facts could be made public. I talked to Pete Khiss at the *New York Times*, and he and Fern called Etling for a comment.

Two days later Etling sent a letter to me stating that Graciliano had been discharged. Apparently a miracle had taken place while he was hiding out in East Harlem; he had become "unretarded" and no longer "defective." He achieved that new status without being treated, examined, or even interviewed by the authorities since his escape from Wassaic. Yet the state had in absentia pronounced him to be cured.

Later, when Graciliano was given an independent IQ test in Spanish, properly administered by a licensed examiner in Manhattan, this formerly classified "mental defective," with an IQ under 60 according to the Wassaic records, scored 115. Later, other inmates were similarly tested, and on average they likely scored higher marks on the IQ tests than did some of their callous and often brutal guards.

Etling evidently thought that Graciliano's release would end the matter. A reporter or two agreed that the matter had been successfully concluded. I considered Etling's precipitous action to be a confession of wrongdoing by the state, an admission that a young man had been falsely imprisoned. In my view, our modest effort to learn all of the relevant facts had just begun.

We continued our fact-finding efforts, and Fern communicated some of the results to the authorities. Finally, in an effort to convince us that all was well and that "those children are mentally defective, but they have active imaginations," Dr. Etling invited Fern and me to visit him in Wassaic.

During the interview in his office, Fern informed him that we had been told that the dining room was locked and the patients were not allowed to talk to one another. I was surprised that she revealed that information, since I thought she may have precluded our hopes of seeing the dining room while the inmates were present. I had great respect for Fern, and while I did not favor the ambush interviews that have now become common, I did believe that it was too early to reveal to Etling all we had discovered.

It soon became clear we approached the inquiry from different perspectives. Fern was a liberal reporter of integrity, and she, her editor, and her publisher maintained cordial relationships with those ultimately responsible for the almost unfathomable misconduct, including the Democratic governor and the much-praised state commissioner Hoch. I had less trust in the authorities and more faith in the words of my young clients. Fern's approach to Etling soon proved to be the path to entry.

Etling denied the charges. "Of course it is not locked. The patients wander around as they choose, and they chat quite a bit in the dining room." He invited us to have a private lunch with him in his own dining room attached to his office.

I said that we wanted to eat with the patients. Fern agreed with me. Etling tried again, stating, "I'm sure you will find the food better here and the atmosphere more relaxing." I assured him that I had no reason to disagree with his evaluation but that we felt quite strongly that we should visit the inmates' dining room. Etling reluctantly agreed to our request; he asked us to excuse him for a few minutes.

As we left his office, he picked up his telephone. I presumed he was ordering the guards to prepare for our visit.

We walked to the massive dining room; however, we could not enter since the doors were bolted and locked. There were more than four thousand inmates at the institution then. If a fire had broken out, the inmates would have been trapped. Etling called a guard so that we could enter the vestibule and then called another guard as we were confronted by another set of sturdy doors that were also locked and bolted. While visiting clients in prisons I had often encountered less security, except at a maximum-security prison for the most violent criminals.

We entered into an eerie scene, quite different from mess halls I had seen hundreds of times while I was in the armed forces and those I had visited in prisons. Hundreds of people were eating in absolute silence. The clicking sounds of knives and forks could be heard but not a sound from a human being.

I observed, "No one is talking; why is that, Dr. Etling?"

He said, "I guess that they don't feel like talking. There certainly is no rule against talking."

With that remark what remaining credibility he had with Fern came to a sudden and irrevocable end. Mine had long since fled after meeting with the clients months earlier. Fern insisted upon trying the food. We went to the mess hall line and were served something that we could not identify, and when Fern tasted it she gagged and almost threw up. Etling did not sample the fare. As I saw hundreds of people, most of them young and thin, devouring the food, I felt obligated to eat it. I consumed some of it. I knew then that if I were imprisoned there I would try to escape before the next meal was served.

I walked up to one young man. I asked him how the food was. He looked around in obvious fear and then whispered, "Don't talk. You can't talk in here or they throw you in solitary and beat you." I later spoke to that young man, Reinaldo Otero, after our efforts resulted in his release, and he talked about the day we had met. "I knew you were coming that day. We heard about what you were doing for us on the outside, and we prayed you would come to see for yourself because we knew they were lying to you." I asked how he knew I would be there *that* day. He said, "We knew it because of the food. It was the best we ever had except for Thanksgiving and Christmas." For the first time in that long struggle, I could not hold back tears.

Fern was convinced that conditions at Wassaic were intolerable. Wisely, she also wanted to conduct her own investigation before she wrote about the conditions. She was going to try to make arrangements with Etling to allow her free access to the entire institution. It did not seem likely to me or to Fern that Etling would allow that. Since time was of the essence and the suffering of innocents had not ceased so far as we knew, a public airing of some sort was necessary.

I wrote to the governor of New York, W. Averell Harriman. He was the millionaire son of the last and greatest of the nineteenth-century railroad barons, but unlike his famous Republican father, the governor was a New Deal Democrat. I informed him that conditions at the state institution were "barbaric" and the children were being subjected to "uncivilized treatment." I offered to submit documentation for each of the specific charges that I had made: long periods of solitary confinement for minor infractions, children bound for weeks in restraining sheets unable to move any part of their bodies except their heads, some of them being beaten by attendants as they were lying helpless. Among the infractions that resulted in mistreatment were talking in the dining room, refusal to work at a job assignment that was too difficult for them, or not responding immediately when given an order. Harriman had supported President Roosevelt in 1937 when he sought to strengthen the child labor laws. These were the very laws his state institution was violating almost two decades later. I asked for the appointment of an independent citizens' commission to investigate the accusations. The governor hesitated.

Fern did not; she pressed Etling for permission to visit the institution and to agree that no area in the facility would be closed to her. Of course, since I had written to the governor I was excluded. I recently shared Fern's series with several friends. Each person who read the articles responded with tears or outrage, often both. I would prefer to cite a readily available source, but the *Post* is not a newspaper of record, as is the *New York Times*, and it maintains no archive. It appears that the only place where the articles may be found is through a physical visit to a special section of the New York Public Library in Manhattan.[2]

I quote or paraphrase below portions of the Marja investigative report, a historic series that remains the definitive work that ultimately led to improving the lives of thousands of oppressed children and adults held captive and mistreated by the state.

On August 17, 1955, Fern's first article in a three-part series was prominently published by the *New York Post* under a banner headline: "The Wassaic Horror: Inhuman Treatment for Young Inmates." She referred to my letter to Harriman and stated, "No matter what the outcome, this reporter has witnessed enough to know that overcrowded, understaffed Wassaic is employing treatment techniques that were regarded as cruel and inhuman before the turn of the century." She listed the many accusations that I had made, asserting that children at the institution were regularly and brutally beaten with fists, sticks, chains, rocks, broom handles, and keys. Children, some six and seven years old, had been struck on an almost daily basis; Puerto Rican children, hundreds of them, had not been tested for years and were beaten for not responding to orders promptly, even though they spoke no English and not one of the guards at Wassaic could speak Spanish.

She concluded, "This reporter, given free access to the institution by the Director, Dr. George W. Etling, corroborated a substantial portion of these charges either directly or through conversations with a score or more of the inmates, whose stories checked on every major point."

In the first article, Fern reported that she had visited several buildings while accompanied by Etling. Two of the structures were "maximum security buildings." She asked Etling to show her the seclusion areas. "He took me to two maximum security buildings where the cells were merely airless rooms that were little better than sweatboxes. I walked through a corridor lined on both sides with tile and steel cells about 7½ by 8½ feet and a metal door with a grated peep hole through which the prisoners stared out like animals."

As she was about to talk to one patient, the attendant told her, "He's only been in there a short time." She wrote, "I asked him how long he had been in solitary and he answered, 'one week,'" adding that he was being punished for attempting to run away from the institution.

The General Orders of the Mental Hygiene Department and the laws of the state of New York specify the rules for the use of "restraint and seclusion": "Protective restraint or seclusion is to be employed only for satisfactory surgical or medical reasons, or to prevent the patient from injuring himself or others." Even when a patient, for surgical or medical reasons, is restrained or placed in seclusion or solitary confinement, the law requires "the maximum period of continuous seclusion shall not exceed three hours in the daytime, and the patient shall be visited every hour day and night." Fern reported that while the attendant said that he let the boys in seclusion out of their cells "every couple of hours," the patient responded, "I ain't been out. I ain't been out of here the whole time." The reporter added that neither Etling nor the attendant contradicted him and that the same scenario reoccurred "almost every time I spoke to a patient in solitary."

One patient had been in solitary confinement since April 6, more than ninety days before Fern visited him. When she visited the next patient, the attendant led her away and said that he is "a low-grade. He takes his clothes off."

"Oh yes," said Etling. "That's the one who can't stand to have anything on him. Takes everything off and smears feces all over." Fern said that "the 'low-grade' had been locked in for two weeks."

She visited another patient in solitary confinement. On that occasion Etling asked the attendant, "Why is he here?"

The attendant responded, "He's the boy who took plums from your tree, doctor."

Fern asked the patient if he had anything to read, and he replied, "No, they don't let you read."

Fern turned to the attendant for an explanation. The attendant said, "It's just routine."

Etling spoke to the attendant, saying, "I don't see why they can't read."

Fern wrote:

> In a third cell was a patient who had spent all but six of his twenty-four years in Wassaic. "This is my first time in trouble," he said earnestly. "I know I did wrong." Just what wrong had he done? "I was talking in the dining room. I'll never do it again."
>
> In another room, a chunky youth addressed Etling: "I don't mind getting punishment for things I do, but I don't like to get punishment for things I don't do." For the first time the director sounded a trifle severe. "We don't call it punishment," he said reprovingly. "We call it discipline." "Well," said the boy, "I got one week of discipline for not drinking coffee."

When she visited one building she noted that the wards were vast, with three rows of cots and sixty beds in all. Between them there was barely more than a foot or two. The sour smell of sweat was overpowering. In the August heat the only window, opaque to prevent the prisoners from looking out, was shut tight.

On August 18, Fern's second article was published under the banner headline, "Young Inmates Tell of Horror at Wassaic."

> This is the story of six boys; but there is only one story, since the facts are almost identical. Each of the youngsters spent from seven months to eight years at the Wassaic State School for

Mental Defectives between 1942 and 1955. Interviewed separately, they filled out individual questionnaires that checked out on every major point.

All had been locked in solitary confinement at least once as a disciplinary measure, with one youth reaching such an acute state of depression that he attempted suicide.

All but one had been beaten by attendants, one so severely that he still carries a head scar. All but one had been immobilized in restraining sheets for days at a time, for real or imagined violations.

All had witnessed widespread homosexuality, and one had himself contracted VD after having intimate relations with a fellow patient.

Five of the six are Puerto Ricans who had serious language handicaps at the time of their commitment. Their IQ could not be adequately determined, since the test was given in English, and they spoke Spanish.

The lead editorial published by the *New York Post* that day was entitled "The Wassaic Horror." It began, "Surely no editorial should be needed to supplement Fern Marja's exposure of wretchedness and inhumanity at the Wassaic State School for Mental Defectives." It ended, "No routine investigation by state officials will be an adequate answer to these revelations. What is needed is an independent inquiry by a special commission whose members are free of any compulsion to cover up. Each day such an inquiry is delayed compounds the state's crime."

The last of the series of three articles was published on Friday, August 19. Although Harriman had not replied to my letter, he responded to both it and the articles by appointing Hoch to secretly investigate the charges made by many inmates and former inmates against the institution for which he was ultimately responsible. I was doubtful about the outcome since the inquiry was being conducted behind closed doors and by the bureaucrat with the most to lose. At best I was cautiously hopeful.

While Harriman had ordered "a full scale investigation of conditions at the Wassaic State School," he apparently ignored the fact that many of the criminal acts at Wassaic had taken place during Hoch's administration; Hoch had never visited Wassaic.

Hoch at once stated, "I will stop immediately the use of solitary confinement and restraining sheets for disciplinary purposes."

While I was relieved that he issued that edict in terms of its impact upon the many tortured children at the institution, the statement by Hoch was bizarre because it merely stated that the state would stop violating the law. In fact, Hoch had been the chief research psychiatrist at the New York State Psychiatric Institute before he had been appointed commissioner. It was at that institute that eighteen of the twenty doctors "received their psychiatric training from an eleven month, one day a week special course given to them after they went to work at Wassaic."

Hoch added that personnel from his department had questioned "physicians, supervisors, and all ward employees who had supervised the patients." No one from Hoch's office had ever sought to speak with the patients who had made the numerous specific statements that I referred to in my letters to the governor or who were interviewed by Marja.

Months of work began. I worked with former inmates and their friends; we located additional witnesses, almost all fugitives from Wassaic, in addition to some who had been discharged or who were on authorized leave.

Nevertheless, it was not surprising when Hoch issued his report to the governor on October 27, 1955, stating that after "an exhaustive investigation" by his department, he had determined that there was "no substantial evidence" of the abuse of mental patients at Wassaic.[3] One had to question his standards, since one child had died after having been beaten.

We met that evening at my office, Graciliano and a few of his friends, still fugitives, a couple of trial lawyers, and the psychiatrist who had assisted us. There were some high-level professionals and a number of courageous kids in that room. Before our struggle with the state was over, each of us had contributed our services over a period of more than a year. No one was compensated or had out-of-pocket expenses reimbursed. None of the abused young men ever suggested that they would like to sue the state. Everyone was there in an effort to challenge and possibly change a barbaric system committed to covering up its crimes. The false imprisonment and mistreatment of hundreds, still ongoing, were beyond our ability to alter. That evening was a meeting of the defeated.

In an act of desperation and with little hope that we could prevail, I wrote an open letter to the governor stating that I should at least be permitted to appear before some person with authority so that our side could be heard. Pete Khiss from the *New York Times* and Fern Marja made sure that the authorities knew of the letter and the reporters' interest in the issue and that the public was informed as well. The state agreed to allow me to make a presentation at its offices in New York City, but the public and the press would be barred from our meeting.

Since the state considered the case closed and wished to maintain that status, their first error was agreeing to meet with me. A more serious mistake was the decision to exclude the press about such a serious public matter. The date and place were set, November 17, 1955, at 270 Broadway in Manhattan, the office of the deputy commissioner of the state mental hygiene agency, Arthur W. Pense, who would meet with me.

I suggested to Pense that instead of my telling him what the witnesses would probably say, it would be better if a couple or more met with him. He was reluctant at first; he was a doctor, not a lawyer. I asked him how the excluded public and press would react if they learned that the person conducting the inquiry favored hearsay over direct admissible testimony. The state reluctantly agreed; they didn't want me to be there in the first place, and they were less inclined to allow their victims to be present. But so long as it was all confined to their offices, and they would not allow a transcript to be prepared, they felt adequately protected. Certainly neither the public nor the press would be admitted. We could speak, but we would only be heard by a state official who had already characterized the allegations as nonsense and who had praised the commitment to excellence exemplified by two distinguished doctors, Hoch and Etling.

I invited the press and the public to the hearing. I said that we were faced with a somewhat ambiguous situation; there would be a public hearing except for the fact that the public and the press would be denied admission by the state. Rule one of a list of one rule: *Never tell the press that they cannot attend.* Even a story of little interest to the media becomes irresistibly fascinating when the press is banned.

We created a quasi-public hearing from a decision that there would be no hearing. Build it and they will come. They came. The media—television crews, newspaper reporters, radio interviewers—all tried to crowd into a small reception room while many more filled the corridors.

A state authority exited the hearing room to announce that the press was banned, and he ordered them to leave. Of course, no one left. I responded to the press that every ten minutes I would take a break, leave the hearing room, and make a full report to the media as to what had just transpired. It would be "breaking news."

I did so for the entire day as witness after witness spoke. The witnesses were all, except one, former inmates who had been brutalized at Wassaic and who had witnessed almost countless acts of outrageous conduct. The final witness was Fern Marja. The facts were out.

We proved that one woman, sent to the institution from the time of her birth because her mother was not married, was confined there for more than forty years, never tested, and never released. Her IQ was slightly over 100. We demonstrated that a number of the guards were sadistic and routinely engaged in torture, including sexual torture by holding the genitals of young men against extremely hot radiators and raping young women.

The case, closed by Hoch at the end of October, had been reopened three weeks later by the victims, the witnesses, and the attention of the *New York Times* and the *New York Post* as well as numerous radio and television stations. Reporting that Hoch had said that there was "no substantial evidence" of abuse, the *Times* provided a meticulously accurate summary of the testimony before Pense, demonstrating substantial repeated abuse.

During our continuing inquiry, I stayed in an isolated motel near Wassaic. Unable to sleep one night, I went for a short walk. I heard a sound behind me and turned to see Pete Khiss lumbering behind me in the shadows. I stopped, and he walked up to me. My look said, *What are you doing?* He shrugged. "You know, from the viewpoint of the attendants you are threatening their jobs. You shouldn't walk around here alone."

Former patients and parents of children still incarcerated came forward with additional facts. Many corroborated what others had said; some added gruesome new evidence. I discovered an eyewitness to the beating and kicking of a fifteen-year-old African American boy by a guard. According to a witness, the boy had asked the attendant to open a locked door, and the guard kicked the youngster in the stomach "as hard as he could." The victim collapsed, doubled up in pain, and then vomited. He remained in bed for three days, crying and unable to move. No medical care was given to him, not even an examination. He was then moved to the hospital where he died. The Dutchess County district attorney's office said it was investigating the possible homicide. The records of the State Department of Mental Hygiene had listed the cause of death as "natural." And that was not the first time that Hoch had covered up a death.

Hoch, when questioned by the *New York Times* about the death and other allegations of brutality, said, "These things have to be looked into. I don't like to make detailed statements before the thing is finished or investigated. Many incidents go back several years. I really don't know what went on there four or five years ago."

Those remarks were published by the *Times* on December 3, 1955, just over a month after the *Times* had printed Hoch's statement about his "exhaustive investigation" and his conclusion that there was "no substantial evidence" of abuse.

The state denied everything as long as it could do so feasibly and, as is the way with great bureaucracies, a little longer than decency allows. In the end restraint was ended, solitary confinement wards were demolished, and reading rooms and libraries took their place. Books were made available, and tests were administered in Spanish for the first time in the history of the state. Many guards were fired, and some were prosecuted.

Above all, many hundreds of inmates were released. They had been confined illegally and improperly at Wassaic as well as at other institutions throughout the state. That was our qualified victory, brought about by the resolve and courage of those who had been brutalized.

In the end there was no real victory and there were no heroes, except the survivors and two reporters, Fern and Pete, who were just doing their jobs, as the lives of so many innocents could not be adequately restored. No one in charge of the institution or charged with the responsibility of monitoring it was ever prosecuted. No official was even reprimanded.

|||||||

The faces of those tortured children and adults were with me for years and now revisit as I write this painful chapter. I have also wondered about their tormentors—not the poorly educated, vulgar, and underpaid guards; my thoughts have turned to Etling and Hoch.

Etling was undecipherable for me. Did he really know nothing about the institution to which he allowed free access to Fern and to me? Did he not know that even a cursory inquiry, in which he was complicit, would prove that all of his assurances to us were fabrications? He remained as director at Wassaic for another eighteen years, at which time he retired with honors and effusive praise from the state officials.

A few months after the stories about the homicide at Wassaic were published, Hoch was honored by the International Rho Pi Phi Pharmaceutical Fraternity for his "outstanding leadership in the research and treatment of mental illness, and his dedication to the welfare of its victims." He was given the organization's prestigious Man of the Year Award. Perhaps Hoch's greatest accomplishment was his ability to hide his past. He was a paid CIA consultant for MKULTRA, the agency's illegal creation charged with discovering new methods of mind control. For MKULTRA, Hoch performed a lobotomy on a conscious victim, injected others with drugs that either permanently destroyed their ability to function or in some cases killed them, and tested various "warfare agents" on unsuspecting patients, and then covered up the cause of death with false certificates. The full extent of his criminal activity will likely never be known, since the CIA destroyed most of the relevant files after a committee of the US Senate sought to examine them. Sufficient evidence survived so that Hoch could have been prosecuted for murder and numerous other crimes. Instead, he was given the authority to govern all of New York State's mental institutions for many years, having been reappointed by Rockefeller in 1959. He remained as the commissioner until his death on December 15, 1964.

Mid-Harlem Community Parish   5
||||||||||||||||||||||||||||||||||||||||||||||||||||||||||||||||||||||||||||||||||||||||||||

After Wassaic, I returned to my office and my clients in East Harlem. On one wonderful day I made the acquaintance of Reverend Eugene St. Clair Callender when one of his parishioners in the central Harlem church was arrested for some minor offense. I met with Gene, Johnny, the young man who was fifteen years old, and his mother.

I talked with the relevant witnesses and concluded that the defendant probably did not do the deed and that in any event would likely be acquitted at trial. The defendant, his mother, and I arrived at the Criminal Courts Building at 100 Centre Street in New York County at ten minutes after nine, anticipating the judge's scheduled entrance in twenty minutes. In my lifetime of practice I have never been late for an appearance except on November 22, 1963, when I learned of the death of John Kennedy. Judges are never late either. It is not a courtroom until they arrive, and thus even should a judge arrive several hours after the appointed hour, he is always just on time.

We were to be arraigned before Judge J. Randall Creel, a judge who could have been assigned from central casting in Hollywood both in terms of looks—tall, distinguished, patrician, gray hair, with chiseled handsome features—and in terms of his knowledge of the law, equal to that of any aspiring starlet. It was generally accepted that the judge, a kind of legally trained dilettante, was the heir to some soap or cosmetic fortune.

The episode went something like this after our case was called.

Judge: Mr. Lane, your client will write an essay about Jackie Robinson or Ralph Bunche. It should be about four hundred words. Do you understand that, Mr. Johnson?

Client: Yes, sir. [*Aside to me*] What's an essay? What's a bunch?

Judge: Mr. Lane, you and the young man will return before me so that he can read the essay in about four months' time. The clerk will give you the exact date. Thank you. [*To the clerk*] Next case.

Lane: A moment please, Your Honor.

Judge: [*Firmly*] Was I not clear?

Lane: Very clear, Your Honor.

Judge: Then what is the problem? I have a busy calendar.

Lane: That is the problem. You clearly stated that my client, who is presumed to be innocent at this moment, was not given a chance to enter his plea of not guilty to the charge; instead he was assigned a task to do. Innocent people should not be given assignments, even enlightened ones.

Judge: Mr. Lane, explain to your client he is to write the essay.

Lane: I can't, Your Honor, since I don't understand how you can impose a punishment before a finding.

Judge: [*Getting very angry, appearing red in the face and much less patrician*] He won't write the essay? [*Now almost shouting*] He won't write the essay?

Client: I'll write it. [*To me*] He's getting mad.

Lane: [*To client*] You don't even know what it is. [*To judge*] I have explained to this young man how our system of justice works. He cannot be ordered to do anything at this stage except enter a plea and then stand trial. If convicted, an essay would be an appropriate punishment. At this stage it is impossible to square your order with his constitutional guarantees.

I had made the unforgivable error. I had mentioned the Constitution in an American courtroom. The judge was justifiably enraged.

Judge: That does it. [*To the clerk*] What is the bail in this case?

Clerk: Five hundred dollars.

Judge: Bail increased to one thousand dollars. Bailiff, remove the defendant.

Client: [*To me*] I'll write it, whatever it is.

Johnny was desperately looking about for a pencil to start writing something. His mother was sobbing. I agreed that the essay would be written. The judge smiled and reduced bail to five hundred dollars, and Johnny was released by the two officers who had just been about to drag him off to the dreaded Tombs.

I called Gene to apprise him of the events. He was a soft-spoken man with a rich voice and a gentle manner. It was generally not easy to determine if he was upset. However, he seemed quite agitated as he heard my report. Finally he could maintain his feelings no longer; he said quite firmly, "No essay should be written." I agreed, but I added that Johnny and his mother had one objective, to keep the young man out of jail. Gene said he would raise the additional funds for bail if the judge was about to modify his order. The reverend met with his parishioners, mother and son, and explained the matter to them, and they agreed that no essay would be written. I was to inform the court on the return date of their decision.

Many weeks later on the appointed day, we were greeted by an unprecedented courthouse scene as we tried to make our way toward the courtroom. Scores of young men, almost all African American or Puerto Rican, each holding a few sheets of paper, crowded the corridors, the anteroom, the witness room, and every available space outside the courtroom. Most were speaking aloud, rehearsing for the big judicial audition.

The courtroom was bursting with humanity. Scores more young men with scripts, reading quietly to themselves, lawyers, newspaper reporters, and curious observers filled every seat and stood in every available space. Judge Creel, smiling benignly, was flanked by a group of well-dressed ladies and gentlemen who nodded with obvious approval as each defendant stumbled through a prepared text about some black or Puerto Rican person of note.

I approached the clerk in an attempt to learn when our case might be called. "Won't reach yours for a couple of hours," he growled. I saw Jack Roth who covered the crime scene for the *New York Times*. "Some zoo, huh, Mark?" Before I could respond he said, "It's my fault. Now I know how Dr. Frankenstein felt when the monster began to move on its own."

I asked Jack what was going on. He explained. "Do you remember the story I did about half a year ago about the kid who wrote a song for Judge Creel?" I did vaguely remember an odd story about a young man who was both very musical and clearly guilty of some misdemeanor. After he had been convicted, the judge, instead of imposing some more routine sentence, such as probation or time in a reformatory, had ordered him to write a song about how crime does not pay. He had complied and performed it in court, and the judge had been praised as an innovative jurist. "So," Jack continued, "Creel has stored up all of these kids, invited the board of education, professors, city council members, every big shot in the city, to watch these kids read their stupid compositions."

When he asked what I was doing there, I told him what had transpired and what I had planned. His face lit up. "Terrific! I'll get your case called at once. I gotta be out of here soon." The case was called within minutes.

Judge: Good morning, gentlemen. How are you this morning?

Client and lawyer: [*In unison*] Good morning, Judge. Fine, thank you.

Judge: [*Consulting a file*] And, Mr. Johnson, do you have your essay ready?

Fear had set in again. Johnny was trying to answer. I held his arm to contain him and spoke.

Lane: No, Your Honor. No essay.

Judge: Well, that is all right. Would your client like a little more time?

Lane: It's not a question of time, Your Honor. My client is innocent. He is presumed to be innocent. He should not be required to accede to any form of punishment. I have instructed him not to write an essay. [*Gasps from the assembled officials*] We are prepared to enter a plea of not guilty and to go to trial. We are entitled to a speedy trial. I believe that has already been denied. No essay.

Judge: Well, Mr. Lane, that is perfectly fine if that is the way you feel. No compulsion was ever intended. I'm sure you know that. [*Smiles and nods from the elite galley*] So if the clerk will just set a date for trial we'll move on to the next case.

We were about to leave. I reluctantly rejected the thought of responding to the "no compulsion" assertion since the case was finally back on track, when the judge, feeling quite secure and very much in control of the situation, unctuously added:

Judge: [*Looking at his colleagues but addressing me as well*] Very well, but it would have been better if Mr. Lane had presented his view of this matter at the outset instead of waiting four months. Thank you. Next matter.

The temptation was too great to resist.

Lane: Well, I did just that, Your Honor. I told you at the time of the arraignment that, with all due respect, it was improper for you to act in violation of my client's rights. You responded by threatening to throw him in jail at once for exercising his constitutional rights.

A silence ensued, broken only by the *tsk-tsk*ing of the privileged panel, whose members shifted uncomfortably, glanced at the judge, and then looked away. Some began to look at their watches, and many suddenly remembered other pressing engagements and excused themselves from the embarrassing scene. The judge looked at me as if he would never forget the episode and my role in it. Jack Roth wrote, and the *New York Times* published the next morning, an accurate account of the affair. The attempt to transform the criminal courts building into the downtown annex of the Juilliard School for the performing arts had been precipitously terminated.

As we left the courtroom I noticed that my client had some writing paper in his hand. I asked what it was, and he showed it to me. It began, "Ralph Bunche, orphaned at an early age . . ." I said, "Orphaned at an early age?" He said, "That's what it said in the book I copied."

A few weeks later the case was tried before Judge Creel. He gave the impression that he had forgotten the incident. His rulings were fair; Johnny was found not guilty.

After that Gene Callender and I became a team. The most reverend Eugene St. Clair Callender arrived in central Harlem during the 1950s. I became the attorney for his oppressed parishioners; we soon became fast friends, and, Batman and Robin-like, together we sought out and confronted evil and discrimination wherever they lurked. And in our world, they lurked a lot. One nearby church memorialized the continuing nature of the problem with a permanent notice on its bulletin board that read PROTEST MEETING EVERY THURSDAY NIGHT. We were good friends immersed primarily in the struggles of the people of Harlem. I could not have wished for a better partner.

It did not require much insight to conclude that most of the problems involving criminal conduct were related to illicit drugs. A heroin habit was an expensive addiction, and heroin in our community was a problem of epidemic proportions. Robbery, burglary, or enlisting in the drug trade were the leading available options to those who were controlled by their addiction.

Those seeking assistance to fight their addictions had remarkably even fewer options. If the addict was a minor he could surrender to the Riverside Hospital in New York City, the only institution for treatment of those with a drug addiction disease. For an adult, there was no facility available in New York State. In fact the only place available was a prison located in Lexington, Kentucky. The addict was required to pay his own fare to get there in order to enter a strange world in a strange area. Over the years I met a number of young men and women who were arrested for robbery in an effort, they said, to obtain funds for that roundtrip.

Gene and I thought that there must exist a better way. After numerous pleas to state and federal authorities went unanswered, we resolved that we would invent a free clinic in our community and staff it with professionals. The facts that we were not doctors, had no access to medicine, and no license available to us were considered challenges, not deterrents. We did have a plan.

We would utilize some rooms in the upper floors in the tenement building that housed Gene's church, the Mid-Harlem Community Parish, which was, as the name indicated, set in a central location at Seventh Avenue and 122nd Street. We would pick one evening each week to invite addicts to come for counseling. They were required to bring at least one chaperone who was committed to staying with the applicant for ninety-six continuous hours. We would have nurses and doctors who would dispense sleeping pills to sedate the patient in the evening and pills to awake and energize the patient in the morning. No other drugs would be allowed. After four days the major physical grip of the habit would be broken, although much additional work would remain. Social workers and psychologists provided assistance.

A placement program would be instituted in an attempt to find jobs for the recovering patients.

Federal and state police agencies, having heard of our plan since we broadcast it widely in the community, began to investigate. The most popular talk show in New York at that time was the Barry Gray radio program. I had been a guest there many times, and when I called Barry asking if Gene and I could have an hour to discuss our plans, he asked if what we were doing was legal. I said, "Probably not."

We announced our plan to an audience of hundreds of thousands, and challenged the authorities to take action by setting up professional clinics and to refrain from interfering with us until they did.

It was a free clinic—really free as no fees were charged of those seeking help and not one minister, lawyer, doctor, nurse, social worker, or psychologist ever asked for any payment. Gene and I were there every day and evening for months. Numerous men and women were successful in kicking their habit. The police never interfered. Among the first to graduate were Teddy Richardson and James Allen. Both of them played important roles during the early days of the clinic.

Teddy became my paralegal even before that term was known. He was extremely knowledgeable, as he had some experience dealing with policeman from his shoplifting days, and I learned more from him during our association than he did from me. He also was a pretty good bridge player, and he joined in our contests, which began late each evening after the clinic closed and often continued until breakfast.

James was a very thoughtful, quiet, and sweet man who believed that God had given him his life back so that it could be devoted to service. He thought that he should assist others seeking to detoxify. Eventually both Gene and I moved to other work in other places. James Allen remained and became the director of the Addict Rehabilitation Center after he kicked his habit at the clinic. He has continued that work for over forty years. During that time and under his leadership more than twenty-five thousand men, women, and children have passed through the now professionally run institution funded by a foundation and grants from the state.

When the recovered addicts sought employment they faced many difficulties. Almost all had criminal records, due to either possession of drugs or the commission of thefts to satiate their habits. Robbed now of an opportunity for another chance, they were even ineligible to work as garbage collectors for the city, and so were vulnerable to recidivism.

Jackie Robinson had become personnel director of Chock full o'Nuts, a quality chain of fast-food restaurants. Gene Callender and I met with him to discuss the matter. He listened during the lengthy meeting, made a telephone call in our presence, and then asked if he could call me the next day. He did call the following morning with the news that his company would hire all those who had graduated from our program and that he would work with them and us to ease the transition.

In my view Jackie Robinson's historic and public efforts to remake America on the baseball field for which the nation has belatedly and posthumously honored him were rivaled by his private acts of compassion.

Gene Callender and I played tournament bridge as partners. We were the only interracial team around since Gene was the only African American. Some thought it was an odd team primarily because one of us was an ordained minister and the other a trial lawyer.

One day in my office, Gene mentioned another pro bono case he was asking me to take. A young member of his church had been arrested and charged with several felonies. The boy was fourteen, and the case should have been assigned to children's court because of his age and because no one had suffered a grievous injury. I met Reggie, my new client, the next morning; he looked as though he were twelve, although I admit that with each passing year all those younger than me seem to be much younger.

Since he had wanted to purchase a candy bar and was without funds, he approached a slightly smaller boy and demanded a nickel.

The kid said he had no money. Reggie said he would settle for two cents. The youngster said again that he had no money, nothing, not even a penny. Reggie reached into his own pocket and found a safety pin. He took the boy's hand and pricked one finger with the pin. It did not bleed. Nevertheless, Reggie felt that the message had been delivered. He said, "When I see you next time you better have a nickel for me."

Reggie was charged with criminal assault, extortion, and various other related felonies as an adult. I told Gene that either a mistake had been made or the prosecutor was deranged. Further inquiry revealed that no mistake had been made. The prosecutor was a young lawyer named Mr. Nadjari. We never got to the stage where we exchanged first names, much less did either of us consider employing them.

The judge was a gentle and studious man. It was rumored that he was the nephew of former governor Herbert Lehman. I asked that the case be reassigned to children's court, an institution that had been established in New York in 1902. The *New York Times* had reported that the court was designed as a judicial experiment to save juvenile delinquents from contacts with crime and criminals. Apparently Nadjari had missed that issue. The judge agreed, but Nadjari strenuously and most histrionically refused to consent. A trial date was set for the case.

When I saw Mike Solomon in court later that day, I asked him about Nadjari. Mike suffered from few inhibitions and was generally willing to share his opinions on most subjects if coaxed. In this instance no pleading was required. "That prick," he said. "I just tried a case with him." Nadjari was, he told me, a young, ambitious, and unprincipled man in a great hurry. He was assigned to the Court of Special Sessions where three judges acting as both the court and the jury heard misdemeanor cases. That summer he had been permitted to try a felony case in the Court of General Sessions with a real jury since the experienced assistant district attorneys were on vacation. Mike was, unfortunately for him, his first adversary. During the trial Nadjari had taken some liberty with the facts, and in closing

Mike referred to "the shoddy tactics of a summertime DA." Nadjari erupted; Mike's client was acquitted.

Reggie's trial lasted but one day. During the proceedings I made a relatively modest procedural motion to which Nadjari objected. The judge sustained the objection, saying to me that the fact I had referred to was not in the record and "if it is not in the record, then it never happened according to legal fiction."

The victim testified as if he had been well rehearsed. He recounted the facts adequately. Cross-examination of a minor must be done carefully. I sought to sympathize with him and to try to establish in the minds of the jurors that the prosecutor may have overstepped. I told the victim that I was sorry that he had suffered in the incident. I asked him to look at Reggie and to try to remember if he had ever seen him before the incident. Nadjari objected to the question; however, since there was no sound basis for the objection, it was overruled. The witness said, "No, I never saw him before or after." I asked him to look at Reggie closely since this was a very important question and a boy's whole future might be decided by his answer. Nadjari said he objected to the question, again to no avail since I had not yet asked a question. I then asked the witness if it was possible that he had not seen Reggie that day, but another boy who looked like him. The witness said, "Yes, that is possible." Nadjari was on his feet, loudly demanding that he be permitted "to redirect this witness, to get the truth out." The court reminded him that he would have to wait until I had completed my questions. I inquired, "So you are saying that Reggie may not have been the boy who demanded a nickel from you?" The answer was, "Yeah, maybe it was not him."

The prosecutor, in a most authoritative manner, reminded the witness that he had said he was sure it was Reggie earlier that day. The witness agreed. Nadjari demanded that the witness testify that he was sure it was Reggie. The witness complied as the jury studied both the witness and the demeanor of the prosecutor. My recross consisted of one question. "Is it possible that Reggie was not there that day?" The witness looked at Nadjari, paused, and said, "I think it was him, but I'm not sure." Nadjari repeated his question and was satisfied with the answer, and I was more than satisfied to let the case end there.

My closing argument was basically a request that the jury try to imagine how the prosecutor acted when he was alone in his office with the young boy since we had all seen how he acted in public. Nadjari objected. I withdrew my invitation to speculate.

As Nadjari passed my table to make his closing statement to the jury, I whispered so that only he could hear me, "Now the shoddy tactics of a summertime DA." He turned and looked at me, no doubt recalling with fury his defeat at the hands of Mike Solomon.

With both hands he held the rail in front of the jury box, too outraged to speak. Then he began by pointing at me and saying that the jury should disregard everything said "by that shyster." I asked for permission to approach the bench, where I asked the court to order Nadjari to withdraw that remark and apologize for having made it. The judge shook his head at the prosecutor and said, "You will apologize, and you will never say anything like that about a lawyer again when you are in my courtroom." Nadjari refused to comply. The judge addressed the jury and said that the prosecutor's statement was stricken from the record and that the court apologized to me on behalf of the prosecutor. I thanked the judge.

While the jury was out the judge called me to the bench. He asked, "What did you say to him before he blew up?" I could have told him the truth, but that might have been inconvenient. I could have said that I did not remember or that I had said nothing to him, but either of those statements would have been untrue, and I would not do that, thus permitting me now, many years later, to say that I have never sought to deceive any judge.

I responded, "Let's read back the record, Your Honor." He responded, "It's not in the record; you probably whispered." I said, "A very distinguished judge recently reminded me that if it's not in the record then it never happened. That's a legal fiction, Your Honor." He smiled.

The jury found Reggie not guilty. A number of the jurors, led by Mr. Goldberg, the foreman, spoke with me in the courtroom. Some asked for my business card. Mr. Goldberg took me aside and said, "That Arab hates Jews, doesn't he? You know 'shyster' is an anti-Semitic statement." I said that I hoped that his concern about the prosecutor's statement had no impact upon his decision to find my client not guilty. He assured me that it did not. I did not have the courage to tell him that I had heard that Nadjari was a Sephardic Jew who was devoutly religious while I had not been in a synagogue since I was thirteen years old.

There are law school professors who tell their students that a trial is a search for the truth. Not even close. A trial is an extemporaneous drama played in a theater we call a courtroom to a rather small audience generally of about twelve members, and each participant—judge, lawyers, witnesses, and defendants—are actors, and as such, you must never bore the jury. They are captives, so walking out at intermission is not an option, but they are not powerless; they can act against your client. Further, if possible, try to present evidence that will cause the audience to admire or like or at least not be hostile to your client. If that is not something that can be accomplished, then attempt to entertain the jurors so that they might, in turn, try to please you.

The extent that the jurors must like your client or you is relative to the extent that they dislike the prosecutor. If they like your client or you just a bit, then their dislike for the prosecutor may become decisive. Once the jurors decide to help, it is vital to give them a place to hang their hats or, in this case, to maintain their self-respect by actually finding a basis with some legal authority for their decision to acquit. For example, an eyewitness who is not certain.

During 1957, Gene and I read about the work of Martin Luther King Jr., a little-known minister chosen because of his moderation, among other traits, to lead the Montgomery bus boycott. Dr. King was just touching a small portion of the national conscience. He had never spoken in Harlem and never addressed a large group in New

York. Few people would have recognized him had he walked down the street. We decided to change that.

Dr. King accepted the invitation to address our community, and our work began. It had to be an outdoor meeting since we had hoped to attract two to three thousand people and since admission was to be free and we had no funds for renting a large room. The location was set for 125th Street and Seventh Avenue, near the Theresa Hotel.

We thought of constructing a small stage on the sidewalk running into the street. That too would be beyond our budget, since we didn't have one, and it might prove to be too flimsy in case the audience surged forward. The comptroller of New York City, Lawrence E. Gerosa, was connected to a large trucking company involved in construction and hauling heavy products. He was a conservative Democrat, but he knew where the votes were, and I knew him. He provided a huge flatbed for the stage.

Gene provided the public relations through announcements at churches and through civic organizations. We needed electrical power. A large generator might have worked, but it would have been noisy and expensive. I paid a visit to Sugar Ray Robinson's nightclub nearby. Ray was believed by many in the industry to be the greatest boxer of all time. In his retirement he had opened an establishment that featured legends of jazz including Miles Davis and Charlie Parker. I explained our problem. Ray had heavy duty electrical lines installed by union members running safely from his establishment to our stage.

We thought that some preliminary low-key entertainment, a folksinger who would perform while the audience gathered and not ask for a fee, might be fine. Gene, thinking in grander terms, contacted famous bandleaders who agreed to bring their orchestras and be our opening acts.

I never much did care for the almost meaningless explanation "you had to be there" because the advice conceded a linguistic inadequacy and the speaker's paucity of imagination. What did Dr. King say that so inspired, educated, and mesmerized that audience? Well, you had to be there, because words cannot encompass the power of that moment.

I remember that when Dr. King said, "I must close now," the audience responded with pleas to continue. It was a Beethoven symphony where the audience wanted to hear more, almost needed to, and the artist felt the same way but in resignation knew that all things must end.

There must have been a previous moment in the experiences of the thousands of people standing in the street in Harlem and looking up at an average-appearing man on a flatbed truck that equaled that epiphany. But I doubt that any of us could recall it just then.

East Harlem Politics

6

IIIIIIIIIIIIIIIIIIIIIIIIIIIIIIIIIIIIIIIIIIIIIIIIIIIIIIIIIIIIIIIIII

The political history of East Harlem is colorful and, more than that, illuminates the powerful, and sometimes conflicting, forces at play in the community. East Harlem in the 1950s was a ghetto largely inhabited by Puerto Ricans, with a dwindling number of elderly Italians still residing on its northern fringe. Harlem, populated almost entirely by African Americans, was to the west. To the south was all-white Yorkville. From 1923 to 1933, East Harlem had been represented in Congress by Fiorello La Guardia, who later became the most jovial, irreverent, and likely the best mayor in the history of New York City. Both his enthusiasm and his courageous commitment to innovative reform (taking on organized crime through his order to arrest Lucky Luciano and his personal participation with a sledgehammer in the destruction of Frank Costello's slot machines, as well as his restoration of New York's economy through massive public works programs) made him a beloved figure. As the city's chief magistrate he often served as a volunteer judge in municipal court. In one misdemeanor case La Guardia ruled that a man who had stolen a loaf of bread because his family was starving should be fined ten dollars. He also issued another order. He announced that he was fining every person in the courtroom fifty cents "for living in a city where a man has to steal bread in order to eat." After the hat-passing ritual, he presented the $47.50 in fines to the defendant.

Vito Marcantonio had served for ten years as La Guardia's voice in East Harlem, responding to the needs of the constituents and working in Fiorello's campaigns. Marcantonio was subsequently elected to the House of Representatives where he became a voice for civil rights and liberties. He won successive reelections by first winning primary elections in the major parties and also running on the American Labor Party ticket in the general election.

Marcantonio's constituents for the most part lived in Harlem and East Harlem. In 1944, his district was gerrymandered; Harlem was removed, and Yorkville replaced it. Still Marcantonio won. Leaders of both the Democratic and Republican parties passed the Wilson-Pakula Act of 1947, which stated in essence that party leaders, not the registered voters, would decide whom their candidates would be. After Marcantonio spoke out against the war in Korea, James Donovan, a former undersheriff in Manhattan for seven years and a man with very conservative views, was endorsed by the Republican Party, the Democratic Party, and the Liberal Party. During the campaign in 1950, at the start of the McCarthy era, Donovan accused Marcantonio of being "the only member of Congress who consistently followed the Communist line." Donovan was elected; Marcantonio died of a heart attack four years later.

When Donovan ran for reelection in 1954, Casper Citron ran against him. Citron did not live in the district and had neither ties to it nor a reputation for service to its residents. But he was ambitious, and he sensed a chance to defeat a thoroughly unpopular candidate. Donovan won.

By 1956 the Democratic Party recognized that Donovan was vulnerable. Citron again announced his candidacy. By then it was clear that Donovan's voting record would have disqualified him for further service if anyone published it and if the voters became acquainted with it, two unlikely events.

Citron called me and asked if I could help him. We talked, and I agreed to organize his campaign, without any fee but with the understanding that I thought he would probably lose again and that if the Democratic Party nominated a suitable candidate I would likely support him. Citron agreed, stating that he was sure that Donovan would be endorsed again by the Democratic Party.

The campaign was taking shape when Citron said that it was urgent that we meet for breakfast. I thought that the agenda would be my strong opposition to his claiming that he was Casper "Cintron" when he campaigned in East Harlem in order to mislead Puerto Ricans into believing that this white American boy from out of the area was one of them. Casper had another plan.

We met in the dining room of a fashionable East Side hotel. The breakfast was memorable for three reasons. It was the first time I ate eggs Benedict; it was the first time I had a meal paid for by a credit card—it had been issued to Casper's father; and then there was the discussion that ensued.

Casper said that a friend of the family had heard that I was running the campaign and also that I had been a member of the progressive National Lawyers Guild. He advised Casper *not* to ask if I was at that time a member of the guild. This was the inception of the Don't Ask, Don't Tell policy for the Eighteenth Congressional District. Instead, Citron was directed to tell me that I would report to him within a few days about my then-present status with the guild and that if I had resigned by then that would be acceptable.

I finished the eggs, thought I must have them again in more amiable surroundings, and said, "Casper, I would not resign from an organization that I believed in for the purpose of being elected to Congress, much less to volunteer my services for a candidate who was almost certainly going to lose a primary election and who, if elected, would be but a minuscule improvement over the incumbent." I thanked him for the hospitality, said I really enjoyed eggs Benedict, and left. I never saw him again. I did call the guild offices in New York and discovered that I was no longer an active member since I had not paid annual dues for some time. I asked how much I owed and immediately sent a check to renew my status.

Some weeks later the local Democratic Party leaders decided to abandon their plan to move New York state senator Alfred E. Santangelo from Manhattan to Staten Island to become the borough president in that mostly Italian enclave. They decided that he should be the candidate for their party against Donovan, whose atrocious voting record troubled them less than his growing unpopularity with the voters. Soon Senator Santangelo called me.

"Mr. Lane," he said, "I wondered if you heard about my situation here and if you could give me a hand."

We met, and I was convinced of his sincerity to provide services to the constituents. I told him about my last meeting with Casper, leaving out the eggs and focusing on the guild. I asked, "Would that be a problem for you?"

He laughed. "I think I was a member there for a while myself."

I became the de facto campaign manager, and we spent election eve together. Freddie, the name by which he was addressed by all who knew him, won by an overwhelming margin; Citron just edged out Donovan for second place. The new congressman-elect, a glass of scotch in his hand, offered a toast to Casper, saying, "Well, he got what he was after. He beat Donovan."

When Representative Santangelo assumed office, he asked me to organize in the community for him. I suggested that we follow the path of La Guardia and Marcantonio by opening two community offices where he would be present one day of each week to meet with constituents. I would be available every day at my own law office or at his community office. We agreed that no fees would ever be charged for any services that were provided.

One huge office was opened in Yorkville close to where I lived, and another in East Harlem close to my law office.

In addition we formed a committee of community leaders comprising activists in the Puerto Rican community, the Irish areas, and the black neighborhoods, representatives from tenants' councils in each community, local and citywide trade union leaders, parent-teacher members, civil rights group leaders, residents of the city housing projects, and religious activists with places of worship in the area. The committee became the voice of the people in the Eighteenth Congressional District with whom the congressman met regularly. They made proposals, some of which became bills and even, in some instances, new laws.

Whenever Freddie had what I thought was a really bad idea and I could not convince him to abandon it, we agreed that the community would be heard. One of the most prominent and influential members was A. C. "Cook" Glassgold, a very sophisticated and distinguished representative of a union of hotel and restaurant workers.

During the late 1950s Freddie returned from Washington with what he thought was a splendid idea: a bill to build fallout shelters against a forthcoming Russian nuclear attack on New York City. The project would materially increase the national debt. When he presented the idea to the community, each person who spoke opposed it and suggested that funds were needed for schools and hospitals and for the repair and maintenance of the infrastructure, not for structures that would not even work in the event of a nuclear attack.

Finally Freddie turned to his trusted colleague for whom he had great respect. "Cook, what do you think?" Glassgold hesitated a moment and then quietly and reluctantly said, "Freddy, I am afraid I must say I think the idea is atrocious." Our congressman listened to the people of the district; the proposed bill was not drafted. Of course, Freddie did not, could not, and would not, even if he could, bring up each bill before he voted or even before he introduced it or agreed to cosponsor the proposed legislation. But often major issues were discussed at the meetings, and often Freddie respected the insight of his constituents.

||||||

We established regular hours when people with problems could meet with us to seek assistance. The matter of "the Cat in the Project" was brought to my attention by Miss Hall, a charming black woman with a youthful face and benign countenance who visited me one evening at my storefront law office in East Harlem. She was a bit coy about her age, which I could only estimate was between sixty and eighty. She was cheerful, asked about my practice and loved ones, and then sat in silence, as if unwilling to bother me with her mundane concerns.

"Can I help you, Miss Hall?" I asked.

She smiled and said, "Just talking with you is so nice, it takes my mind off my trouble. And I do thank you."

Only when I pressed her to share her troubles with me did she reluctantly reach into her pocketbook, take out a legal document, and hand it to me without comment. It was an eviction notice from the New York Housing Authority. Miss Hall lived in a low-income project in East Harlem. The notice said that she had done violence to the rules that govern the housing projects. One could hardly imagine a more caring person who respected the rights of her neighbors. I read on through the legalese. The clause, referred to by rule number and lettered subdivision, alleged my new client had violated the prohibition against having pets in the project.

"Do you have a pet?" I asked.

"Not exactly," she replied.

I was puzzled. Dissembling was not a characteristic I associated with Miss Hall. Either she did or did not have a pet in the project.

"Maybe it's just there part-time?" I offered.

Shaking her head from side to side, she said, "No, Mr. Lane. Sheba is there all the time."

"Is Sheba a pet?"

Miss Hall paused. "Well, sort of."

"What is Sheba?" I asked. "A dog, a cat, a fish, a bird, or a person?"

Miss Hall smiled and said, "She is a cat. But she is also a servant. Really more a servant than a cat."

When I asked her to explain, Miss Hall said, "I have the arthritis. I can't move quickly anymore. The most important thing for me is when my grandchildren call me. I don't hear all that well these days either. So when the telephone rings, Sheba runs to the phone, knocks the receiver off with her paw, and then jumps off the table and goes *meow, meow, meow* into the phone until I get there. If it wasn't for her I would miss so many calls from those angels."

I thought I had spotted a flaw. "Does Sheba also meow into the phone when you're not home?"

"Oh, no. She only does it to help me. When I'm not there, the phone just rings and rings, and she doesn't answer."

The next morning I called Representative Santangelo in his congressional office in Washington. I briefed him on the case of *New York City Housing Authority v. Hall.* He laughed and asked if there was anything serious I wished to discuss with him.

"Do you think I could have invented such a story?" I responded.

He paused and then said, "Yes, but I guess you didn't. Tell the lady to see me at our First Avenue office on Saturday morning. Tell her to bring the cat."

At nine o'clock Saturday morning, I was with Freddie in his Yorkville community offices, a huge space located on First Avenue, which was filled with scores of constituents. Among them were Miss Hall and Sheba. When her name was called, Miss Hall entered the private office, carrying Sheba.

Miss Hall introduced me to Sheba; I introduced them both to Congressman Santangelo. Freddie said, "Can this cat answer the phone right here?"

Miss Hall asked, "Do you mean now?"

"Yes, now. Right now," Freddie insisted.

"We could try. She never was asked to do this outside of my own apartment."

I gave the signal to a receptionist in the outer office. The telephone on the congressman's desk rang. Sheba looked up. She looked at Miss Hall, who tried awkwardly to rise from her chair, and surveyed the scene: the ringing telephone, Miss Hall's halting movement, the inaction or indifference of the rest of us to the sound emanating from the telephone. Suddenly she sprang onto Freddie's desk and knocked the receiver off the hook with one practiced stroke. She crouched down, her mouth at the talking end, and insistently said, *Meow, meow, meow.*

That morning I drafted a letter to the leaders of the Housing Authority, the mayor of the city, and various other officials stating that the eviction notice must be withdrawn. Sheba was not just a cat but a servant who provided essential services for the resident and constituent. It added that we would resist any effort to evict Miss Hall with all the legal and moral force we could gather. It was on the stationary of the US congressman and was signed by Representative Alfred E. Santangelo. The eviction notice was withdrawn.

Almost fifteen years later I met Miss Hall in a coffee shop in East Harlem. She said she was still living in the same apartment, although Sheba had passed on.

||||||

My office in East Harlem was then located on East 116th Street, just around the corner from a small and almost secret sweatshop that employed blacks and Puerto Ricans from the neighborhood. One day, without the assistance of any union organizer, the workers put down their tools and quietly began to picket, holding signs saying that the conditions were horrible, that the hours were so long they violated the law, that the pay did not even reach minimum wage, and that no matter how many hours were worked no overtime was ever paid. They had also been threatened with violence if they considered protesting or trying to join a union.

I returned to my office intending to call the congressman, but he called me first and said we had to meet. I began to tell him about the demonstration, but he interrupted to tell me that he knew about it and was flying back to New York at once to talk to the workers. He said, "I know you won't like this, Mark, but I am going to order them to go back to work."

I began a protest on my own, and he said he would see me very soon and explain.

Later that day, he was in my office. He did explain. "Mark, I knew that I might lose you if I did this. I have no choice. If I thought that I would lose the next election, or even never be elected again to anything in my life, I would do this anyway. I have no choice. I have only orders that I must follow. I value our friendship, and I need you to be with me for the work. But I have no choice."

He spoke to the workers and told them he was not with them and in no uncertain terms said that they must go back to work. The little strike collapsed.

I sent my resignation to Freddie that day. I said that I did understand what he told me but that his action had been so inimical to what I believed that I could no longer ask the community to support him. I said that I would always be his friend.

In fact, we rarely talked again, and in our last conversation I told him that I was thinking of running as an insurgent in the 1960 Democratic primary for the state legislature in the center of his congressional district.

He sighed. "You'll find it very lonely out there." We shook hands, and as I left he said, "I will not support Kelly against you. I will be neutral." He kept his word.

Bill Dufty, a talented writer, volunteered to write a pamphlet endorsing my campaign. It was a brilliant and innovative piece of work that materially contributed to our efforts. One day after work, he invited me to join him and Maely, his wife, as they visited Billie, a dear friend who was in the hospital.

Billie was the godmother to Bevan, Bill and Maely's son, and Maely had been Billie's best friend for many years. Bill coauthored Billie's autobiography, *Lady Sings the Blues*, later a film with Diana Ross. I was about to meet Billie Holiday.

In spite of her international fame, Billie was penniless and addicted and had no choice but to seek treatment in Metropolitan Hospital, a city hospital. Denied drugs or a substitute due to hospital rules and the law, her body, suffering from liver disease and heart problems, was engaged in a battle aggravated by the trauma of heroin withdrawal.

Billie was in a hospital room. Her ill health could not obscure that incredible voice or her optimism. An echo of her vibrant and tough and elegant persona, the Lady Day, was also present, although muted by her pain. Billie had been under arrest since June 12, 1959, for possession of narcotics; police officers were standing guard at the door to her room at the hospital while she was dying. We talked with Billie for half an hour when Billie began to tire. I left the room so that the three good friends could share some private time.

During dinner at a famous Manhattan delicatessen perhaps an hour after we had left the hospital, Maely suddenly froze. Bill asked if she was all right. Maely cried out, "Oh, my God. She is dead. Billie just died." Maely ran to a public telephone to call the hospital. A nurse told her that Billie had just passed. She died on July 17 at the age of forty-four.

In 1994, the US Postal Service printed and circulated the Billie Holiday postage stamp. This tribute was given to her by the same government that had harassed her and refused to protect her from racial and sexist attacks during her lifetime. In 1987 she was posthumously given the Grammy Lifetime Achievement Award, an award that might have had some positive effect upon her if bestowed when she was alive. She was inducted into the Rock and Roll Hall of Fame, also after her death. Yet there had been few supportive voices when her recording company, Columbia, refused to record "Strange Fruit," a powerful and brilliant reminder to America that our recent past included lynching.

And when she sang with the Artie Shaw band, she alone was required to enter the hotel through the back door. This was not the nineteenth century, and it was not in Mississippi. That degradation took place in 1938 in New York City at a hotel in Manhattan named for Abraham Lincoln.

The Campaign in East Harlem

IIIIIIIIIIIIIIIIIIIIIIIIIIIIIIIIIIIIIIIIIIIIIIIIIIIIIIIIIIIIIIIIIIIIIIIIIIIIIIIIIIIIIIIIIIIIIIIIIII

During the 1950s, it became clear that the Democratic Party in New York State was under the influence and, in many respects, the control of organized crime. The confluence of these forces, organized crime and the Democratic Party, was apparent in the person of Carmine DeSapio, the leader of the Democratic Party in New York City. John Merli, a district leader in the Tenth Assembly District, which included Yorkville and East Harlem on the East Side of Manhattan, and Frank Rossetti, a district leader of the Sixteenth Assembly District, in East Harlem, were his loyal cohorts.

In Yorkville, the families that had been there for years living in modest four- and five-story buildings were almost all Irish or German. Those who lived in the large, higher-rent apartment buildings—built after many of the smaller buildings had been demolished to make a space for them—were white, and no ethnic group predominated. Many were young professionals who paid the rent by sharing living space.

In East Harlem, almost all of the residents were Puerto Rican; some were black and others Italian, although many Italian families had left for homes in Long Island. Many of those who remained lived in apartments in old but fairly well-maintained buildings. The blacks and Puerto Ricans lived in city projects or in overcrowded rat- and roach-infested tenements.

At that time I had been practicing law from my East Harlem storefront office for almost a decade. A few of us thought we might try to change things and a reform movement was established so that people in the community would have a voice and not be controlled by a few leaders, some of whom had associations with organized crime. I would organize, as part of our citywide reform movement, a Reform Democratic club in East Harlem. There were few reform clubs in existence, and until then every one had been in white middle- or upper-class areas. We would try to raise money for rent for a headquarters as we went along. I had sufficient funds for one month's rent and a security deposit.

We formed the East Harlem Reform Democrats (EHRD) in a small storefront. Many of the people I had met over the years, including a number of those whom I had represented, joined. A sign stated in English and Spanish: THIS IS THE DEMOCRATIC PARTY WHERE ALL ARE WELCOME—AQUI SE HABLA ESPANOL.

Paul O'Dwyer, a decent and good man and also the brother of the former mayor, William O'Dwyer, and I were the only leaders of the reform movement with concerns about including blacks and Latinos, then primarily Puerto Ricans, in our effort to bring about change.

At one meeting of the East Harlem Reform Democrats we discussed the integration efforts going on in the South. In Greensboro, North Carolina, some young black men and women requested food at the counter of a Kress store. The managers said they could stand and buy a sandwich and a drink and take their purchases home or enjoy the refreshments on the street corner outside of the store. They could not sit at the lunch counter. That elite privilege was reserved for whites only. A number of the kids sat on the stools anyway. They were not served; they remained sitting, and soon they were arrested.

National five-and-ten-cent stores such as Woolworths, Kresges, and S. H. Kress predominated in the country during the 1950s and 1960s. For many years Kress stores were everywhere, a profitable chain with locations in most cities and towns in the United States. These stores were truly democratic regarding whom they would sell their merchandise to. The color scheme in corporate headquarters favored green, while black and white were irrelevant.

Yet the executives were confronted with an important decision when the civil rights movement in the South, at first demanding equal transportation and the right to vote, gave some thought to dining at the popular fast-food marts of the day, the lunch counter at the local five-and-dime.

I was familiar with the process. Years before, some students at Howard University in Washington, DC, decided that in the nation's capital they should be permitted to eat in a restaurant of their choice. The students had worked out a plan. Some white men and women would sit at the counter for breakfast, order a cup of coffee, and drink it slowly for an hour or two until the proprietor decided to let a black person take their place and be served a regular meal. The only flaw in the plan was the shortage of white people willing to be arrested or beaten. A couple of us in New York were asked to volunteer. I never drank coffee so slowly again. It was the first of many times that I was arrested.

We knew that our neighborhood enjoyed the presence of a very popular Kress store at a busy intersection. Integrated dining was not an issue there. Kress management was willing to bow to the customs in place in each community. I was delegated to call upon the national office of the powerful chain and request that they permit all of their customers to partake throughout the country. The CEO mentioned "state's rights," "local options," "regrettable in a way," as well as other phrases popular at the time and often employed to direct attention away from the central question. In short, the chain had decided that it would preserve its bottom line in the modern world by adhering to concepts long discredited. No appeal to concepts of decency or fairness moved them.

Three days after the Greensboro confrontation, our little reform club became the first organization in the North to act in support of their southern sisters and brothers. We said that while they were being arrested for sitting in at lunch counters in North Carolina and elsewhere in the South we were going to share that information with Kress customers in East Harlem. We organized an informational picket line and through leaflets and conversations with prospective patrons sent a message to Kress that racism was not acceptable anywhere.

We knew that the message would resonate with African Americans who felt a connection with others of color in the South, where many had previously lived. We were less sanguine that Puerto Ricans would universally respond due to cultural considerations—the hostility or fear that existed among minority groups and the absence of ties to southern blacks. We relied on Ramon Diaz, East Harlem's most persuasive ambassador to those who spoke Spanish, to explain the profound message: in Dr. King's words, "Injustice anywhere is a threat to justice everywhere."

We arrived, about fifty of us, soon after Kress opened its doors. All colors, religions, and political perspectives were represented. The customers—in particular black customers—paused to read our signs, hear our songs, or talk with us, and a number stood with us. Soon we were hundreds.

It was a very busy Saturday morning, and not one black person entered the store. Ramon Diaz had not yet arrived. While many Puerto Ricans understood our position and joined in the boycott and even in the picket line, a substantial number patronized the store.

Ramon finally arrived to cheers from most of us and a few shouts of "It's about time" or similar jibes in Spanish from those who knew and loved him best. The modest-looking man, not impeccably dressed and apologizing for his tardiness, evaluated the situation in a moment. He entered the store and quietly talked to each shopper, singly or in family groups. They all left the store quickly and waved to the picketers who cheered them. Those who had lined up at the cash registers dropped their packages as well. The store was empty with the exception of the manager and the clerks. It remained without customers all day.

Our modest reach was greatly enhanced when we were joined by Eleanor Roosevelt and former US senator and New York governor Herbert Lehman. Mrs. Roosevelt told me that she knew of my efforts in East Harlem, and she hoped one day that I might run for office. Almost immediately after our conversation, I called my mother and told her that I had actually talked with Eleanor Roosevelt. My mother later said that had been one of the greatest gifts she ever received.

The *New York Amsterdam News* devoted a front-page headline to our effort. Eleanor Roosevelt issued a public statement in support of the principles involved. Her words were widely carried. Within weeks a movement that had started as a regional effort in the South had reached into all forty-eight states that at that time composed our Union. The people of East Harlem rejoiced at their contribution, and some, despite living below the poverty line, talked about raising funds to send to the South.

Later, over a beer or two in an East Harlem bar, I toasted Ramon. I told him I had never seen a more effective job of on-the-spot community organizing. I marveled at how he had taken a complex situation and, apparently utilizing all of his considerable intellectual skills, resolved it so quickly. He smiled shyly into his beer.

"What?" I asked.

He drained his glass, put it down, and then looked directly at me.

"Ramon, what did you say? What did you tell them?" I asked, hoping to discover the magic of his quick mind and silver tongue that perhaps we could replicate in the future.

He ordered another beer, and when it arrived he sipped a bit, put the glass down, and said, "I told them there was a bomb in there."

John Harrington, one of my closest friends, was an Irish lad, a bit older than me and decades wiser politically. He was a churchgoing

Catholic married to a woman who was even more religious. He had worked with Marcantonio. He was also part of the regular Democratic organization in Yorkville run by Martin Kelly. Kelly had anointed his son, Martin Kelly Jr. (who was still in law school at the time), as the assemblyman. John held a patronage job as a clerk in the court system. It had been given to him by the regular party organization. I met with John to discuss the possibility of running as an insurgent for the New York State Assembly in the Tenth Assembly District that comprised Yorkville and East Harlem.

"Should I run?" I asked him over a couple of scotch and sodas in a lounge he favored in the East Fifties, where his primary allegiance was to the jukebox.

"Do you have any money, any at all?" John asked, although he knew the answer was no. "Do you know anyone who can contribute something to start?"

The same hopeless reply.

"Is there any organization in East Harlem that might help out?" No.

He added, "I know there is no group in Yorkville that will endorse you, and Old Man Kelly will fight for his son."

We sipped our drinks and listened to Billy Eckstein.

John looked at me and smiled. "Yes."

"'Yes' what?" I asked.

"Run."

John would try quietly, in deference to keeping his job, to pull some people together in Yorkville. Garnering support from the established reformers was very difficult. I was an inexplicable figure to them. I had fought the House Un-American Activities Committee as soon as I was admitted to practice. The liberal reformers did not much like HUAC, but they were not enamored with those left-wing people who took action against it. They were uncomfortable with my early public opposition to the war in Vietnam, a place most of them at that time had never heard of. Those who were knowledgeable discounted the presence of a few American "advisers" there as a problem and said that my early warnings of a likely wider conflict were misplaced and foolish, if not downright unpatriotic. Above all they were offended by my pleas that the citywide movement must include all residents of the city if it was to proclaim itself reform.

Nevertheless, there was a large and enthusiastic base of support for our reform efforts, most notably Mrs. Roosevelt, Governor Lehman, and Senator Eugene McCarthy. Students from almost every college in New York City, led in numbers by the Sarah Lawrence College contingent, many high school students, and, above all, the until-then voiceless people of East Harlem, turned our small club into a vibrant and ever-growing chorus for change. On many days and nights I was by far the oldest person in the room. I was thirty-two.

I expected to win the endorsement of the group I had organized. I was their unanimous choice. But other neighborhood liberal clubs had some questions.

"If you are offered a judgeship, who will replace you?" No one, since I will neither seek a judgeship nor accept one if it is offered. That assertion was received with skepticism from the group of ambitious lawyers who were present. I probably was dissembling, they thought; if not, then deranged.

"What will you do if you are elected?" Fight to increase the minimum wage of the working people in our state and to decrease the wages of the members of the legislature, introduce legislation to abolish capital punishment, introduce a bill to authorize literacy tests in both Spanish and English (if I failed to eliminate them as prerequisites for registering to vote), create tenants' councils throughout the city (the landlords already had their conglomerates), prosecute police officers who had violated the law by brutalizing those they arrested, prosecute the captains of each police precinct where such conduct was routine (starting with the Twenty-Third Police Precinct in our district, where such conduct took place each day and which was referred to by the residents as "the Slaughter House"), and build a consensus in the district to elect as my successor a member of the

East Harlem community. The all-white and native-born residents of Yorkville emitted audible gasps at my last idea.

"When will you be leaving?" The question held its own anguished contradictions and hopes. As soon as my first two-year term was up. I would hold that seat only to ensure minority participation in our democracy.

"There never has been a Puerto Rican elected to the assembly from the Tenth District. Did you know that?" This said with increasing volume and rancor. Yes, I was aware of the history. I knew it was time to break from the past. I asked, "We are reformers, right?"

One club voted 82–3 in my favor. One of the three negative votes was ardently cast; she, a club coleader, resigned from the club in protest. The other club demanded to know the details of my "close association and friendship" with Marcantonio, a man they considered to be too liberal. In fact I had never even met Marcantonio, a privilege that I said I regretted having missed.

Having completed and survived the reform endorsement rituals, I was ready to run for the state legislature from the Tenth Assembly District. In the primary campaign in the Democratic Party, I was opposed by the incumbent. I owned a very small convertible, a Morris Minor. It consumed little gasoline and could accommodate four people, if they were not too large and rather good friends. A couple of college students in our campaign majoring in engineering assembled a reconstructed speaker system, attached it to a battery, and installed it in the open vehicle. That was our sound truck. It always worked.

Eleanor Roosevelt endorsed me, posed for campaign pictures with me and Governor Lehman, and made a recording on my behalf. I met with former New York governor Lehman at his home in Manhattan. He said that he would like to see our office and go for a ride around our community sometime. He arrived one evening in the backseat of a town car. Quite small in physical stature, he appeared a bit frail. As I was greeting him curbside, a group of about ten men arrived, almost all very large Italian men, getting on in years but still looking quite formidable. They had been Marcantonio's loyal supporters and worked in the trenches of the political wars in East Harlem as his loyal advocates. When they saw Lehman they shouted, "It's the senator!" or "It's the governor!" and rushed to him to shake his hand.

A few members of the East Harlem Reform Democratic Club asked if they could meet with Mrs. Roosevelt. When I conveyed the request to her and asked if there was any time that she might be in Manhattan, she said, "Why don't we just invite them for lunch at Hyde Park?" We set a date, and she asked me to tell her well in advance how many people would be coming to their home in upstate New York. We then notified the membership and the community of the opportunity and asked for those who wanted to make the trip to sign up within the next two weeks. About eight people volunteered. I reported that information to Mrs. Roosevelt, and on the morning of our departure from the club, those eight people arrived, as did almost a hundred others. I called Mrs. Roosevelt, expecting that she would accept my advice that we just cancel the event. She laughed and said, "Bring them all, Mark. We have a lot of room up here." We hastily organized buses, station wagons, and anything else that might be able to make the trip.

At Hyde Park, Mrs. Roosevelt was gracious and welcomed each person individually. She spoke to the group about politics. She said that she had endorsed Mayor Wagner, whom she believed to be an honest man, not beholden to the worst elements of Tammany Hall, the Democratic political machine that controlled New York. One woman told her, "We don't have any bright streetlights in our community, and we have a lot of crime. When you go downtown from East Harlem, across East Ninety-Sixth Street, where the white folks live and the wealthy people live, the streetlights are a lot brighter."

Mrs. Roosevelt said, "I think you should meet with Mayor Wagner. Tell him what it is you would like him to do if he is reelected and see if he will promise to do it. Politicians sometimes forget their promises, and that's where the people have the responsibility to remind them what they said before Election Day." It was clear, it was simple, and it conveyed eloquently how a democracy is supposed to work. I don't think that Mayor Wagner would have considered it to be a stirring endorsement.

Her words, unencumbered by rhetoric or ambiguity, were a lesson for all of us. In a direct and honest way she had told us that we alone were agents of change and that the hope for a better life was in our own hands. She never discussed tactics, dirty tricks, or the methodology of dividing us for political profit.

During this period Mrs. Roosevelt wrote to me, stating that she had received a letter from a person who had apparently been unjustly accused and imprisoned; she asked if I might be willing to look into the matter. I examined the official records, made inquiries, and interviewed some witnesses before reporting to Mrs. Roosevelt; how could I have done otherwise? On irregular occasions for some time, Mrs. Roosevelt referred other obviously pro bono cases to me.

Some lawyers unlawfully employ "runners" to secure clients for them, paying secretly, often in cash. I once told Gene Callender that I was honored, yes, blessed, by two of the most wonderful unpaid runners, Eleanor Roosevelt and him, a distinguished minister, and if I could just find a third I would be able to declare bankruptcy.

||||||

In addition to the series of reform club caucuses, the primary and the general elections followed each other so closely that there was one extended campaign. I won the primary by defeating Kelly and became the official Democratic Party candidate for the state legislature.

That designation was not dispositive as far as the Democratic Party warlords were concerned. The stakes were too high for them. They did not want an independent voice in Albany. Their establishment, not the Democratic members of the senate and the assembly, decided how votes were to be cast there, and they thought that I would attempt to challenge that process. They were correct; that was my plan.

A far greater threat was that if I was elected I would support candidates who opposed their delegates in the north and the south.

Those posts were the real seats of power. It was through the district leaders that organized crime held the Democratic Party in its hands. Their fears were well grounded. Although they were planning to offer personal incentives to me, they thought that I might not be interested.

At that point the regular Democratic clubs in the Tenth Assembly District endorsed and worked for my Republican opponent. Carmine DeSapio, who was the leader of the Democratic Party in the city and also a district leader in Greenwich Village, played a major role in coordinating the plan to defeat me in the general election.

The leaders were convinced that I was isolated from the base that they believed they still controlled, since they remained the sole distributors of patronage jobs throughout the city, including judgeships, nominations for Congress, the state legislature, the governor, and who would be the New York State choice for national office, in addition to thousands of other lesser positions. Again they were correct, but only if one discounted the support of thousands of people in the area and literally hundreds of others who volunteered each day and night to make our area the concentration point for the movement for change.

Our campaign took place in the streets of East Harlem and in Yorkville and in visits to the homes and apartments of the residents of the two communities. I opened another headquarters in Yorkville. In both storefront offices scores and then hundreds of young people organized lists, canvassed each area, visited each home, and tallied the responses. I spent time at the headquarters just to greet the volunteers and thank them for their contributions. My sister, my brother, and their friends were among the most diligent and dedicated workers.

I spent most of my time on the street, often driving my makeshift sound truck, speaking day and night on every corner in the district from Seventy-Fourth Street to 106th Street and from the East River to Third Avenue or Lexington Avenue or Park Avenue. The odd-shaped district had been gerrymandered in a bizarre fashion to benefit the incumbents and to decrease the impact of minority participation.

In East Harlem every corner became an extemporaneous rally, sometimes with large numbers singing along in English, while others made hasty translation into Spanish. The residents had heard my almost shouted words sufficiently often that when I said, "Ninety-Sixth Street is the Mason-Dixon Line of New York, and housing is more segregated here . . . ," the audience chanted back "than it is in Jackson, Mississippi."

Mrs. Roosevelt toured East Harlem with me in my open convertible, and many hundreds of people filled the streets and windows and rooftops to applaud her. One person, standing on a roof, threw a can of beer at us. It struck me in the head. Head wounds have a tendency to bleed profusely. I took a handkerchief and pressed it to the wound and asked the driver to put the top up on the convertible and to take Mrs. Roosevelt quickly back to our headquarters. I said a hasty good-bye and ran to Metropolitan Hospital, a short distance away. There, I learned firsthand of emergency room operations in the ghetto. Blood was streaming down my face, and I was told to wait. Finally, a doctor came out of a back room, recognized me, and rushed me into a treatment facility in the emergency room. Soon there were several doctors, all acting quickly and competently, to stop the bleeding and to sew up the wound. One of them asked if I was impressed with their efficiency. I thanked them. I was also impressed, though not favorably, with the distinction with which they treated patients and their ability to provide excellent care for a white male quasi-celebrity.

After that incident we received a number of death threats. I was naive enough to consider them just nuisance calls. One threat delivered through an anonymous telephone call specified the date, close to Election Day, and general area in East Harlem where I was going to be killed. On the specified date, at a location within that area, I was speaking from our sound truck when witnesses heard what they thought was a gunshot. People fell to the ground or ran into hallways, and I called the police and reported the assault. When the press arrived I reminded them of the Scottoriggio case, one of the most publicized political murders in recent history. The murder of the election district captain had taken place very close to the location where I was standing.

The police then provided protection until Election Day. The police were efficient. The protection was absolute. Detectives drove unmarked cars, taxicabs, and pickup trucks. I was never out of their sight for a moment, and an observer would never know they were there. Officers in plainclothes sat in cars or walked around our club. Others were stationed near the apartment building where I lived, and one stayed in my apartment. The only fatalities that last week were my social life and my privacy.

Registration of those who had never voted, had never registered, and had lived in New York for many years was our primary goal. For years every previous effort in the city to involve Puerto Ricans in the voting process had failed. In 1957 the large and well-financed Council of Spanish Organizations estimated that only 85,000 of the potential 266,000 Puerto Rican voters were registered in spite of its efforts.

One of the major deterrents to participation was the literacy test, which had a long history as an effective means of controlling votes. It required the applicants to read and write effectively in English even if that was not their native language and even though they had not been afforded an education. In 1790 only white adult male property owners had the right to vote in the United States. A half century later, property ownership was eliminated as a requirement. Five years after that, Connecticut adopted America's first literacy test for voting, and two years later, during 1857, Massachusetts passed the same law.[1]

We declared war on the New York law mandating the tests. I spoke against them on radio programs and to the press. I said that we would abolish it in our community. When asked how I would accomplish that feat, I replied that I was going to get the tests each day, answer the questions in writing, and distribute the questions and answers by the hundreds while broadcasting the answers on every street corner in East Harlem. When asked what the authorities would do about this blatant violation of the law, I answered that I had already informed the US Attorney's Office and the FBI of my intentions and that those questions should be directed to them.

That night FBI agents monitored my activities and continued to do so each day when registration offices were open, taking copious notes. They were present each day of registration week. I was not arrested. My opponent not only reported but distorted my work in East Harlem to the Yorkville voters. He did not dare to openly oppose registration efforts in East Harlem; the paid registrars, taking orders from those who provided their jobs, the bosses of East Harlem who were also the Democratic district leaders, did their best on his behalf.

In Yorkville, a priest at my campaign manager's Catholic church endorsed my opponent Kelly and urged the congregation not to vote for me. When my manager, John Harrington, learned about the sermon, he confronted his priest.

"Father, I have attended this church all my life. I was married in this church. Goddamn it, I will not see my church used to oppose my candidate. When you enter politics and tell people how to vote you are a disgrace to the collar, especially in this case." When the priest began to apologize, John interrupted to say, "I want you to withdraw your remarks on Sunday." The father did, and the next week he apologized to the congregation.

Yet the damage had been done. In one Irish pub that I visited, I received a precedent-breaking cold reception. I had represented many tenement dwellers in Yorkville over the years in an effort to prevent their eviction from buildings that developers wanted to demolish so that luxury apartment buildings could be erected. In the past my entrance had been greeted with a muted form of Norm's arrival in *Cheers*.

I bought the lads a round and asked what the trouble was. Mr. McGinty, the apparent leader of the rebellion, said that violating the literacy laws so that "those spics and niggers can vote is the problem. If they want to vote, let them learn to speak English that everyone can understand." I asked if he knew why literacy laws were first designed. He said he was no historian but that he knew what was right. I told him that they were first created a century ago to prevent Irish immigrants, probably his grandparents, from voting, since they did not speak the King's English well enough.

The silence in the bar was broken by my comment, "Timothy, I knew you were an active supporter of the IRA, but I never knew that you were so loyal to the king." There was laughter, and Tim bought me a drink.

In one week 3,115 Puerto Ricans in our district registered for the first time. Some of them had lived in the city for fifty years. In addition the drive enrolled 1,110 other new voters, most of whom were black.

|||||

During my own campaign, I was also engaged in the campaign to elect Senator John F. Kennedy president. Many in the reform movement were not pleased that he had been nominated. They had supported Adlai Stevenson, who I thought was a good and decent man. The liberals said that *others* would not vote for a Catholic. The *others* were never defined, but they were so committed to the wisdom of their analysis that I suspected that in the secrecy of their homes they confided their more personal concern about decisions that might be made in the Vatican and that the Kennedy clan was in some fashion untrustworthy.

I arranged for a meeting with the West Side liberals and reformers and representatives from Greenwich Village at a posh East Side club to meet with Robert Kennedy regarding his brother's presidential campaign. Bobby's colleague, an acquaintance of mine, suggested an apartment in a fashionable Manhattan building as the site, saying that it was presently unoccupied and maintained by the Kennedy brothers. To my questioning glance he replied, "For the occasional liaison."

I found Bobby to be refreshingly frank at the conference. The question of religion that so preyed on the minds of the liberals was never raised at the meeting.

"If Senator Kennedy should be elected president, what position will he take in the conflict between party leader DeSapio and our movement?" one person asked.

Bobby responded immediately. "I want my brother to be elected president. Once he is elected we will not care if blood runs in the streets of New York."

The audience was astonished and appalled. Later, after Bobby departed, the talk was of his "ruthlessness," his lack of concern for reform, and his inappropriate imagery.

I conceded that he might have replied more delicately, but suggested we look beyond the extravagant allusion and realize that he had said President Kennedy would be neutral as the internecine contests continued. That was a major concession; we could not have expected him to say that he would turn his back on the regular Democratic Party in the city. A few of those present agreed.

Subsequently Robert Kennedy said that there should be a representative from our reform movement and one from the regular organization to jointly help manage the presidential campaign in New York. I was chosen as the reform delegate. There was a photo opportunity at a suite at a hotel where John Kennedy was speaking for every Democratic candidate to have his picture taken with the presidential nominee. DeSapio, through intermediaries, had chosen the photographer, and his office also was obligated to notify the candidates of the event. He had failed to inform a number of the reform candidates who had won primaries. I contacted each of them. John shook everyone's hand, wished her or him good luck, and posed for the picture that would become a valuable asset in each campaign. The photographer informed me a couple of days later that every picture had been developed and printed and sent to the candidates, except for mine. The camera had mysteriously malfunctioned.

When I met with Bobby and some campaign staff members and the DeSapio delegate the following week, we exchanged information and ideas. I never mentioned the camera with the inexplicable malady at the meeting. As we were parting Bobby invited me to join him in another room and asked how things were working with our joint effort. He also asked how the picture with John came out. I said, "It didn't," and explained. He said, referring to DeSapio, "That son of a bitch." He asked me to wait for a few minutes, as he had to make a telephone call. He returned and asked me if I could be at a designated Midtown hotel at a time and date about a week ahead.

He said, "John wants to talk with you. And he said to bring a photographer." Then he paused and said that John's message was, "Tell him to bring two of them."

||||||

Although I had been an early supporter of John Kennedy, I was also inspired by Gene McCarthy's brilliant nominating speech for Adlai Stevenson at the Democratic National Convention in Los Angeles in 1960. I called the senator, told him that I was a candidate, and asked if his schedule might take him to New York and, if it did, if he would speak at a small gathering for me. He was very gracious, and we set a date. I met him at Idlewild Airport, later named JFK following the president's assassination, and we drove through East Harlem and Yorkville discussing the problems and their possible solutions for each area.

When we stopped for dinner I told him how impressed I was with his convention speech. He said, "It did wonders for me." He paused and smiled diffidently. "Poor Adlai, I don't think I picked up a single vote for him."

Gene was a charming and self-effacing gentleman. He made a very generous speech on my behalf. "I have seen Mark's district, the Tenth Assembly District, and East Harlem needs a voice that will be heard."

It was October, and Election Day was nearing. The EHRD continued its work of organizing tenant's councils, conducting literacy classes, and petitioning for a city minimum wage of $1.50, which approximated a living wage. With the help of hundreds of volunteers, that work could continue even as we organized a massive campaign to remind the newly registered voters and the other residents that registering was only the first step. Rallies at street corners were drawing hundreds of supporters, many of whom followed the sound truck on foot for blocks to join in the festivities again.

One day the Republican governor of New York, Nelson Rockefeller, appeared for a brief stop in our community. He spoke from a well-guarded sound truck looming far above the street. A young Puerto Rican boy, raising his voice to almost a shout, asked the governor why East Harlem had such poor services—"dim street lights, irregular garbage collection"—but before he could continue, the governor pointed at him while he looked at a police officer who immediately arrested the youngster.

The charge should have been "attempted freedom of speech," but instead the youth was charged with disorderly conduct. I represented him in the Upper Manhattan Magistrate's Court, set in a slum building in a deteriorated neighborhood. I found Rockefeller at another rally and had him served with a subpoena in the case. Since it had been carefully gift wrapped and bestowed with a handsome red ribbon, he apparently thought it was a present until he opened it. He read the document and handed it to an aide. We photographed the event so that the service could be established.

Rockefeller was not present in court, but his counsel was, resplendently dressed, or overdressed, for the occasion and accompanied by two other attorneys, an assistant, and a chauffeur. His staff served copies of a massive document on the bailiff, the judge's clerk, the judge, me, my client, and a couple of innocent bystanders. A more spartan presentation could have been prepared on one page, since the only point it made was that the governor could not be brought to court to question his official act causing the arrest of a youngster who had annoyed him. However, I pointed out that there was nothing in his job description that mandated that conduct and that therefore he had no immunity from the legal process.

The judge agreed. The governor's staff huddled. The judge asked what I thought he should do. I suggested that he hold Rockefeller in contempt for deliberately refusing to meet his obligation to appear. After another huddle the lead counsel suggested that the case against my client should be dismissed.

The campaign workers at the headquarters cheered briefly when they learned of the dismissal and then went back to work. They were calling upon almost everyone in the community, interviewing all of the families in East Harlem to weed out people who illegally voted in the district despite having moved years or even decades ago. Among them were judges and other office holders still clinging to a former address in order to vote for their benefactor. Getting out the vote was a primary concern; so was preventing former residents from casting an unlawful vote.

Pete Bartone, a retired Marcantonio friend, taught the volunteers how to challenge a vote at the polling center. "He can vote if you challenge him, but only if he signs an affidavit in which he swears he lives at the address." He added metaphorically, "Until he does just sit on that registration book." A young college student asked where the affidavits would be. Pete responded, "A good question, miss. They are supposed to have them there, but they won't." She asked, "Can we make our own affidavits and mimeograph them?" Pete said that was also a good idea. One of the law students researched the election law and drafted the affidavit. Some of the kids made hundreds of copies and placed them in folders with copies of the election law for use on Election Day.

Opposition sound trucks were now everywhere claiming that I was a "pro-Communist who wants to destroy the House Un-American Committee"—they were right, except about my political affiliation—and "Lane is a Jew whose real name is Levine." I said I would answer that allegation at our victory rally on Election Day.

The number of voters on Election Day was unequaled in the history of East Harlem. In black and Puerto Rican districts more than 80 percent of those eligible to vote did so. In Merli's stronghold the vote was down.

Our young poll watchers were quite vigilant. When a judge who had been placed on the bench by Merli entered the polling place to vote, he was warmly greeted by the adoring election officials, and when a twenty-one-year-old college student challenged his right to vote, they laughed. She took Pete's hypothetical suggestion literally and immediately sat on the official registration book. As the police moved toward her, she brandished her affidavit in which she had sworn that weeks ago she interviewed the judge's parents in their home, and they told her that the judge had moved to Long Island eight years ago. She also provided the address and telephone number of the judge's real home. She concluded, "If the judge will sign an affidavit swearing that he lives here, he can vote." The election authorities said they had forgotten to bring the blank affidavits, at which time she took one from her folder and offered it to the judge. He recoiled as if he were a vampire being offered a silver cross. He fled, stating that he would return. Of course he never did; not that year or ever again.

That same scene was repeated at many polling places early in the day. Word traveled quickly in the small community, and later in the day scores of those who had voted illegally and regularly for many years declined to make one more illicit attempt.

That evening the street in front of our office was filled with so many people waiting to hear the results that traffic in East Harlem was brought to a halt. In Yorkville hundreds waited at our headquarters. I knew that the vote from the election district where East 100th Street was located would be significant. Merli had a captain there for many years who had dispensed political favors to many. He had carried his district historically by overwhelming numbers, often ten to one, often padding that figure by offering dollars for votes and with the assistance of the officials who miscounted. We could offer nothing but hope. That night our reform reporter assigned to that polling place called to say that we had won that election district. The votes came in, and in Yorkville and East Harlem shouting, cheering audiences greeted the results as they were written on blackboards. We had won.

In Yorkville, beer appeared and a very large party was held. In East Harlem we marched through the streets, now more than two thousand of us, cheered on by music from our sound truck. When we reached 100th Street, it was filled with hundreds of people dancing in the street and hugging one another and surrounding us. I spoke from the sound truck, "You have earned the right to be represented. All you have to do now is choose your candidate, my successor, when my term is up in two years and work for his or her election. I will be with you in that campaign as you have been with me in this one."

One young man shouted, "Hey, Don Marco, didn't you promise to tell us something tonight? About your name?" I took a number of copies of my birth certificate and gave them to the young man to pass out. I gave one to Reverend Carlos Rios. He read it to the laughing audience. "It says Mark was born in New York on February 24, 1927, and that the name given to him by his parents, Mr. and Mrs. Lane, was," he paused, "Mark Lane." And thus the first birther movement met its justified demise.

||||||

My election to the state legislature did not break the hold of the DeSapio wing of the party in East Harlem and Yorkville, where the powerful district leaders, John Merli in the north and Martin Kelly Sr., the father of the defeated former assembly member in the south, were entrenched. At that time in New York politics the district leader was a powerful force. There were two district leaders for each political subdivision, and they dispensed the funds for campaigns and chose the candidates. For years, when a party district leader entered a courtroom the judges stood up, something they would not do for the governor of the state. DeSapio issued vague but severe warnings that we should abandon our effort to replace the district leaders. John Harrington, Carlos Rios, and I discussed the implications and decided to ignore the threat. We decided that both John and Carlos should run in their districts.

John had numerous contacts in the community going back many years, and almost everyone who had worked on my campaign in Yorkville enlisted in his. I served as his campaign manager. I spent hours each week at Harrington's offices, but since things were so well organized there I was able to spend much more time at the EHRD, where Carlos Rios was the candidate for district leader.

Things were slowly changing, and, during 1961, DeSapio was defeated as district leader in Greenwich Village. He was later indicted and convicted of conspiracy in a bribery case and sentenced to a two-year prison term and sent to a federal penitentiary.

On Election Day, 1962, it soon became clear that Harrington was going to be elected as district leader for the south of the Tenth Assembly District. As the polls closed at 10:00 PM I raced back to East Harlem to find more than five hundred people crammed into our small office and on the sidewalk out front. Within fifteen minutes the votes came in from three districts and showed Merli was leading by a few votes. I suspected then that Carlos had also won. Those districts with large Puerto Rican and black populations had not yet reported. As those returns came in and were written on the club's blackboard, Carlos surged into what seemed to be an insurmountable lead. Then Robert Verdejo, a captain who had worked tirelessly in his election district, one of the most populous areas in the Tenth Assembly District, raced in waving the results. Carlos had carried that district five to one. Carlos became the first Puerto Rican district leader for the north of the Tenth. Carlos Rios was elected to the assembly the following year. He was the first Puerto Rican ever to be elected to the state legislature from that district.

No one better understood the winds of change than did Mayor Robert F. Wagner. He called and asked me to visit him at Gracie Mansion. I thought I might be asked to write another proposal that would interest him to the point of discussing its merits and its pragmatic disadvantages before it was discarded. Instead, it was a meeting to dramatically alter my future.

I was ushered into a small parlor that I had not previously seen. The mayor said that he had heard that the reform movement was going to run a candidate for congress from the Eighteenth Congressional District. The present occupant was Leonard Farbstein, a regular Democrat who had held that seat since 1957. I nodded in agreement. The mayor said that he would prefer that I did not run. I told him that I had not made a decision yet, but even if I declined the reform nomination, some other candidate was almost certainly going to emerge.

"I don't care about any other candidate; they have no chance. I am concerned about your running," he said. I was flattered, but I said that I might not win the reform nomination. The mayor, a political being, surprised me with some advice. "Don't even think of running for the reform nomination. It doesn't mean a thing." He paused. I suspected he may have realized that he was arguing against his own mission. I said I was a founder of the movement and asked how I could now ignore it. "That was then, when the idea was to save the party; this is now, when those so-called reformers are just scrambling for the best jobs for themselves." He was referring to the all-white liberal clubs. I thought, but did not say, that I agreed with him.

He then said that he was going to give me some confidential information that I was not at liberty to disclose. I told him that I would keep his confidence. He said that a poll that they conducted showed that I "might" beat Farbstein and then corrected himself by saying that I "would probably beat the incumbent what with your registration campaigns, your popularity in the district, and the election of two district leaders [Rios and Harrington] in the heart of the district."

"You make it seem as if it were an attractive option for me," I said.

The mayor said, "It will be a dirty campaign. Farbstein is desperate, and there will be no holds barred. You might lose."

I said, "Well then, I might not win, but my life will go on."

Mayor Wagner looked at me, paused, and said, "I have an alternative. You can be a judge. You will be one of the youngest judges on the bench."

For the first time that I can recall, I was speechless.

The mayor raised his glass and said, "A toast to Judge Lane."

I thanked him and said that I would always recall this moment when I was threatened with a judgeship. He asked if I was turning down his offer due to some concept of principle. I said that principle never entered my mind. I told him I was declining his offer due to my fear of never-ending boredom. I explained that when I appeared in court and was required to listen to arguments that were of no interest to me while waiting for my case to be called, I pitied the judge who was required to be there each day for years on end.

I agreed with the leaders of the reform movement to participate in a reform-based primary, members only, to decide who the candidate would be. My reform opponents said that my opposition to the Vietnam War was unpatriotic and demonstrated that I was unfit for office. Since most people did not know anything about the subject, the personal attacks upon my loyalty carried less of a sting than I thought they might. Others said that it was a small conflict, basically a matter for the French, and it could not possibly develop into anything that would involve the United States. One opponent said, "It is absurd to suggest that we might one day send troops to fight there." I said the Israeli-Palestinian conflict might be resolved if both parties agreed to a two-state solution. This, claimed my reform opponents, was a form of anti-Semitism even though I was Jewish, since the West Bank and the Gaza belonged exclusively to Israel and would forever. Many years later the state of Israel advocated the two-state solution. However, during the campaign, my position on the Middle East was widely distributed and attacked in the Jewish communities that comprised large sections of the district. I learned that premature analysis may be exceedingly troubling as nothing is more dangerous than an idea whose time is about to come.

In spite of these positions and the emotional response to them, I won the majority of the votes cast by the members of the reform movement in the district. As it turns out, that didn't matter since the reform leaders had worked out a method by which the members of the newly formed clubs, such as the one in East Harlem and the reform groups on the Lower East Side, also primarily composed of blacks and Latinos, were each credited three-fifths of a vote; the members of the older clubs on the Upper West Side, primarily non-Latino, white members who had elected white candidates to public office, were each given a full vote. None of this "one person, one vote" nonsense. All of these machinations were worked out after I had foolishly committed myself to participate in what had been erroneously called the "reform process."

Congress held some attraction for me, but the methods of the reformers in adopting 1950 Mississippi racial standards in a reform race in New York became a serious detriment to the future development of clubs in minority communities. The reform movement, perhaps inevitably, was beginning to emulate the regular organization in many ways. In 1887, the British historian Lord Acton said, "Power tends to corrupt and absolute power corrupts absolutely. . . . There is no greater heresy than that the office sanctifies the holder of it." Once again, Lord Acton was proven correct. I thought seriously about trying to correct that approach, and I have sometimes wondered about whether I should have made that effort.[2]

Years later, on a cold and wet night in 1982, I was driving from Washington, DC, to New York City in a still serviceable but aging car with a malfunctioning heater. The windshield wipers seemed more intent on making indignant sounds than on removing raindrops. Traffic was heavy, and the drivers moved cautiously through the storm.

In spite of it all, my mood was exuberant, for I was about to have dinner with an old friend I had not seen in years and also catch up on New York state politics, from which I had been absent for a long time.

I had known Bill Haddad since my early days of community organizing and political activity in East Harlem, beginning in the 1950s. A remarkable renaissance man, he founded the Peace Corps and was its associate director as well as an investigative reporter nominated for the Pulitzer Prize and an assistant both to Senator Estes Kefauver of Tennessee and later to Robert Kennedy. He was a kind and generous man and a strong supporter of my various endeavors.

A few days earlier, we had agreed to meet during a telephone call during which he told me that he was doing some work for Mario Cuomo, a candidate in the Democratic primary for New York governor. All the pundits said was it was a hopeless race against Ed Koch, who was well known as the popular mayor of New York City.

I left the main road and pulled into a gas station in search of a telephone to tell Bill I would be late.

A man answered, and I asked to speak to Bill.

"And your name, please?" he asked. I answered, and he inquired, "What is it you wish to speak about with Mr. Haddad?"

I was cold and damp and getting irritable, never having claimed for myself the virtue of patience. "We are having dinner, and I am going to be late—"

He interrupted, "And where do you plan to eat? What kind of food do you prefer?"

"Who are you? And why do you need to know the name of the restaurant and my food preference as prerequisites to handing the telephone to Bill?"

"I am Mr. Haddad's secretary, and I am—" He began to laugh, and I could hear Bill, who took the phone and told me that I had been talking to Mario Cuomo.

With Bill as campaign manager, Cuomo was elected that year, the first of three consecutive terms. In recent years I have gone back to my first conversation with Mario Cuomo and thought about his stewardship of New York and especially his appointments to the New York courts. Had Governor Cuomo, who possessed one of the most brilliant and principled minds in contemporary American politics,

decided to run for the presidency, a matter he had seriously considered, and been elected, the world would have had far better moments.
Had he been responsible for appointing federal judges and justices,
our society would be far more just and transparently devoted to the
rule of law.

The Assembly Line

8

|||||||||||||||||||||||||||||||||||||||||||||||||||||||

In 1961, shortly after my election to the New York State Assembly, a reporter for an Albany newspaper called to arrange a meeting with me at the hotel where he was certain I would be staying. He told me that all of the Democrats were registering in one hotel, a fine establishment conveniently situated just down the hill from the capitol building, while all of the Republicans would be at a more luxurious place a block away.

I called the "Democratic" hotel, identified myself, and was told that no rooms were available. After a search I found a very modest motel more than a mile from the capitol that had a room. With no public transportation available, I knew I would have to hike to work up the hill on icy streets and often through snow or rain and wind. I was young, and it was an inconvenience but not a problem.

Meetings in the evening were sometimes held in the "Democratic" hotel. After one event I met Nick Kissburg, the lobbyist for the Teamsters Union assigned to the state legislature. We had a drink and talked about issues, and when I was about to leave I reached for my coat.

"Where are you going?" he asked.

I gave him the name of my motel. He said that he admired my independence but thought that it was idiotic of me to refuse to stay at the same hotel that the other Democrats patronized. I told him that I had tried but no rooms were available.

He said, "Those petty, pathetic pricks."

"I'm impressed by your instantaneous alliteration, but I don't have the faintest idea what you're talking about."

"The hotel always has rooms for every Democrat elected to the legislature," he said. "It's negotiated long in advance."

I said it was not a matter of importance, and the daily walks were probably good for me.

The next afternoon I received a call from the concierge at the "Democratic" hotel stating that my room was ready. I moved in within an hour. That evening Nick, who was always a presence there, said, "I'm glad you moved," adding that he had been furious. "Telling a man that there is no room at the fucking inn, like years ago."

I tried to shrug it off by asking if he thought that they might now name a religion after me.

He laughed. "Do you want to know how it happened?" Before I could answer, he continued, "I grabbed the manager last night and said, 'You don't have room for Lane.' He said, 'The leadership wants him to stay elsewhere.' I said, 'Well, you got a choice to make. You know I'm the Teamsters. There will be no milk, no bread, nothing delivered as long as Lane is kept out.' He said, 'I understand.'"

The Democratic members of the assembly who had been elected for the first time were summoned to a meeting with the Democratic leadership in the lower house. The first speaker informed us of the perks that would be available. He had all the relevant facts and figures. Lawyers could increase their fees by 50 percent and would attract an estimated 38 percent increase in clients by publicizing their newly acquired status. All would be provided with hundreds of tickets to various racetracks for distribution in their districts. Various committee assignments could, in time, add to the member's income. The speaker went on for some time as he took on the role of a legislative Santa Claus dispensing valuable gifts to all who were present so long as they went along.

Then the Democratic leader of the assembly greeted us and informed us of the time, date, and place of the first Democratic Party meeting with all of the members of the assembly. I asked the leader if we would be informed as to when the meeting was going to transform into a caucus. He asked why I wanted that information, and I told him I had promised my constituents that I would attend all meetings and no caucuses.

At the meetings, all subjects could be discussed, and no member was obliged to surrender his or her vote for the common good of the party. However, during a caucus the members would be instructed as to how the party wanted them to vote, and when a majority went along with the leaders, as historically they always did, all those present were required to vote the party line when the bill was presented. I considered it my responsibility to vote for or against proposed legislation based upon my own evaluation and in the best interests of those who elected me. The caucus was the method employed to permit the corrupt regime to sell or trade our votes.

Before the first meeting began I informed the press that when the party moved into its usual caucus mode I would walk out of the room. That step permitted me to control my own vote. The reporter for the *New York Times* and many others had gathered in the lobby to report upon that development. When the leader said that he thought the caucus should begin, he added, "That is, if it is all right with Mr. Lane." I said that I could not control what they did in my absence and that I was withdrawing from the meeting. He urged me to stay and said that a caucus was not required that day. I remained at the meeting.

The Democratic Party in the New York State Assembly continued to hold regular meetings throughout the next two years without ever convening a caucus. For two years the members were free to vote their conscience; I thought it a shame that so few took the opportunity to do so. The word still came from the machine, and most, but not all, acquiesced.

One of the first legislative matters, the Republican Speaker Joseph F. Carlino stated, was the immediate passage of the $100 million fallout shelter bill. Funds were to be expended to build shelters in public institutions to be used in case of an atomic attack. The Democratic leadership fully supported that effort. There was no need to read the massive bill, Carlino explained, since it had been passed the previous year by the assembly. We just should all vote for it, he insisted, even without reading it. The problem was that the senate and the assembly had passed different versions of the bill that were rushed through the process without an effort made to reconcile the two bills. I suggested that there were a number of us now present who were not here the previous year and that we should be given an opportunity to read the proposed legislation before voting on it. Any member can strike out a bill so that it cannot be voted upon at once. We did not vote that day.

Carlino knew that the governor was almost fanatically devoted to the concept of fallout shelters. Governor Rockefeller had a fallout shelter built in the governor's mansion in Albany. He had one constructed in his apartment building on Fifth Avenue in Manhattan. He ordered that the largest fallout shelter in the country be built in Albany. The $4 million monstrosity was to protect, he said, some seven hundred "key state officials" as well as "businessmen" with jobs in Albany (vital to keep the lobbyists alive) who had been selected in advance. Rockefeller posed for an official picture in his personal fallout shelter. In the photograph he held in both hands a pamphlet about shelters. On the shelves behind him were cans of sliced beets, corn, tomatoes, and other goods, as well as a small first-aid kit that might be invaluable if a hydrogen bomb liquefied the shelter. Present also was a set of silverware in an elaborate box.

Rockefeller talked about shelters incessantly, not just in his annual messages to the legislature but in meetings with far-removed heads of state. The prime minister of India, Jawaharlal Nehru, discussed that fixation after he visited New York in 1960. Nehru said, "Governor Rockefeller is a very strange man. All he wants to talk about is bomb shelters. Why does he think I am interested in bomb shelters? He gave me a pamphlet on how to build my own shelter."

Almost all prominent scientists agreed that the fallout shelters were little more than a hoax; they could provide no serious refuge from an atomic attack. Yet the need for such shelters formed the heart of Rockefeller's addresses to the legislature and the public. President Kennedy stated that he would follow the progress of the proposal in New York before deciding if it should become a national project. The demand for fallout shelters fueled hysteria during the Cold War days, as did drills that taught students to cower under their desks for security from a blast that would level the school, the desks, and the children.

I read the bill and began a public campaign against it. I spoke at meetings throughout the state and called for a march on Albany to oppose it. Under the headline "Speaker Stumbles," *Time* magazine began, "Sleek, sonorous Joseph F. Carlino, G.O.P. boss of booming Nassau County and Speaker of the New York State Assembly, was a leading aspirant to succeed Nelson Rockefeller some day." The newsmagazine continued, "But last week ambitious Joe Carlino was fighting for his political life." The origin of the problem, *Time* concluded, was a "shaggy lone wolf."[1]

I was not really shaggy then, not that there is anything wrong with it. I was six feet tall, weighed 175 pounds, wore conservative dark suits with those skinny ties that were the fashion, and was clean shaven with rather short hair. Photographs at that time support those descriptions.

The march to the state capitol was one of the largest demonstrations there in recent history. Many thousands of people arrived by bus, train, and car, assembling in front of the building, where they heard from scientists, leaders of the movements for a sane nuclear policy, trade union leaders, professors, and one shaggy wolf, no longer alone.

During this period I received a call from a man who said that he had some information that I might consider useful. He seemed reasonable and sane, and I agreed to meet, but by then I had been so immersed in the legislative process with my colleagues on both sides of the aisle that my barometer for making such distinctions was less than acute.

We met, and that brief meeting may have seriously affected both the state and national drives for fallout shelters. He passed me a brochure soliciting investors in Lancer Industries, the only company authorized to manufacture fallout shelters in New York State. This company was set to reap windfall profits from the bill. The very privately circulated brochure stated that the well-paid general counsel of Lancer was the Speaker of the New York State Assembly, the Honorable Joseph F. Carlino. Carlino was also listed as one of the members of the board of directors.

I have never before divulged the source of the damning evidence, since the document needed no one to authenticate it. He authorized me to reveal that he had been the source if I waited ten years. The man who gave me the evidence five decades ago was the owner of the shop where the brochure had been printed.

Since the legislature had no serious code of ethics—the Speaker could have sold the steps to the capitol building without an ethics violation—I called for the adoption of a real code of ethics for members of the senate and assembly. I also called for an independent investigation into Carlino's blatant conflict of interest.

The matter was referred to the Assembly Committee on Ethics and Guidance, a committee that served under Carlino's stewardship, to determine if Carlino had violated a nonexistent code. *L'affaire* Carlino continued for more than a year with new disclosures, new witnesses, and new denials. Carlino appeared before his own committee to present his view, which, as it turned out, was not much different from mine. *Time* reported that when Carlino testified he admitted that he had profited from his relationship with Lancer and that his defense "sometimes seemed limp." Carlino testified that he might in time have had a "conflict of interest problem."

The rumble in the assembly was coming, the media informed New Yorkers. There was about to be a confrontation between me and Carlino. The New York newspapers heralded it as a battle between the silver-tongued Speaker, an eloquent spokesman and phenomenal debater, and me. I appeared at the specified time and spoke on the floor of the assembly. Carlino was silent; he was not even present. Confident that the politicians would absolve him, since many had similarly but less extravagantly and publicly profited in the past, he remained in his office until after the vote. Carlino was found not to have violated the code of ethics by the assembly unanimously, with the exception of my vote in opposition. Editorials in newspapers across the state said kind things about one man standing alone. Another almost useless code of ethics was drafted and approved shortly thereafter. I pointed out, to no avail, the assembly's flawed approach to a serious problem and that the heralded new code was almost as impotent as the one it replaced. The media seemed pleased at the time to endorse the new code.

The fallout shelter bill passed; however, after Carlino's role in the scandal was exposed, public opinion was so opposed to the concept that no funds were allocated for the shelters. President Kennedy then decided to abandon the whole idea. Carlino was defeated three years later when he sought reelection. He then became a highly paid lobbyist for the racetrack industry, a wealthy organization dependent upon the legislature to set its schedule.

Freedom Ride

9

||||||||||||||||||||||||||||||||||||||||||||||||

Prologue

In May 1961, thirteen activists left Washington, DC, for Birmingham, Alabama, a hotbed of racism, with plans to continue on to Jackson, Mississippi. Seven were black, and six were white. They traveled on Trailways and Greyhound buses, testing and supporting the recent US Supreme Court decision that made racial discrimination unlawful when practiced against those engaged in interstate travel.

Before the riders arrived in Birmingham, Eugene "Bull" Connor, the public safety commissioner for the city and a member of the Ku Klux Klan, met with Gary Thomas Rowe, a leader of the KKK's Eastview Klavern #13, the most violent group in the state, to plan an attack upon the riders. Connor told Rowe that he and his group would be immune from arrest. Given that license, the mob slashed the tires of one bus, firebombed it, and then held the doors shut in an attempt to burn the occupants to death. After an explosion, the mob fled.

The other bus was also attacked by Connor and Rowe and their fellow Klan members, who beat the passengers with iron pipes, chains, and baseball bats. Rowe was among the most virulent of the assailants. He was a major player in the attempted murder sequences and one of the most violent members of the mob. He was paid by the FBI, reported to them about crimes he had initiated, and later testified about his fellow criminals. He was further compensated when he was accepted into the federal witness protection program and lived in Savannah under the name Thomas Neal Moore. Alabama investigators uncovered evidence that Rowe had also been involved in the bombing of the East Sixteenth Street Baptist Church in 1963, where four young African American girls died. He later admitted that he shot a black man.

Among those beaten was Jim Peck, an acquaintance of mine. He was hospitalized, suffered a concussion, and required fifty-three stitches to close the wounds to his head. Most of the wounded were refused treatment at local hospitals. They were rescued from a mob by Reverend Fred Shuttlesworth, who had arranged for church members to drive through the screaming crowd of racists and bring the riders to safety.

Many of the Freedom Riders who made it to Jackson were sent to a maximum-security death-row section of the notorious Parchman Penitentiary, where they were abused. They sang freedom songs, and when they refused to be silent, the guards confiscated mattresses, sheets, toothbrushes, and window screens. Swarms of mosquitoes from the surrounding farmland entered the cells. At 2:00 AM the guards hosed the prisoners with DDT. Their only crime had been to travel together in their own country.

On May 24, Reverend James Lawson was arrested as he entered Jackson on a Trailways bus. I did not know Jim then; later we became colleagues and very dear friends. That same day John Lewis, now a member of Congress, was arrested. On June 8 (a day with significance for me, since I spent part of it as a prisoner in a Mississippi jail), Stokely Carmichael, then just nineteen years old, later a movement leader, was arrested at the Jackson train station.

The Ride

After the attempted murder of the young women and men, and their subsequent imprisonment, a movement was created. The perilous trail that they had pioneered became a sacred path, with the Holy Grail located somewhere south of Jackson, Mississippi. Black and white, together they journeyed to demonstrate that democracy might live in a multiracial America. Always threatened and taunted, sometimes struck and wounded, invariably refused service by restaurants and lunch counters at every stop, they were each arrested as they reached the capital of Mississippi. These few men and women were named the Freedom Riders, and the prayers of millions rode with each of them as they embarked upon their dangerous mission.

In Harlem, Gene Callender had left the Mid-Harlem Community Parish to be installed as the minister at the prestigious and powerful Church of the Master upon the retirement of its famous leader, Reverend James Robinson. That church, located on the fringes of Harlem, drew its parishioners not from the down and out but rather from the up and in. Gene often reminded them in his sermons about their responsibility to others.

One Saturday night, as Gene and I played in a bridge tournament, we had serious but nonspecific discussions about the Freedom Riders. I sipped some scotch as I saluted their courage. Casually my friend asked if I had ever considered joining their ranks. I was then a member of the New York State legislature, and I believed no elected official had ever been arrested as a Freedom Rider. I said that in principle I had no objection to the concept of being arrested but that I could hardly go alone, since the point was to illustrate the right of African Americans (I am sure that I then said "Negroes") to travel together with white Americans from state to state.

Gene said, "How about Percy?" He was referring to Percy Sutton, an elegant and accomplished black attorney who had become the president of the New York chapter of the NAACP and who was later elected borough president of Manhattan.

"Percy would be a wonderful companion," I offered.

When the evening ended Gene asked me to be at his church the next morning. I agreed. I suspected that I knew what Gene was planning. Later Percy told me that he had also figured it out.

That Sunday morning was bright and brisk. Gene preached with emotion and skill to a full house. Then he paused, looked about at the audience, and said he had an important announcement to make.

"Two dear friends of our church," he said, "have agreed to set forth upon an historic mission for our nation." His deep, melodious voice took on added timbre. "This morning we acknowledge and honor our colleagues, Mark Lane—please stand, Mark—and Percy Sutton—you too, Percy—as they travel through the southern states of our nation as Freedom Riders, to witness, for all of us, our commitment to freedom and equality. May God speed your way and keep you safe, dear brother Percy and dear brother Mark."

Before brother Mark could even catch his breath, the parishioners were participating in an offering to cover the expenses anticipated for our travel. Several hundred dollars were raised, and as they were pressed into Percy's hands and mine we began the noble task of comparing calendars.

A few days later, the parishioners' impassioned praise still echoing in our minds, Percy Sutton and I arrived at Newark Airport. I had embarked from La Guardia Airport and Idlewild Airport on numerous occasions, but this was my first flight originating in New Jersey. For years afterward, whenever I drove past that airport, I thought of the flight to Atlanta, the gateway to a bus trip through Georgia and Alabama. I thought also of the fear hovering at the edges of my consciousness.

The point was to be together. A nonsegregated taxi ride from the Atlanta airport was not all that difficult to arrange. Accommodations in Atlanta were a different matter, as they were segregated by law. Percy said he had the solution. He gave an address to the driver, and soon we arrived at the all-black YMCA in the middle of black Atlanta. As we walked up the steps, Percy leading the way, a hundred eyes focused upon me. I was, I felt certain, the first white person to enter that ancient building since it had been constructed.

We each requested a small single room. A few elderly men in the small lobby stared and looked toward one another in perplexed silence. The clerk behind the scarred desk hesitated, began to warn me that I must have made some awful mistake, and then finally gave me a key. I reached for my luggage, but Percy, no doubt intoxicated by the moment, grabbed at it first, stating in a voice loud enough for all those in the lobby staring at me to hear, "Dat's all right, Mista Mark, I take it fo' you."

The spectators were puzzled. Mista Mark had brought his Negro retainer with him. Percy could not stop laughing for days. "You should have seen your expression," he often began to say before collapsing into convulsions of howling roars and cackles.

The bus trip to Montgomery, Alabama, was less amusing. Before Percy and I embarked upon our trip, I had called Attorney General Robert Kennedy, with whom I had worked closely during JFK's campaign, to request protection from illegal acts, including attacks by civilians and arrest by those acting under color of state law. His noncommittal reply, "We'll look into it," was less than reassuring. The administration had called for a "cooling off period" and suggested that the Freedom Rides be suspended. Bobby issued a public statement explaining that he did "not feel that the Department of Justice can side with one group or the other in disputes over Constitutional rights." This exchange had been publicized, and therefore news of our visit had preceded us. I told Percy that, in view of Bobby's ambivalence, perhaps his agency should be renamed the Department of Justice or Injustice.

Several large and angry men, responding to the shouts from the crowd—"There they are" and "That's them, the nigger and the nigger-lover"—began to board the bus. I had supported Dr. King's and Jim Peck's nonviolent philosophy in spirit and general terms. Now my commitment to it was to be tested. I stood and grabbed my attaché case, prepared to strike the first would-be assailant with all my force as I looked across the aisle to Percy. He was equally positioned. We agreed, in a word or two, that we would inflict the most grievous bodily harm possible as a matter of self-defense.

The men who had been moving in single file in the narrow aisle toward us stopped as the man in the lead hesitated. Both Percy and I were a bit over six feet, fit, young, armed in a fashion, and clearly determined. There was a discussion. Their name calling and other indicia of bravado increased in volume and intensity as the potential assailants withdrew from the bus.

At the next stop, a larger town, reporters and photographers were present as well as unruly protesters. Percy and I left the bus, pushed through the crowd, entered the luncheonette, and sat down at the counter. The waitress and waiter sought to give the impression that they did not know we were there, but, fascinated by our presence, they continued to sneak looks in our direction. During one of those indiscreet moments I caught the waitress's eye.

"May we each have a cup of coffee, please?" I asked.

She appeared amazed. "Can't. He's a nigger, and you're with him."

It was clear enough. Flashbulbs exploded; photographers jostled one another to get that perfect shot. My request for two glasses of water was rejected with a shrug. I explained that facilities that serve interstate transportation are precluded from practicing racial discrimination. Passengers were boarding the bus, and my arguments were not sufficiently persuasive. Percy and I rushed back to the bus through the disgruntled and muttering crowd. We settled in for the next part of the journey.

I looked at him. He seemed poised, elegantly dressed as usual, professional, and calm. He had been born in the South. He knew its potential for violence far better than I did. Yet he was the personification of grace under fire, which in my mind, then and now, is the ultimate definition of courage. Of one thing I was certain. I could not have been more fortunate in the choice of a companion for the trip down freedom road.

We finally reached Montgomery many stops later without further incident and without a cup of coffee. We had tried to avoid the former; our efforts to secure the latter were universally rebuffed, often in anger but once in a while with regret, and from that small sign we took enormous encouragement.

In the cradle of the Confederacy we were met by a number of young black lawyers. We ate with them, they offered their homes to us, and together we spoke of a new South that might one day result from these efforts. They expressed their gratitude to me, but I knew that my brief, well-publicized trip through the South added but a drop to the mighty river of righteousness that Dr. King said would one day flow.

I knew that the real work for radical change was being done by those who lived there, the women, the men, their children, black and white, who engaged in voter registration drives, who fought each moment of racism that marked each day of their lives, who went to jail, walked to work, boycotted stores, and lived at risk of imprisonment, poverty, and even loss of life. If our trip could help bring further attention to their struggle, the effort was worthwhile.

In the early hours of the morning it was determined that while those who had preceded us were arrested at the Jackson bus station, no one had tested the police reaction to a flight to that city.

"Target the airport," they said. "It will provide a new experience."

It was easy to convince me. The bus trip held no special charm for me. We might even get a drink on the plane, and once we were airborne, confrontation by a mob made up of club-wielding, red-faced, angry villains was unlikely.

We landed in Jackson and entered the almost vacant, modern, relatively small airport building. A few police officers and their chief stood off to one side, silently observing us. Percy said he had to utilize the facilities. We found the white men's room. Percy preceded me as the officers moved slowly toward us. I was in a quandary. If I did not enter the rest room, Percy might be arrested alone for violating some ancient sacred Mississippi statute based upon the purity of white-sponsored urination. If I did enter, I might be arrested for some other crime existent at that time only in the minds of the local police.

I opened the door and said, "Percy, for God's sake, let's get out of here. Do you want us to get busted for disorderly conduct in a bathroom?"

Together we left the now forever-sullied facility and sat down in the waiting room. The chief of police walked up to us. He addressed only me.

"Mr. Lane, we have been expecting you." He paused. "You and this here—man—well, you cannot sit here together."

"Why is that?" I inquired.

"You could incite a riot!" he exclaimed.

I looked about. One woman, perhaps sixty years old, was sitting a few rows from us. She was concentrating on her knitting. She was, with the exception of the two future criminals and the police, the only other person present.

"Chief," I said, "I'm sure you can handle her if she gets out of line."

"I hate to do this, Mr. Lane," the chief said, "but you and—well—your friend, you both are under arrest."

Percy had remained silent as he observed our little ritual exchange. He was precluded from it by reason of birth. I looked at him, filled with respect. He had come home to the South. He had made his silent witness.

The chief sat in the front passenger seat, Percy and I in the backseat.

"Are you really a member of the legislature in New York?" he asked. I said that I was.

"You ever see our state capitol?" I said I had not.

"Drive past the capitol," the chief instructed the driver.

It was a magnificent building; I said so.

"Take him past the old capitol. It's not much out of the way," he said.

The old capitol building was charming; I said so.

I felt odd about our conversation. For an attorney, a cheerful and civil series of exchanges with the enemy was not unprecedented. What was disturbing was that Percy was excluded.

"You know, Chief," I began, "we have been together for several days. That is how we've been making our point."

"So I heard, Mr. Lane," he replied.

"On the bus for days, in the Negro YMCA, in homes in Montgomery, on the plane ride here, and even in your waiting room at the airport," I said.

"Negro YMCA?" he asked incredulously.

"Yes. But we never could figure out one problem."

"What's that?" said the chief.

"How we could get an integrated ride from the airport to the center of Jackson. Chief, we both want to thank you for that," I said.

The chief, who had been turned around in his seat, slowly looked forward, never addressed another word to me, and was in fact silent until we reached the city jail except to say to the driver, "Let's go. Put on some speed." We were charged with disorderly conduct by improperly "congregating" and placed in separate and segregated cells.

When the barred door slammed shut, I experienced strong feelings. I was powerless and, therefore, fearful. I was aware that many people, including the attorney general and colleagues in the media, knew where I was, which was a comforting thought. I also knew that I was alone in a jail cell in Mississippi. I thought of Percy and how much more terrifying it might be for him. I would never find out, for Percy would likely, in retrospect, dismiss the event as a nuisance.

Later two guards came for me. No, one of them said, I was not being released. They took me to a small office in the jail. There was a chair, a desk, and a telephone. A guard told me that there was a call for me. A *New York Times* reporter wanted to interview me. We spoke for a few minutes; I suggested that he call Percy also, and he said the *Times* had tried but was informed that he was unavailable. As I was escorted back to my cell I asked why Sutton had not been permitted to answer his call. There was silence, except for the slamming of the door.

Several minutes later the *New York Post* called, followed immediately by a radio station asking for a live interview. After that third interview, the guards told me it would be the last one, although dozens of other media representatives persisted. I did not object. I had never known of any prisoner in a New York jail who had been allowed to conduct a single media interview on the day of his arrest. Later, Percy and I were released on bail pending appeal, after having been convicted without a trial and sentenced to four months' imprisonment. Each state does things somewhat differently from others, none more so than Mississippi.

When we returned home we met with Gene and his parishioners in New York. Calls from lawyers in Alabama, Georgia, and Mississippi and from other Freedom Riders told us that we had contributed by publicizing their struggle. Percy and I, however terrified we had been at various moments, knew that we had been privileged travelers, not brutally beaten as had been Jim Peck and so far not thrown in prison, a far different environment than our relatively safe jail cells, as had those who preceded us.

Later in New York City, a meeting attended by more than one hundred Freedom Riders was convened by the Congress of Racial Equality (CORE), the organization that had largely financed and organized the campaign. Percy and I were among the very few who had covered their own expenses or had been given traveling funds privately. CORE was broke, we were all told. It had exhausted all of its funds in the effort. Therefore, since the state of Mississippi had set one day for us all to return to face trial, the CORE leadership had determined that "when we are down there we will abide by all local ordinances."

When a young student asked what that meant exactly, he was told, "In the courthouse Negroes use the 'colored' restrooms and drink from the 'colored' fountains, while whites will use the 'white only' facilities." Percy and I were less than pleased, and we said so. We had not embarked upon that long and challenging journey to capitulate in the end to degrading southern customs. The CORE leaders argued that further challenges meant further arrests, higher bail, and more return trips to court, all of which cost money, and none was left for the continued struggle.

Percy said that he and I would return to Jackson, would violate indecent laws, and would remain in prison if need be until the movement could afford to continue the effort or until the walls of racism came tumbling down. The two of us, filled with bravado in public, returned as the fearful advance army to the scene of battle. A friend met us at the airport and drove us to the courthouse. Before entering the building, we shook hands, and I said, "It could be a long time." We were prepared for a four-month stay in some unknown Mississippi farm prison.

Percy said, "I know it. Do we have a choice?" It was not a question.

We entered the courthouse together. Every COLORED ONLY and WHITE ONLY sign had been removed by the authorities. In their place were newly stenciled cardboard plaques that read MEN'S ROOM, DEFENDANTS and LADIES' ROOM, DEFENDANTS. The state of Mississippi, too, was running out of funds and could no longer afford the confrontation.

I said, "The signs are temporary. They'll be down soon." Percy answered, "Yes. The cardboard signs will go now—but one day soon all the other signs will disappear also."

On March 29, 1962, our trial began before Hinds County judge Russell Moore. Almost at once the prosecutor, Jack Travis, moved for a directed verdict of acquittal because, he said, Percy and I were "not congregating" with other people when we were arrested since we were "alone" at that time. Judge Moore dismissed the charges, and we were free. Of course, those facts had been known before we were arrested, fined, and sentenced all without a trial. We had been jailed and then released on bail with pending prison sentences. The only newly discovered fact was that we were prepared to continue the struggle against segregation.

||||||

About two decades later, after I gave a lecture at a college in a town in Alabama about the assassination of John F. Kennedy, I asked one of the students to drive me to the bus station. The same luncheonette was still there, although it had not aged gracefully. I sat at the counter and read the menu. I thought of Percy. For a moment he was with me, smiling now, as I saw a couple of black teenagers enter the restaurant, order hamburgers and Cokes, and laugh about some private matter. They had no idea of the drama that had been played out on this spot twenty years ago. A waitress handed me a menu. I glanced at it. I left without ordering. There was nothing else that I wanted.

I saw my mug shot, taken by the Jackson Police Department in 1961, now published in this book, years later when Julian Bond found it in the files of the Mississippi Sovereignty Commission and sent it to me. That state agency, led by the governor, the lieutenant governor, the Speaker of the House, the attorney general of Mississippi, and a former special agent of the FBI, had been created in 1965 to oppose decisions of the US Supreme Court, the Civil Rights Act of 1964, and the 1965 Voting Rights Act—in other words, to preserve racism and segregation in the state. Through the Sovereignty Commission, the state collected and sealed the names of eighty-seven thousand "suspects," including all of the more than four hundred Freedom Riders.

In spite of the state's efforts at secrecy, many years later, in 1989, a federal judge ordered that the documents be made available. The Mississippi Sovereignty Commission had been empowered "to perform any and all acts deemed necessary and proper to protect the sovereignty of the state of Mississippi." Apparently, among those "acts" was murder.

Included in the records was proof that the investigator for the state agency, A. L. Hopkins, obtained identifying information about three civil rights workers, including the license plate number of the automobile they were using. He provided that information to the Neshoba County sheriff's office. That office was involved in the murder of James Chaney, Andrew Goodman, and Michael Schwerner near Philadelphia, Mississippi, on June 21, 1964. The federal judge trying the case referred to the civil rights workers as "one nigger, one Jew, and a white man." They had visited the state to help register African Americans who wished to vote. Not one of the state government officials was ever prosecuted.

The commission also planted informants in the offices of attorneys who represented those framed by the state and secretly financed the White Citizens Council with a substantial portion of the state funds provided to it. The files of the commission reveal that it continued to follow my activities in matters bearing no relationship to the state of Mississippi for a number of years after the false charge against me had been dismissed.

Fifty years later Oprah invited all of the surviving Freedom Riders to be honored on her television program. It was a joyful moment for many of us, but my traveling partner and many others had died before the honors arrived. The city council of Jackson issued an award to each of us for excellence as outstanding citizens. The state of Mississippi passed a resolution celebrating our contribution to the civil rights movement and stating that we had "called national attention to the violent disregard for the law that was used to enforce segregation in the Southern United States." They also planned a theme park based upon the efforts of the Freedom Riders in order to promote tourism in the state.

During May 2011, the president of the United States signed a proclamation stating that the Freedom Riders had "sent a resounding message to the rest of our Nation that desegregation was a moral imperative" and that through "unflinching bravery and unyielding commitment" the Freedom Riders inspired "many of those involved to become lifelong activists, organizers, and leaders in the civil rights movement." He added, "Because of their efforts, and the work of those who marched and stood against injustice, we live in a country where all Americans have the right to dream and choose their own destiny." Actually, although Percy did not and the young people who suffered from state-inflicted brutality may not have, I did flinch a few times.

Rush to Judgment: The Journey Begins

10

The judge had recessed for lunch, and I was returning to the criminal courts building in Manhattan. It was November 22, 1963. Small crowds had gathered around radios to hear the incredible news reports that President Kennedy had been shot. In court, over my objection, the judge directed that the trial proceed. At the end of that day, as I raced to a subway station to return to my apartment, I knew less about the facts than most Americans.

On November 24, 1963, Lee Harvey Oswald was shot to death in the basement of the Dallas Police and Courts Building while surrounded by Dallas police officers who were there, they said, to protect him. The murderer was Jack Ruby, who had performed services for the FBI and who had worked for Representative Richard Nixon by looking into "un-American activities." Ruby also had friendly relations with numerous police officers for whom he provided special services, including, but not limited to, free drinks from an elite, special area set aside for them when they visited his crude and raunchy Dallas bar. Previously, Ruby had been seized by the police in Chicago as a suspect in the murder of a union leader. While the information about Ruby's background was not publicly available and was later suppressed by the Warren Commission, the circumstances of the murder of the suspect on national television raised serious concerns. The Dallas district attorney, Henry Wade, who had regularly assured the press that Oswald was guilty to a "moral certainty" and that he would be prosecuted and executed, felt called upon after Oswald's death to outline his case at a press conference. The *New York Times* provided a transcript of Wade's accusations, which consisted of fifteen points that he said proved his case. Wade, who had formerly been employed by the FBI, said that he had presented "the evidence, piece by piece, for you."

I studied the document. Some media reporters had been impressed. But those covering the story had gone to Dallas as White House political correspondents and had little experience with criminal cases. Had Wade presented his views to reporters who covered the crime beat, he likely would have been confronted by many searching questions, and his piece-by-piece charges might have received a far different reception.

At that point I had been a defense attorney in criminal cases for a decade, including murder cases, and I knew that an indictment always seemed impressive. Yet defendants are subsequently acquitted in some cases. Cross-examination is the heart and soul of our judicial system and the engine that drives our concept of due process. During direct testimony the rehearsed statement of the witness is presented and almost always seems persuasive. It is during cross-examination that the story is tested and the truth often emerges. Wade's uncontested allegations had not been scrutinized.

I made a decision that had implications well beyond anything that I might have anticipated. I decided, after wondering why no one else had done so, to write and seek to publish a response to Wade. The writing was time consuming, a ten-thousand-word analysis, but not difficult, since everything Wade offered was speculation, consisting of statements rebutted by the witnesses or clearly false or misleading information. Unlike the Wade proclamation, the evaluation I wrote was understated and offered no speculation and no conclusion. I suggested that a comprehensive review of the evidence was required.

The difficulty arose in having it published. I offered the article, specifying that I asked for no fee for it, to almost every publication in the country. *Fact* magazine, a publication that asserted it was a magazine of controversy, declined to publish it, stating that it was "too controversial." The editors reached that conclusion without having read the article, demonstrating that the subject, not the analysis, was the basis for the rejection. That same result followed letters and discussions with the editors of *Look, Life*, the *Saturday Evening Post*, the *Nation*, and dozens of others. James Aronson, the editor of the *National Guardian*, called. He had heard about my article and was interested. I told him that I could send it to him but that I did not want him to print it, as it was controversial enough on its own and I did not wish to complicate the matter further by having a newspaper of the left be the original publisher. He read it and called within the hour; the *Guardian* was eager to publish. He said the article was a historic document and that it would be unprincipled for me to withhold it based upon the publication's politics. I was unable to offer a logical rebuttal, since his argument was not without merit, especially since I had offered to it *Time* and *Life*, two magazines of the right. Since my own political preferences were closer to those of the *Guardian*, I had to question if I was seeking protective political cover for the cause, that is, the article, or for myself.

I met with James Wechsler in his office at the *New York Post* to discuss the matter. Wechsler had belonged to the Young Communist League for three years during the mid-1930s. He later renounced that allegiance and testified at a hearing conducted by Senator Joseph McCarthy at which time he named others who had been Communist Party members. Later, as a liberal, he became the editor of the *New York Post*, likely the only daily in the city that could be fairly classified as somewhat liberal and somewhat crusading.

Wechsler did not react quietly to the request by the *Guardian* to publish the document when I asked for advice. He said it would be far better to bury the article than to allow them to have it. "Better that no one ever sees it if you can't get a non-lefty." Wechsler was a friend. The *Post* had published so many articles about my work—representing civil rights activists and Puerto Rican and black kids who had troubled backgrounds, seeking to prevent the eviction of many hundreds of tenants, and attempting to reform the court system, the state mental system, and the Democratic Party—that one letter to the editor suggested that the paper should change its name to the *New York Lane*. His vehement analysis, not his conclusion, was telling. (After the *Guardian* published my work, neither Wechsler nor his associates ever spoke with me again.)

I called Jim Aronson, and, embarrassed by my hesitation, I offered him the right to publish any part of the article he wished as I believed that the weekly twelve-page publication could not accommodate my entire response to Wade. That, I believed, was the end of my participation in the Oswald Affair.

On December 19, 1963, less than a month after the murder, the *Guardian* published the article in full; not a word had been edited. It comprised more than half of the entire issue. It was also circulated among members of the press and the broadcast media worldwide. In the United States, only the *New York Times* made reference to it, but that was enough to sell out every newsstand in the city and for numerous additional demands to be made. The *Guardian* reprinted tens of thousands of additional copies of the article in a tabloid-sized pamphlet, and, since their costs were low, they sold copies for fifteen cents, seven cents each if purchased in bulk.

The response in Europe, Asia, and Latin America was more impressive. The *Guardian* reported that in Rome the largest evening circulation newspaper, *Paesa Sera*, printed the entire article in Italian, as did *Oggi*, an Italian national magazine with a circulation of millions. *Liberation* in Paris reprinted the story. Japanese news agencies, magazines, and newspapers also sought and were granted permission to publish the document, as did magazines and newspapers in Mexico and South America. Many millions of people throughout the rest of the world had access to the response to the district attorney's false charges; in the United States relatively few did. Walter Cronkite, the stentorian voice of CBS-TV, lamented the fact that Europeans and other foreigners were "conspiracy minded" instead of reporting that they had access to another view not generally available in the country where the assassination took place.

Many years later, when I brought a lawsuit to recover classified documents, I discovered that the FBI had placed its own imprimatur upon my article quite literally by stamping TOP SECRET on all copies it could collect. The bureau had never heard of, or was determined to ignore, the rule that it is easier to squeeze toothpaste out of a tube than to put it back in.

The *Guardian* asked me to speak in several cities where it was able to organize large meetings. It was an exciting and exhausting time, and I was about to return home from the tour when I was asked to make one more stop. A number of union members had asked their officials to invite me to speak with them, and I agreed. At the airport I was met by a man in a well-kept car that was well over a decade and a half old. He invited me to dinner, but I said that I would rather take a nap if there was time. He drove me to his very modest apartment. I told him that I was not prepared for another day on the road and, since all of my shirts in my suitcase were badly wrinkled, I hoped my appearance would be forgiven. When I awoke, he was in the kitchen ironing my shirt, which he had just washed by hand. When I asked if he worked for the union, he said he was the president. I told him that I knew union business agents in New York who were provided with a new automobile by the union at least every other year and who lived in very comfortable homes. He laughed and said, "Well, welcome to the UE [United Electrical, Radio and Machine Workers of America]. We have an agreement with our members. No union official, including the president, can be paid more than the median wages for our members. Also, we have no benefits that they don't have. No cars as gifts."

I spoke that evening to a large and enthusiastic audience and went out for a beer or two with several rank-and-file members after the talk. I learned that the policies, expenditures, and contract negotiations must all have prior consent from the members. The union was the realization of a dream, the New Deal reforms, democratic and progressive. It had been a target of the right-wing members of Congress, from Martin Dies and his House Un-American Activities Committee in 1938 through the McCarthy era and beyond. I am not naive about union abuses, and I know that many unions have been manipulated by corrupt officials and that many are run autocratically. I do not recall with specificity many of the places I visited on that first hectic and groundbreaking national tour or the details of most of the events. My most vivid memory of that time as I look back over a half century is the support from the UE leaders and members and their commitment to justice for their colleagues and their nation.

Of the people in the United States who read the article, none was more important to the continuing narrative than Shirley Martin. She lived in Hominy, Oklahoma, with her family. Shirley did not know Marguerite Oswald, Lee's mother, but she thought it would be comforting for her to read the article and sent her the publication. Mrs. Oswald then called and asked if I could meet her in Dallas to consider representing her and her son. She added that she had no income and no savings and would be unable to pay any fee or even expenses that I might incur. She also said that her son was innocent and that he had worked for an American intelligence agency, although she could provide no clear evidence for that conclusion. I agreed to meet with her but cautioned her that I would be unable to represent her for many reasons, not the least being that I saw no proof at that time that Lee Oswald had been an agent or informant. Further inquiry would substantiate her views.

We met in the lobby of the Dallas hotel where I was staying. She was with a reporter for the *New York Times* and insisted that he sit in at the meeting. I told her that having him present eliminated any attorney-client privileged communication that she might wish to rely on at a later time. She was adamant, and the three of us talked for hours. When she asked what she could do about her son's murder, I suggested that she might explore the Texas wrongful death statutes with local counsel. When she said that she knew no lawyers in Dallas, I said that perhaps the local bar association or the ACLU could help her find one. Finally, I agreed to take one more step; I would ask the Warren Commission to allow me to look at its evidence against her son and report to her about it. The *Times* ran an article about the meeting.

The most sinister menace, aside from more than two hundred death threats that I received, came from the bar associations. Lewis F. Powell Jr., then president-elect of the American Bar Association, sent a letter to J. Lee Rankin, the general counsel of the Warren Commission, stating, "There ought to be some way for the bar to discipline people like Lane, as he is certainly bringing serious discredit to the legal processes of his country." Later Richard Nixon appointed Powell to the United States Supreme Court.[1]

Rankin acted on Powell's suggestion, and the Association of the Bar of the City of New York instituted a proceeding against me threatening to result in disbarment. As John G. Bonomi, the bar's chief inquisitor, put it, I did not have sufficient faith in the conclusions of Earl Warren, who was the chief justice, and that I had "solicited" a case. Technically, Warren was not acting in his judicial capacity; he was a political appointee to a political commission in which the majority of the members were politicians serving in the Senate and House.

Setting aside that misrepresentation, lawyers regularly question the decisions of judges. The bar association was formed in 1870, following the Civil War, because, according to the bar's own published history, "errant judges" and "unsavory politicians" took advantage of the "troubled times." What was required, said the American Bar Association, were independent lawyers who would provide a public service by "defending liberty and pursuing justice."

Bonomi was undeterred by history, and committed to taking action against me. He told me that if I ever discussed the complaint he would institute additional proceedings against me. I knew that the raison d'etre for the rules of secrecy was to protect a lawyer to whom the privilege ran, not to shield the unconscionable acts of a politically motivated prosecutor. I also knew that my adversaries were powerful. Bonomi would not have initiated a procedure aimed at disbarring me without having been authorized. While I was confident I had not acted improperly, the frightening thought that justice and precedent might not prevail in the hysteria was more than troubling. I also believed that a subsequent appeal to a federal court while Warren was both the adversary and the chief justice was not a comforting option.

The charge that I solicited a case was based solely upon the *Times* article with reference to the potential wrongful death case. Three people had been present. Bonomi had never bothered to ask any of them what had transpired; he merely assumed that I was seeking to represent Mrs. Oswald in a Texas court. I explained to him that I had suggested that she retain local counsel. He said, "So you are saying the *New York Times* article was false."

"No," I replied, "the article was truthful, your inference is false, and your implications are irresponsible." Bonomi demanded to know why I had not written a letter of complaint to the *Times*. "Because the article, which merely said we discussed a wrongful death action, was accurate, and because the reporter was not obligated to publish a transcript of the very long meeting in his one column piece." I added that I might write a letter of complaint to the bar about his misconduct.

Bonomi said, "This is just the start. We will pursue this complaint vigorously."

I consulted with Edward J. Ennis, who had served as general counsel of the ACLU for many years and also as its chairman. Ed was a true friend with an unsurpassed devotion to the values of the Constitution. I offered to retain him and said we should discuss his fee. He smiled and waved my suggestion aside, saying, "Mark, how could it be anything but pro bono? It will be my pleasure and my honor, and I don't think it will take very long."

At the next bar association hearing to discipline me, Ennis, a quiet and serious advocate, reviewed the complaint and, looking directly at Bonomi, offered a one-sentence conclusion. "I think you have substantial cause to feel ashamed of yourself."

Bonomi was stunned. After a period of silence that probably seemed longer than it was, Bonomi stood, picked up his papers, and said, "This hearing is over. I will notify you of the next date."

I never heard from him or the bar association again.

I established the Citizens' Commission of Inquiry (CCI) in a very small office on lower Fifth Avenue and raised funds for trips to Dallas to find and talk with witnesses. Later I began to talk about the case at a theater in Manhattan and to arrange appearances at colleges throughout the country.

During this time, a letter arrived from London. This was of interest, since I did not know anyone in London.

It was an offer of help from Lord Bertrand Russell, a leading philosopher of his time as well as a respected historian, logician, and mathematician.[2] He wrote that he supported my efforts and was eager to assist me. I later met with him several times at his home in London and his retreat in Wales. I also met Ralph Schoenman, his executive secretary, who played a part in forming the Who Killed Kennedy Committee in Great Britain. It was chaired by Russell and composed of members of parliament, Nobel Prize winners, well-known authors, playwrights, film directors, religious leaders, publishers, and professors. Committees were also established in Denmark and France, and journalists, publishers, professors, and attorneys in a number of other countries including Germany, Italy, Sweden, and Spain made similar offers.

The time spent with Bertrand Russell remains for me a treasured memory. When we met for tea in his home, I addressed him as Lord Russell. He said, "Please call me Bertie." It was his only request that I was not able to convince myself to grant. I do not believe in titles, inherited or obtained in any other manner, and I would have been happy to abandon the "Lord" part, but to call a world figure whom

I greatly admired and respected and who was approaching ninety "Bertie" was a step too far for me. In meetings with Ralph and all others who knew him and worked with him he was exclusively referred to that way, and I, bearing the smirks and delighted shrugs from my British allies, was the lone and obviously out-of-touch American who called him *Lord Russell*. I finally succumbed and allowed myself to refer to him as Bertie in conversations with others but I found I could never refer to him that way directly.

On one winter's day, after a wee drop, Bertie was adding a log to the roaring fire in the living room fireplace, rejecting my offer to help with, "I like you very much, Mark, but some things are too important to trust to a young man." At Ralph's urging he began to tell a story or two from his colorful past.

Other more important issues were also discussed. Bertie was quietly responsible for the release of many hundreds of political prisoners held in numerous countries including China, where he was venerated for his wisdom and age, the Soviet Union and countries under its sphere of influence, and several emerging African nations.

When I told Bertie that I was interested in talking about the case in Europe, he suggested that the Peace Foundation he led could set up meetings in various countries. Plans were made, and I visited several countries to discuss the issues. I learned from reporters that the American embassy in each country I visited was actively seeking to sabotage the meetings with false notices sent anonymously to the press stating that the meeting had been cancelled and with calls to the embassies of other nations notifying them that the United States would be affronted if any of their personnel attended. I thought then that there was no designed effort to silence me, but rather that overzealous individuals were acting on their own. Had I grasped the enormity of the organized governmental opposition, I might have withdrawn from the conflict. Probably not.

I spoke at a meeting in Vienna on December 18, 1964. It was the first lecture sponsored by the Vienna Branch of the Bertrand Russell Peace Foundation. Present was an undercover representative of the US Information Service of the American embassy in Vienna. I was unaware of that person's presence until many years later when I obtained a copy of an FBI report dated February 19, 1965, numbered 1869, which revealed that information and described the invaluable assistance I had received from an attendee, Hellen Battle.

My talk was given in English, and a middle-aged woman volunteered to translate as I paused every minute or so. She seemed to have a command of English, and German was her mother tongue. Apparently her interpretation bore little relationship to my remarks, judging by the audible and irritated reaction of those in the audience who were conversant with both languages. Each time she spoke people shouted *Nein*—that part I understood—and then explained in German how wrong she had been. One very attractive young lady, who later introduced herself as Hellen Battle, tried gently to intercede between the translator and the audience. She spoke perfect English, and the audience certainly appeared to understand her German. I asked her if she would translate, and she did so commendably. After the talk she joined me for a late dinner at a little place that served fine food and excellent desserts and coffee. I thanked her for saving the lecture, and she said she had been puzzled that the translator seemed to be so deliberately misleading.[3]

A literary agent whom I did not know approached me with the suggestion that I write a book about my investigation into the facts surrounding the assassination. He said that he knew a publisher who would be eager to accept it. The publisher had reviewed the proposal and the supporting documents and had agreed to publish the book.

I had never written a book and was hesitant. I finally did agree, and the publisher paid me an advance of $1,500 for all rights to *Rush to Judgement*, hardcover and paperback, in the United States and throughout the world. Actually, the agent was given that check, and he deducted his fee of $150 and sent me a check for $1,350.

Three weeks later the representative of the company called to state that they could not publish the work. That journey was replicated more than a dozen times with leading publishers thoroughly examining the documentation, accepting the manuscript, and later withdrawing.

One insisted that I should guess about who killed the president, another sought assurance that the publisher would be safe from "unfair attack," and yet another wanted a guarantee that the book would sell five thousand copies, enough copies to break even. I would not speculate about the names of the assassins, I could not exempt the publishers from "unfair attacks," but I could, and did, agree to return any advance I had received if a single statement in the book was proven to be inaccurate, and I did agree to take out a loan and purchase the first five thousand copies. Nevertheless, all the publishers declined.

Later I learned that officers of the FBI and the CIA had visited publishers and told them that it would be unwise for any company to publish my book. FBI agents also called upon local radio stations almost immediately after I had been interviewed; sometimes they passed me in the studio hallway as I left and they arrived. Their visits were to advise the management that I should never be allowed to appear there again.

During that period CCI volunteers, including students, housewives, and teachers who traveled to Dallas, were harassed by the local police; some were arrested as soon as they arrived. Later we learned that the FBI had tapped our telephones and placed listening devices in our office, thus resolving for us the mystery of how the local police knew that volunteers were on their way.

After lecturing about the assassination at academic institutions in England, Scotland, and Denmark, I returned to the United States on a flight to JFK International Airport. I was temporarily prevented from entering my own country and the city where I was born by orders of the government that directed that I be held until the FBI, the Department of Justice, and the US attorney general were "telephonically" notified that I had come home.

Later, I went to London, tattered manuscript in hand, and found a conservative, venerable, and respected old firm, the Bodley Head.

The manuscript had been mimeographed on legal-sized paper, 8½ by 14 inches. Two holes were punched in the left column, and I used a black shoestring to bind the pages, well over a ream, together. Very few copies were made. I still have the original document that I submitted to the publisher that day, now many years later.

The British company, unlike its American counterparts, did not find it necessary to consult with, or seek the permission of, the CIA or the FBI about the propriety of publishing the work. Instead, they sent the manuscript to a leading historian and author, Hugh Trevor-Roper, the Regius Professor of Modern History at Oxford University. Congressman (later President) Gerald Ford, a member of the Warren Commission, had written something called *Portrait of the Assassin*, and that professionally prepared manuscript had also been submitted to the Bodley Head with a request by a proper American literary agent that it be published. The company sent Ford's work to Trevor-Roper as well. While it was not clear that either book would be published, it was certain that both would not be accepted by the same publisher.

Professor Trevor-Roper reviewed both works and reported upon his conclusions to the publisher. The Ford book, he asserted, was of no value, almost a child's view of the Warren Commission Report. He strongly suggested that it was not worthy of publication. Later, when I met him, he told me that he was about to write that if the Bodley Head did decide to publish Ford they should also provide a package of crayons but that he feared that such a remark would appear unprofessional.

Regarding *Rush to Judgment*, he advised the publisher that he believed it would be a classic when published. He added, "Mr. Lane has the right, which in America has often been denied to him, to a fair hearing." He added that he so enthusiastically supported the work that he would be honored to write the introduction to it. And so it came to pass that this American story about the death of an American president found its first publisher in a foreign country.

I learned all of this when James Michie, a young executive at the publishing firm, invited me to lunch to congratulate me. I was at that time almost penniless, unable to pay any rent, and I rarely enjoyed a full meal. I lived in a room on the King's Road, near World's End, London, in a large flat owned by the Bertrand Russell Peace Foundation. I was, of course, ecstatic about the news and almost as pleased about the wonderful lunch.

I told James that I wanted to rewrite portions of the manuscript and that I would need to check all further entries against the Warren Report and the twenty-six volumes of its evidence. A young American, Michael Lester, had worked with me both typing the manuscript and checking out certain references to government documents. James was not surprised, since the manuscript that I submitted began with this note: "This is an un-corrected, un-conformed and un-edited original mimeographed copy of the manuscript. It is intended as a publisher's document and is NOT intended for publication or release in its present form." That page also bore my signature.

I began to write the final version of the book. Comparing the printed work with the earlier manuscript reveals that very few changes were made. I spent a great deal of time writing to Mike, who was in New York, and waiting for his reply about a citation I sought. When I received a small portion of an advance from the publisher I invited Mike to join me in London and to bring all the relevant documents and volumes. I asked Lord Russell if Mike could stay at one of the rooms on King's Road, and he was more than gracious and welcoming. The team was reunited, and Mike began to type.

Since there were no personal computers, Mike employed a portable typewriter. If he made a single mistake, even at the end of the page, even placing a period where a comma belonged, he ripped the page out rather than place a comma over a period, and started anew. When I submitted the final manuscript, the executives at the Bodley Head were astonished. They agreed that it was likely the most perfect submission they had ever read. They were referring to the typing.

While living in London during that time I attended a small party of about a dozen people. One of them was Paul McCartney. He walked up to me, offered his hand, and told me his name. The introduction was hardly necessary as he was one of the most famous people in the world. He seemed very young and remarkably modest. That was because he was twenty-two years old, and he was not impressed with his accomplishments. He said, "I understand you have written a book about Kennedy's assassination. I would like to read it." I told him that it was still in manuscript form and that there were only two mimeographed copies, one at the publisher's office and one at the flat where I was staying. Paul said, "If I could just borrow your copy I would keep it safe and get it back to you in a few days." I agreed. The next day a man in a chauffeur's outfit arrived and asked if I had a package for Mr. McCartney. He took it.

Several days later he returned with the manuscript, neatly wrapped. I took it to my desk, opened it quickly, and began to search for the note that would be my first review. There was no note; I was very disappointed and thought that evidently he had not been impressed or perhaps, I hoped, he had just been too busy to read it.

Early that evening while I was in the throes of editing, the telephone rang. The caller said, "Well he could'na done it, could he?"

I was irritated by the interruption, the obscure message, and the failure of the caller to identify himself. I said, probably in a less-than-generous tone, "Who is this? And who could not have done what?"

He replied, "Sorry. Paul, Paul McCartney, we met the other night. And I meant that Oswald could not have killed President Kennedy." I may have been one of the very few people on the planet who would have failed to recognize that most famous voice. Paul seemed not at all put out. He said, "Could we have dinner together to talk about it? Maybe tomorrow?"

A few days later he invited me to his home, suggesting that I drop in at about noon. He opened the door and showed me to a parlor, asking if I minded waiting a few minutes as he walked into another room where John Lennon was seated at a piano. Paul called out, "Mark, this is John. John, this is Mark." We each said hello, and the two of them continued working on a song. They hummed, they sang, and they played the piano and Paul played the guitar. When they were satisfied, they agreed to call their associate who was going to write it down. Neither Paul nor John could write music. Then we had lunch prepared by a woman who worked there. It was sliced white bread toasted and covered with baked beans, apparently a Liverpool favorite. Paul's very large English sheepdog stayed outside, guarding the house.

Paul, of course, had a very busy schedule and said he would call when he could. He did a few days later and suggested a late dinner at a place I might recommend. I told him about a Polish restaurant where the food was excellent, and since all the diners and staff were ancient and spoke primarily Polish, he might not be recognized. The owner seated us near a window and then returned in a few minutes and nodded toward a table where an obviously wealthy woman in her nineties was seated.

"Madame Slovenskia wondered, Mr. McCartney, if you could sign her menu, which she would like to present to her granddaughter."

Paul smiled and wrote, "Happy dinner, Paul McCartney, friend of Mark Lane." The owner was bemused, and his customer was bewildered. Paul smiled and said, "I guess they heard of the Beatles in Poland."

As our dinner continued past the closing hour it was fortunate the door was locked. Paul had been spotted. Before long, the crowd grew to more than two hundred. The owner showed us a seldom-used back door, and we ran to Paul's car. He drove me to my apartment in a rather deserted section near World's End. No one was on the street. Paul brought out a guitar, and we walked just a few steps before a young couple appeared. She screamed, ran up to Paul, and ripped a handkerchief from his pocket as we ran to the building. We settled into the den and caught our breath.

||||||

During a meeting at my London publishers, James Michie mentioned that there was an American named Ben Sonnenberg who was eager to assist me as a volunteer quasi-editor. I met Benjamin Sonnenberg Jr. and Wendy, his charming wife. Ben appeared to have neither a job nor a profession but was accustomed to a very rich lifestyle because of the largesse of his father, a multimillionaire who had practically invented the profession of modern public relations. His suggestions for the book were uniformly without value, and some were counterproductive. I ended our professional relationship, and my publisher agreed when I stated that I was accepting none of Ben's concepts or language. I considered Ben to be well meaning but not competent, and my parting gift to him was words of appreciation for his efforts, since I did not want to do him harm, either to his ego or his future prospects. I likely would have been less gracious if he had not waited so many years to write his autobiography.[4] In his memoirs Sonnenberg admitted, really boasted, that he was working for the CIA when he attempted to edit *Rush to Judgment*, all the while reporting back to his CIA contact about its contents and how to alter them to protect the agency.

While I was working with and against Sonnenberg, Bodley Head was engaged in finding an American publisher. They were finding it a struggle until Arthur A. Cohen, editor in chief of Holt, Rinehart, and Winston, requested a copy of the manuscript.

Arthur primarily, almost exclusively, was responsible for the publication of *Rush to Judgment* in the United States. After it was printed Arthur called to tell me that the *Herald Tribune* in New York (then in combination with other leading national newspapers) was going to review the book and had decided to ask Norman Mailer or Arthur Schlesinger to write the piece.[5] I did not know of Mailer's view on the subject, but I was aware that Schlesinger supported the Warren Commission and had publicly and vehemently denounced me for questioning its work. I called Norman and asked if we could meet. Norman lived in a townhouse in Brooklyn Heights not far from Manhattan, where I was. However, he also owned a house in Provincetown, Massachusetts, where he was at that time. He invited me to share dinner that evening with his family, and within hours I was driving north.

Dinner was fine, but the discussion frustrating. Norman said that he could not take time off from his disciplined life to interrupt work on his novel in progress. Soon there was a party. Many young women and an assortment of pills and other chemical substances were available. In the early morning he told me that he just could not undertake the review, but he did invite me to stay the night, or what was left of it, and have dinner the next night.

Just after dawn Norman was awake and on his way to someplace in the neighborhood where he wrote. He was there all day and arrived home sober and serious at dinnertime. We had a conversation that I am too embarrassed to recount, even to recall, in detail, but some groveling on my part was certainly involved.

He raised a glass to me and to my efforts. We drank. He simply said, "If they ask me, I will do it." They did, and he did. It was published nationally, and it was more than a favorable review.

The publication date for *Rush to Judgment* was August 15, 1966. My publisher scheduled a three-week tour to begin on August 16. Traveling around the country, appearing on hundreds of radio stations and television programs, and meeting with innumerable print media reporters were exhausting experiences, since I never rejected any invitation. One memorable event began during my first trip to the West Coast. I checked into a hotel in San Francisco and discovered that the success of the book had encouraged my publisher or the hotel to provide an enormous and well-appointed suite. In order to be on time for the first television appearance of the day, I tossed my unopened suitcase on the bed and rushed to the studio. After numerous appearances on radio and television programs and meetings with print reporters and the book editor of the *San Francisco Chronicle* through the day and evening, I took a taxi to Jack London Square in Oakland for a late-night radio program. The host, Joe Dolan, was also an attorney who had studied the Warren Report and my book. He said that he was a strong supporter of my work. I thanked him, gratefully accepted his offer of coffee, and asked how long the program was going to be. It was to begin in thirty minutes and would continue for many hours until just before dawn. I said that I was too exhausted to stay for more than an hour. He explained that the only sponsor of the program was Brentano's bookstore in San Francisco. Brentano's was a major store that reported to the *New York Times*. Every commercial on the show would urge the listeners to call operators who would be standing by all night to take orders and that the large glass storefront windows displayed hundreds of copies of *Rush to Judgment* and no other book. Of course, I said I would stay, asked to be awakened two minutes before show time, and fell asleep on the couch.

Callers bombarded us with questions, praise, and suggestions, and many asked what they could do to get the government to tell us the truth. We also sold enough books that morning so that if not another copy was purchased in America we would have been on best-selling lists that week.

At dawn I rushed back to my hotel room, took a shower, changed, and then ran to the next interview. I was at it all day and evening, again arriving back at the hotel just in time to pick up my suitcase and catch a plane to the next city. I looked at my suite for a moment, the most luxurious accommodations I ever occupied and never slept in.

As *Rush to Judgment*'s success grew, I continued my exhausting but exhilarating book tour. I landed in St. Louis, and, after nonstop meetings with editors and writers and appearing on television and radio programs, the long day was nearing its end with a two-way late-night radio show with a well-informed host. The opening interview was followed by a series of calls from interested listeners.

As midnight neared one caller asked the producer if he could speak with me off the air. During a commercial break I agreed. As soon as the program ended he called again. I asked how I could help him, and he said that he wanted to help me and that he had some information that was of the greatest importance to me. He said that he could not talk with me unless we were on a secure line and that a telephone at a radio station did not qualify. He seemed normal in manner, although his words were rather unusual. He asked me to drive to a telephone booth at a location some distance from the station and said that he would call me there when I arrived. For some reason that I cannot now fathom, I followed his instruction.

I took a taxi to a deserted and destitute section of the city. I asked the driver to wait; he was reluctant, and when he heard that I was there to receive a telephone call he was even more doubtful. I understood his position; it was not unlike my own. The telephone rang, and the same caller thanked me for cooperating. He then directed me to another telephone booth a few miles away. I was tired and getting more than a little impatient, and I said that if the second booth was inadequate we should probably just end the charade. He sighed and said that the matter was of vital importance, a matter of life or death, and that the next call would be the last one. The driver said that he would take me to my next location, but that he would not wait for me there. I acquiesced. The neighborhood was not inspiring. I walked up to the booth as the taxi departed.

I thought of novels and films with unlikely scenes that often seemed to me to be poorly constructed since the fictional hero, I was certain, would never have placed himself in such a risky predicament. Yet here I was, after having received numerous death threats via telephone and in letters always demanding that I abandon the search into the facts surrounding the death of the president. I looked around apprehensively, thinking that the caller was likely near, since he had known exactly when I had reached the previous destination.

The telephone rang. "Here is the story," he began. "There will be plenty of details, and you can check them out in the morning." He asked if I knew where I would be on the book tour on a specified date in the near future.

I said that I had no idea since my schedule was sent to me periodically by the public relations office at Holt, Rinehart, and Winston, my publisher in New York.

He said, "You will be in Chicago." He gave me the name of a well-known hotel where I would be registered and the room number to be assigned to me.

I said that rooms were not assigned in advance.

He laughed and added, "It's an intelligence-maintained room with listening devices so we will know when you leave." He added, "King stayed in that room when he was in Chicago." He told me the precise time I would leave the room, enter the lobby, and then cross the street to go to a nearby studio for an interview. "At that time, a mechanically enhanced pickup truck will speed around the corner from your right and hit you. You will almost certainly be killed." He paused, sensing that I had a great deal to process. "The driver won't be found, the local police will have been warned off, and the stolen truck will be located in a nearby town."

The prediction was calmly related with a countenance that seemed credible. I recovered and asked how he came across the information.

"I was assigned to drive the truck," he responded with just a touch of bravado.

"And you are telling me this why?" I asked.

"I am a patriot, I love my country, and I almost always follow orders. I am an American, and I have killed for our country. I have even killed Americans, and I have killed people in America. But I have my own code; I will not kill an American while he is in America. Do you understand?"

Well, not fully, I thought, but said, "Yes, I very much appreciate that you can see the distinction. So you won't be the truck driver?"

He responded, "When I tell them I quit they might assign someone else, but they'll probably be concerned that I may have blabbed to you, although I will deny that. If so, they will call it off."

He provided the name and time of the program I was destined to miss and the address of the station. I asked if he had any advice. He said that he could see that I was without a ride and he would send a taxi to take me to my hotel in a few minutes. He named the hotel. I said that I had meant to ask if he had any advice about what to do in Chicago.

"If you actually go there, then follow the advice your mother probably gave you long ago: look both ways before crossing the street and then cross quickly."

I thanked him and said good night. A taxi arrived at once; the driver knew my destination.

Every death threat had some impact upon me. Most of them seemed foolish, designed to frighten but not to kill. This one had a different feel; for the first time the threat was real enough to prevent me, exhausted as I had been on the tour, from sleeping soundly. The next morning before breakfast I checked with my publishers. The book was doing well and paperback offers were flooding the office. They thought it odd that I brushed the good news aside for specific information about my upcoming Chicago visit. The hotel had just been booked. My putative assassin had been right about which one it would be. I asked if any specific room had been assigned to me. The answer was a trifle condescending, something like, "No, silly, they don't assign a room until you arrive."

"Any media operation I'll appear at near the hotel?" I asked.

"As a matter of fact, we just have arranged for you to be able to walk from your hotel right to the studio, across the street. You must be psychic."

"At what time is that show scheduled?" I asked and then offered a guess.

"You *are* psychic" was the reply. "You hit the time on the head."

When I arrived at the hotel and checked in, I had written on a piece of scrap paper the room number my informant said was the sound studio for special guests and placed it on the counter.

The clerk was astonished. "How did you guess? That is your room number." I told him that I had recently been informed that I was psychic.

I entered the room, did not unpack, and looked without reward in the usual places that spy films had taught me: the lamps, the phones, and behind the pictures. Technology had apparently out-stripped Hollywood. I visited reception again and said that the room was unsatisfactory and if it was all they had I would move to another establishment. The receptionist seemed confused, but I was finally assigned another room. In the morning I ordered some food to go, slipped out a side door of the lobby, and took a circuitous route to the studio, at all times on the lookout for a primed vehicle. I arrived quite early and dined in the green room where, to my surprise, there was excellent coffee.

|||||

When I appeared on local radio stations or network programs, I could hardly avoid the conclusion that the questions formed a familiar pattern. In most cases they focused less upon the inconvenient facts and more upon matters irrelevant to the central issues, areas intended to demean me and my client, Marguerite Oswald, Lee's mother. I confess that at the time I believed that there was no master plan directing the interrogations and that my hosts had merely parroted the same lines that others had previously pursued. Later I discovered that there had been a master plan set in place by the CIA with specific instructions to their assets in the news media about how to question me, what accusations to make, and how to review my book.

Less than one month after the book was published it made its way onto the *New York Times* bestseller list. During November 1966 it became the number one bestselling book in the country. It remained on the *Times* and *Time* magazine bestselling lists for six months, and the next year became the number one bestselling paperback book according to the *Times*. It also became a popular book throughout Europe, Asia, and South America and the basis for plays, screenplays, and conferences. It was never published in the Soviet Union or in any of the countries under its control. However, during the Prague Spring, when it appeared that the oppressive Soviet regime was to be overthrown, a lengthy interview with me by a reporter covering the United Nations for Czechoslovakia was published as a small book and was awarded a national prize. Later he was imprisoned for taking a part in attempting to free his nation from domination by a foreign dictator. A police department in the United States utilized my book as a training manual regarding how to investigate a crime.

One afternoon, I received a telephone call from Emile de Antonio, a man I did not know but whose work I had admired. He was a famous film director when I met him, although he had been credited with directing only one film, the successful *Point of Order*, about the Army-McCarthy hearings. He suggested that we join our talents, his as a filmmaker, mine as an expert on the assassination of President Kennedy, to make, as he often said, "a stark and didactic documentary." I agreed to his terms. He would direct; we would both be producers; I would locate and interview all of the willing and crucial witnesses while he decided what would be innovative and filmic. We would each try to raise funds for the project. I never knew how "stark and didactic" would be applied to a film comprising a series of interviews.

"D" and I became friends and for many weeks discussed the project. We visited a few bars and ate at inexpensive restaurants. His circle of friends included Jasper Johns, Robert Rauschenberg, and Andy Warhol.

At one party Andy approached me with a tape recorder in his hand. He was at that time a very low talker, and I could barely understand what he was saying. He was making an audio of a day in his life. He said, "Just talk, about anything," and then nodded. I rambled on for a few minutes; he seemed satisfied and walked away. I don't think he even knew my name.

He and D, as well as a number of their friends, were attracted to a lifestyle of living on the edge; their lives were, they said, performance art, and therefore ordinary rules did not apply to them. D had for years made a living by renting the film classic *The Blue Angel*, starring Marlene Dietrich, to colleges and other groups, stating that he owned the film. He had rented one copy and had others made from it, and he did in fact own the actual copies. He did not own the rights. Andy agreed to lecture at a college, and, after receiving the fee, he asked a friend who did not look much like him without makeup to appear as him. The group talked openly about these actions as being the ultimate in counterculture protests.

D was charming, I thought loyal, and always interesting. I worked hard at overcoming my differences with him about some of his concepts that I could not share or even fully comprehend.

We rented an old wreck for seventy dollars a week, no mileage charge, which was all that our budget would allow, and drove south to Dallas to make the film. De Antonio was at the wheel as I was just awakening after having driven the first shift.

"D, that's the skyline of Chicago," I said, to which he replied, "Couldn't be. It's not on the route." D was not always right, but he was never in doubt, and although he alone remained in a state of denial, the rest of us were in Illinois. His final comment was, "We just need to make a left."

As he was driving us along the coast at the southernmost part of Mississippi, still seeking the elusive Dallas via an unknown shortcut, the rest of the plans were going well. Dan Drasin, an expert in editing and all things related to film, was in New York awaiting our daily exposed film to have it developed and put in some order for editing. Robert Primes, an excellent cameraman, arrived before we did, as the pilot of the commercial airplane had no difficulty in finding and closing in on Dallas. I had a written agreement with D, and his primary contribution was to come up with the idea of using my work for the film and to invite Dan to edit it.

I thought that locating key witnesses and convincing them to tell us on the record what they had seen, after they had been strongly advised by FBI agents and the Dallas police not to talk to us, was the great challenge facing us. It was, but the courage of ordinary people who had seen history and knew that the government was distorting the record was always present and always inspiring. One of the first witnesses I interviewed was S. M. Holland. He had been a Dallas deputy sheriff for seventeen years and an employee of the railroad companies even longer. He was standing on the bridge, the triple overpass, to watch the motorcade as it approached his vantage point. He was a spectator, but he had also been asked to keep an eye on everyone on the bridge to make sure no one threw anything toward the president's open limousine. At least one shot came from behind a wooden fence on a grassy knoll to his left and in front of him. He heard the shot and then looked toward the fence, where he saw puffs of smoke. The president's head was driven backward and to his left by the fatal shot. All those with him had the same experience, and all were convinced, these men who were avid hunters and owned numerous weapons, that the assassin was on the grassy knoll. We interviewed others at that and other locations, and their memories were identical.

I asked Holland if he had been told about us. He said he had. "They, the police, warned us not to talk to you. Really, warned us." He said, "I might even get fired for this interview." I asked why he was speaking to us. "When the time comes that an American sees his president being killed and he can't tell the truth about it, that's the time to give the country back to the Indians"— he paused, looked at me with eyes that glistened with tears, looked down and then back at me, and said—"if they'll take it." He refused to accept a small sum as an interview fee and for taking so much of his time. He made one request. "One day America might know what actually happened that day, and I would like to have a copy of my interview to give to my grandchild."

I tried to raise funds for the film while in London. I knew that Tony Richardson was part of a progressive film group, but I could not locate him. Instead I found a wonderfully talented artist, Vanessa Redgrave, who was still married to Richardson, but that union was failing. She gave me his numbers, suggested how I might approach him, and said that it might be better not to mention her name. I followed her advice, and Richardson and his group invested half of the budget.[6]

I met with Paul McCartney at my flat. He asked about the film, and I described it. He asked if there was going to be music, and I said that the director and I had not even thought about that yet. "Well," he said, "I would like to write a musical score for the film, as a present for you." I was astonished by that generous offer and speechless for a moment. I thanked him, but then I cautioned him that the subject matter was very controversial in the United States and that he might be jeopardizing his future. He added, "One day my children are going to ask me what I did with my life, and I can't just answer that I was a Beatle." It became clear to me that he had not grasped the enormous contribution he had made to music and to the lives of young people everywhere. During that meeting, Paul said he had just finished composing a song and he wanted me to hear it. "You'll be the first," he added. I told him that I really enjoyed his music but that I was practically tone deaf and not the person who should give him the first review, that he should play it for someone else first. He laughed and took the guitar out of its case.

He played the melody and sang bits of the lyrics he had composed. I didn't really get it; it had a haunting and sad sound. I said, "I think this is a little complex for me the first time hearing it."

"You don't like it?" he asked.

I said I did, but I would have to give it more thought.

He added as a joke, "I gave you your first review, and it was much more favorable."

The next morning Mike Lester, who was staying at the flat, asked what Paul was playing. I didn't remember the name, but I recalled that it had a refrain about all the lonely people and that some father was darning his socks at night. I had apparently been the first person to hear "Eleanor Rigby." When it became a huge hit, my friends made sarcastic remarks about my musical ear, suggesting that I might consider giving up the law for a new career as a music critic.

Paul called and said, "What do I have to do to write the musical score for the film?" I arranged a meeting at the King's Road flat for Paul and D and myself to discuss the subject.

D asked Paul, "What have you written for us?" Paul politely said that he wanted to see the film and then compose. D ruled that reasonable suggestion out. Paul then asked D how the film would begin, and D described a scene where the plane landed and the president and his wife walked to the tarmac. That had not been discussed as the opening scene and was not used in the film. D said, "So play your music for that scene."

Paul said, "You want me to audition now?"

D said, "Yes, right now."

There was a long and awkward silence broken when Paul picked up his guitar and created a bit of music. D, even less musically talented than I was, immediately said, "No good. It's boring."

Paul laughed and agreed by saying, "I tried to match the scene you had described."

I argued with D about the musical score to no avail. He insisted that a score by Paul McCartney would not increase the film's popularity or reach and would prevent it from being "stark and didactic," a phrase that I still did not comprehend and one D could never adequately explain.

The film without a musical score was stark enough and was moderately successful. Its debut was on BBC in 1967. I was there for the showing of the film with two Warren Commission lawyers, Arlen Specter and David Belin. It was then the longest studio-originated broadcast in the history of BBC.[7] In the United States the documentary debuted at the Carnegie Hall Cinema and was reviewed by Bosley Crowther, the film critic for the *New York Times*, who wrote that if the "purpose of this film is to rouse its viewers into having doubts about Oswald's total guilt . . . then it eminently succeeds."[8]

Chicago, August 1968 11

Likely no year in recent history was filled with more open political internecine conflict, chaos, hope, and commitment from a new generation opposed to war and racism and influenced by the death of our political and moral leaders. It was 1968.

In Vietnam, the Tet Offensive began during the first month. Guerrilla warfare was transformed by the Vietnamese Revolutionary Forces and the National Liberation Front into a series of coordinated attacks upon the military of the United States and their allies in numerous cities and villages throughout South Vietnam. The US embassy in Saigon was penetrated. The onslaught reverberated in the United States.

In March, hundreds of students at New York University demonstrated against the presence on campus of recruiters for Dow Chemical, the manufacturers of napalm, a toxic chemical burning agent that US planes were dropping and which causes great suffering and death as well as the predictable destruction of the environment for decades to come.

On April 4, the moral leader of the nation, Dr. Martin Luther King Jr., who had unified the antiwar movement and the civil rights movement, was assassinated. He was building a consensus for a massive campaign for economic justice starting with a permanent encampment for change in the nation's capital. Riots in black communities in many cities across the nation were followed by student protests against the war and student-faculty strikes at educational institutions.

In June, Robert Kennedy was assassinated. In August, the Democratic Party convention was converted into a war waged in the streets and parks of Chicago by the Chicago Police Department, the National Guard, and the US Army against antiwar students and other protestors.

The Democratic Party was divided between those led by President Lyndon Johnson, Senator Hubert Humphrey, and Senator Ed Muskie, who favored continuation of the war against Vietnam, and those who favored a peace plank, including Senator George McGovern. In the Democratic Party primary in New Hampshire, Senator Eugene McCarthy, the candidate who opposed the war, won 40 percent of the vote against President Lyndon Johnson. Senator Robert Kennedy entered the race. Johnson announced that he would not seek reelection. Thousands of demonstrators coalesced in the city.

Mayor Richard J. Daley unleashed 11,900 police officers to augment 7,500 US Army troops, 7,500 Illinois National Guard members, and 1,000 US Secret Service agents in the city. He ordered tanks placed in strategic locations. In addition to the student demonstrators, noninvolved bystanders were attacked. News reporters and doctors and nurses offering help were severely beaten by the police. The young people were terrified and filled with despair. They chanted, "The whole world is watching," while television cameras captured the five shameful days of carnage and suffering.

The National Guard was armed with powerful M-1 rifles, Browning automatic rifles, and gas grenades. The military of the United States was armed with numerous weapons including both .30-caliber air-cooled and .50-caliber water-cooled machine guns. The local police were armed with gas, sidearms, rifles, clubs, brass knuckles, and blackjacks. In coordinated efforts they herded the demonstrators, primarily armed with rhetoric, into Grant Park and Lincoln Park where their actions would be observed by fewer reporters and photographers. I knew many of those weapons quite well and had fired them at ranges during World War II. I had been assigned my own M-1. I never thought then that I would see one pointed at me in an American city.

Many of the demonstrators were forced to flee to Grant Park to escape the tear gas and police clubs. There the brutality and cruelty were most vicious, and I, along with many others, was beaten and gassed. In a book I wrote just after the events, I described the terror.[1]

My dear friends Carolyn Mugar, Dick Gregory, columnist Murray Kempton, and I were there together with about three thousand others. Carolyn was making a historic photographic record of the events at great personal risk. When the authorities said that we could not continue our peaceful march and that we would be arrested if we took one more step, Dick Gregory said to me, "Stay with Carolyn. Get the photographs," and he stepped forward and was arrested. Murray was not only a well-known journalist, he was a delegate to the convention. His convention badge was the magic pass allowing him to proceed. He turned to other delegates who were present and said, "Hell, I'm taking off my badge and going to dinner with Mr. Gregory." He took his badge off, placed it in his pocket, stepped forward, and was arrested. Almost every delegate present followed his lead, as did ministers and priests and the president of the State University of New York, Harris Woffard, who was also a former White House aide, all of whom had been our walking companions until then.

As Carolyn and I neared Grant Park, a unit of the National Guard, rifles held at ready, some pointed at us, moved in. We stood at the very front of the line at that moment, and we saw and recorded the cause of the riot. One guardsman began to mumble, and then he screamed and moved toward the demonstrators. A lieutenant ordered him back, but moments later he again broke ranks, charged toward a young couple, turned toward me and then back to the couple, and struck one of them with his rifle. The young man tried to push him away, and another guardsman moved in, swinging his rifle. Before then, Carolyn had made a photographic record of the anatomy of the riot.[2]

At one point a guardsman had reached for her camera, and she tossed it to me. I continued to take pictures. The command "Gas!" was shouted; the troops retreated a few steps, put on their masks, and fired gas grenades that exploded among the demonstrators. One tear gas canister struck me as it exploded. This was my first experience with a direct hit. The reaction of my lungs was frightening; they felt as if they were suddenly frozen. I began to gasp for air even as I remembered the warning, "Take short breaths." But there was no clean air to breathe, only clouds of gas.

I could not see the gas, for I was totally blind. My eyes burned, and tears were running down my face. My nose burned and ran. I could not catch my breath; I could not speak. I tried to say, "Are you all right, Carolyn?" She understood and answered that she was blind.

"Don't touch your eyes," I said as I grabbed her hand. We ran in what we hoped was a northerly direction. I stumbled as my feet struck someone stretched out in the street. I could not see but heard the Guard move toward us. I heard a rifle butt strike flesh and bone very near to me.

"Are you all right?" I asked again.

"Yes, are you?" she answered.

We heard screaming ahead of us following the explosion of more tear gas canisters. We were running from the area as quickly as we could. With my left hand I held Carolyn's; my right hand extended in front of me hoping that I would touch a tree or some other obstacle before I crashed into it. I began to discern shadows, but within a moment we were forced to run through additional concentrations of the gas to escape bludgeoning by the rifle-swinging guardsmen.

We ran, blind and crying, from the advancing soldiers and mounted police. The exertion caused by running forced us to breathe more deeply, but our lungs burned intolerably, feeling as if they would burst. Hoping for some fresh air, we sped on, and I crashed

Mark Lane during World War II, United States Army, 1945.

The leaders of the Democratic Reform Movement. Mark Lane with Eleanor Roosevelt and Governor Lehman, who campaigned for him for election to the New York State Legislature, 1960.

Mark Lane with Senator John F. Kennedy. Lane was a campaign manager for New York in 1960.

With John Harrington and Adlai Stevenson in 1960.

Mark Lane arrested as a Freedom Rider in Jackson, Mississippi. Police Department photo, June 8, 1961.

Arnold Toynbee reviews the manuscript of Rush to Judgment *with Mark Lane, Scotland, 1965.*

Mark Lane and Bertrand Russell: Lord Russell established the British "Who Killed Kennedy Committee" to support the work of Mark Lane, London, 1964.

Campaign literature for the 1968 Gregory/Lane presidential campaign.

DESIGNED BY DICK GREGORY

During the Wounded Knee trial. Russell Means, Dennis Banks, and Mark Lane at the federal courthouse in Saint Paul, Minnesota, 1974. CAROLYN MUGAR

Dennis Banks and Mark Lane addressing the media after their victory in federal court, 1974. CAROLYN MUGAR

James Earl Ray testifies before the House Select Committee on Assassinations. Mark Lane, his attorney, exposes the false charges leveled by the committee against Ray. MEMPHIS VOL. XI, No. 10, JANUARY 1987, P. 45. UPI/BETTMANN NEWSPHOTOS

Television artist draws Mark Lane cross-examining E. Howard Hunt in the case against the CIA for the assassination of President Kennedy, federal judge James W. Kehoe presiding, Florida, 1985.

Mark Lane meets James Richardson on death row in Raiford Florida State Prison, Florida, 1968. Lane carried with him a small spy camera.

MARK LANE

James Richardson and Mark Lane as Richardson walks out of prison after twenty-one years, five of them spent on death row, Arcadia, 1989.

© SARASOTA HERALD TRIBUNE, APRIL 26, 1989

First morning of freedom for James Richardson. Richardson and Mark Lane walk on Daytona Beach. © Orlando Sentinel, April 27, 1989.

into a post of some kind in what was total darkness for me. At Sixteenth Street we paused.

A voice commanded, "Open your eyes." I tried to as a stream of fluid washed over my face. The voice repeated, with some annoyance, "Damn it, open your eyes. We don't have any water to spare." I opened them further. Within seconds I could see again, although my vision remained blurred for some time.

I led Carolyn, still blinded, to the medic, and her eyes were also washed of the toxic substance. As soon as her eyes cleared, she took pictures of the medics pouring water in the next patient's eyes. Three medics knelt over a girl stretched out in the street. They had carried her from Seventeenth Street. She had stopped breathing, in what appeared to be a traumatic response to the gas. They began artificial respiration. She gasped, and the doctor sighed with relief. Soon she was breathing regularly. But another tear gas canister exploded thirty feet from us. The medics helped her up and carried her, trying to escape the spreading gas.

A young man was bleeding freely from the head and mouth. Medics tried to lead him away from the gas. Another man, bleeding from the scalp, was aided and water washed the gas from his eyes. A network television crew, wearing gas masks and helmets, arrived and interviewed him. Another young person, beaten and unconscious, was carried off on a stretcher while a police officer, club raised, watched. Tanks began to rumble near us.

We were tired, near exhaustion. Many were vomiting in the street. The gas had not affected me that way yet. Several people came from an alley into which they had run to escape the fumes. A girl cried out, "Stay out of the alleys. The cops are beating people in there."

At a hotel lobby, a medic begged for water. A police sergeant, brandishing a club, chased him away. We walked west one block to Wabash. For the first time since the attack began, the air smelled fairly clean. I recalled my first contact with toxic and nontoxic gas. It came during the war when I was taking basic training. We were required to enter a Quonset hut in which various gases were released before we were permitted to put masks on. In this way I became acquainted with the smell of different gases and proficient in placing a gas mask on quickly. As it developed, however, the training was not necessary. The Nazis did not utilize gas in combat. They reserved it for their killing camps. The Chicago police and the National Guard techniques were more universal.

Subsequently, it was revealed that an undercover Chicago Police Department officer, Robert Pierson, was Jerry Rubin's bodyguard in the streets of Chicago and precipitated some of the acts of violence. Rubin was one of the Chicago Eight defendants and an organizer of the protest. When the convention ended Mayor Daley praised the Chicago Police Department for their deportment and discretion; he also gave them a raise.

Actually the whole Second City adventure was a mistake on my part, or at the very least it was not something that I planned. I had not gone to Chicago to participate in or observe the Democratic Convention or its context. Dick Gregory had just announced that he was running for president. He needed a vice-presidential candidate, and he reached out to me. I told him I had always enjoyed visiting Washington, and I thought that living there for four years might be interesting.

Clearly it was going to be a protest vehicle for us to discuss the war and racism, and we needed to meet to draft a platform. During a telephone call, each with his appointment book in hand, we tried to find a date within the next couple of weeks when we would both be available for a few days. We settled on a time near the end of August and agreed to meet at Greg's home in Chicago. Just before the call was concluded, Greg said, "Oh yeah, Mark, you ought to make hotel arrangements soon since there is going to be a convention in town around that time unless they move it to Miami, which they are considering." Thus I went to Chicago not because of the Democratic Convention but in spite of it.

Our relaxed meeting took place later in an apartment in New York's Greenwich Village.

Greg was designing our campaign literature. Of course we had no funds, but Greg had no shortage of imagination. The literature was in the shape and size of a dollar bill, and it began "For President of the United States." It featured a picture of Gregory, had a peace symbol, and was signed by "Dick Gregory, President and Mark Lane, Vice President." It concluded, "ONE VOTE—Cannot Be Bought Sold Or Purchased."

The small item was widely distributed and soon developed a cachet of its own. Collectors added it to their political acquisitions. People taped it to the windows of their homes and automobiles. Then the federal police struck and seized all of the bundles that were stored at one location, claiming that they were counterfeit one-dollar bills. I told a network television audience that I had lost confidence in the talent of our police agencies, since apparently they were unable to distinguish between George Washington in a white powdered wig and Dick Gregory. Walter Cronkite took up the matter. He reported that he had tried to insert the bill into a change machine at the CBS commissary in New York and that it had been summarily rejected.

Greg and I spoke at rallies throughout the nation in opposition to the war in Vietnam. Our two opponents had appeared on the Johnny Carson show. I requested equal time for Greg, and when denied, I notified the network that I intended to file a complaint. The Carson show then decided to invite Greg, but as he had a previous speaking engagement he asked me to appear for him. Joey Bishop was a guest host that evening, and, after a one-sentence introduction, Bishop said that the audience, not he, would interview me.

"Many people also want us to end the war but think there is no way to get out. What do you propose?" a member of the audience asked.

That was a frequent line then that has been recycled for our wars in Iraq and Afghanistan, among others, where there has been inadequate planning and no endgame considered other than an illusory military victory. I told the audience that Greg had a trade that most people were unaware of. "He has an engineering degree, and he has discovered that the ships that brought the GIs to Vietnam have a reverse gear. Load them up and bring them home."

One middle-aged woman from the Midwest was outraged at the prospect of a black man being president. She had no objection to me, but I was only running for vice president. "Couldn't something be done to stop it? I mean, what would it look like if he was president?" she asked.

I thought that perhaps one day we would know. We have that answer now, and it looks relatively gratifying to me and to most of the rest of the world. We were not elected, but you probably knew that. It was in all of the newspapers at the time.

I appeared as a witness at two trials in Chicago. One was the Chicago Eight, then Seven, trial, in which I played a small and largely irrelevant role. The other, in which Carolyn Mugar also testified, was the trial of Professor Sidney Peck, who served as a principal negotiator for the demonstrators with the Daley machine. On the evening of August 28 he was attempting to arrange, with Chicago police deputy superintendent James M. Rochford, for a place for the demonstrators to march, when he was brutally beaten by Chicago police officers. Sid was arrested and charged with four misdemeanors. He was offered a deal by the state's attorney's office; if he pleaded guilty he would be given a ninety-day sentence. Sid refused, and the notorious prosecuting attorney Edward V. Hanrahan upgraded the charges and indicted Sid for two felonies.

Later Sid, Carolyn, and I met to discuss the case. When he described the events in detail we realized that we had probably witnessed it from a considerable distance and through mists of gas, so far away that we could not have recognized Sid, whom we knew. At the time Carolyn, of course, had taken pictures of the encounter. Carolyn and I examined all of the many pictures for hours until she located photographs of the event. It was not a motion picture, but it appeared to demonstrate that Sid was the victim, not the aggressor, but it was not dispositive.

Rochford's perjured testimony was based upon the exact time that he said the encounter had occurred. He was absolutely sure of the time. While studying the pictures Carolyn noticed a large steeplelike building in the background. She quickly enlarged it, and it proved to have a clock. The time was visible. It demonstrated that Rochford had lied about the time. That was quite enough for the trial judge, who acquitted Sid of both felony charges. Rochford was promoted and became the superintendent of the Chicago Police Department.

James Joseph Richardson

||||||||||||||||||||||||||||||||||||||||||||||||||||||||||||||||||||||||||||||||

W hen I left Chicago for Florida during September 1968, I thought I was just fulfilling a commitment to give a lecture and participate in a panel discussion, but fate apparently had another plan. If there was a plan, I knew that it was not mine. I was not seeking another windmill.

My days in Chicago had tired and frightened me, and I was looking forward to a more bucolic period of speaking at academic institutions and quietly practicing law with clients who might actually pay a fee. I spoke at a university in San Francisco and had two free days before another lecture in Los Angeles. I stopped for a night at the legendary Big Sur Inn. The most recent magazine available was a one-year-old copy of *Newsweek* with an early article about the events in the Richardson case. About thirteen months earlier, the dead bodies of James Joseph Richardson's seven young children were found in Arcadia. They had been poisoned. It was for a moment a major national news story, and I remembered the television images of the distraught father, an illiterate black farm worker, crying and demanding that the white sheriff find the cause. Arcadia, Florida, was a racist community, and I was struck by the bravery of that arrogation. The nation was still attuned to the mass killing of the little children when Sheriff Frank Cline, a white law enforcement officer, almost immediately arrested Richardson and charged him with murdering his children. For a reason I cannot define or explain the charge had a disquieting effect upon me, and I thought I should visit the area and look about. Other events interceded, but since I was to speak in Tampa in a few days I planned to ask about the case when I got there.

I participated in a panel discussion at the University of South Florida in Tampa with Margaret Fischer, the dean of the school, and John Frasca, who had recently won a Pulitzer Prize as a journalist at the *Tampa Tribune*. During lunch I asked if they knew about the final resolution of the Richardson case. Richardson had been convicted and sentenced to death. Both of my companions stated that they had uneasy feelings about that resolution but were not sufficiently knowledgeable about the facts to articulate their doubts. Soon I was tilting again and facing the overwhelming challenge in which the life of an innocent man on death row was placed in my hands.

I called John S. Robinson, the trial attorney for Richardson, certain that he would have additional information. We did not know each other, but he was familiar with my work in the assassination investigation of President Kennedy, and that was helpful. In our first conversation Robinson told me he was convinced that his client was innocent and that he had been framed. He invited me to review the record. I rented a car and drove across the state to Daytona Beach, checked into a motel, and then met him at his office.

Later I met Richardson on death row. The state had refused access to James in spite of many requests from reporters to interview him. The officials knew I was a lawyer and were impressed that I had been a member of the New York State legislature. They were also proud of their death row operation. I had a very small Minox B camera in my pocket that I was about to place on a counter just before entering the electronic screening apparatus when the senior official said, "Well, Mr. Lane, you-all don't have to go through that being that you were a state representative in New York."

James and I talked at some length and I was convinced of his innocence, and, feeling the need to help him, I called Carolyn Mugar. She joined me, and for the next eight months we drove through the state in search of witnesses. We interviewed more than 150 people in fourteen cities and towns traveling on Florida's fine highways and just as often on its winding and dusty back roads. At the end of that journey we knew a great deal more about how the children had died and how justice functioned in that part of our country when the jury is white, the sheriff and the prosecutors are unscrupulous, and the defendant is a penniless black man without powerful friends or influence.

I wrote a book titled *Arcadia* about our investigation even though there was no hope that James would ever be released from prison since all appeals had been exhausted. My good friends at Holt, Rinehart, and Winston agreed to publish it so that evidence establishing the innocence of my new friend James could surface.[1] A picture of James confined to death row, clandestinely taken with my Minox camera, appeared on the back cover.

Our work led Coretta King and many other civil rights leaders to demand a new trial for James. That book detailed the unconscionable conduct of local and state law enforcement officials in the deliberate frame-up of a man they knew to be innocent.

The state's claim, repeated over and over, that James murdered his children for the proceeds of an insurance policy was never established since the state did not call the insurance salesman as a witness. But the judge allowed that false allegation to reach the jury. I located Gerald Purvis, the door-to-door insurance salesman who had called upon James uninvited. He said that James did not purchase a policy and that there was no insurance. He said he had told that to the lead prosecutor, Frank Schaub. Schaub ordered Purvis to court to frighten the defense, he said. Purvis remained in the witness room and was never called to testify. The only two potential witnesses on that subject were James and Purvis; they both agreed that there never was an insurance policy. The jury had been convinced by unsupported and uncorroborated statements by Schaub and Cline in the absence of any evidence that a policy existed.

I interviewed Richard Barnard, the chief of police of Arcadia, and Lieutenant Joseph Minoughan, the two men who had conducted the original investigation. When it became clear to them that Richardson was innocent, Cline, who fabricated the case against Richardson, had them removed from the case with the apparent assistance of the governor, who wanted the matter quickly resolved. The crimes of the state in this matter were not committed only by local authorities.

The murder weapon was parathion, a deadly poison developed by the Nazis prior to and during World War II. It had not been perfected for use before the end of the war. In Florida it was used as an insecticide. The state said that Richardson had mixed it in the food to be served to the children and in body powder and sugar so that he could kill his wife as well. The body powder belonged to James and was used only by him; he alone in the family added sugar to his coffee.

According to the state, a neighbor, Bessie Reese, heated the cold breakfast and then served it to the children. They all died painful deaths. It was not possible to claim that James or his wife, Annie Mae, had served the breakfast because numerous witnesses knew that early that morning they had been taken in the bed of a pickup truck with many others to work in the fields.

Our investigation revealed that Bessie hated James since the time that James and Bessie's third husband traveled to Jacksonville, where he met a woman who was a relative of James's and decided not to return to Bessie. That decision probably saved his life. We also discovered that Bessie had been convicted of murdering one husband. She also poisoned another husband. She was a murderer who had used poison, she said that she would get even with James by destroying his family, and she had served the food to the children. She was never a suspect.

The Richardsons had not agreed to allow Bessie to babysit. Bessie's attractive grown daughter, rumored to be a favorite of Cline's, had said she would care for the children, serve breakfast, and prepare the older ones for school. After James and Annie Mae left, Bessie insisted that she would take care of the seven children and had sent her daughter away on an errand. She heated the food, added the parathion, and served it.

All the police officers and others who arrived as the children died stated that the smell of the poison gas in the house was overwhelming. If the poison had been placed in the food before it was heated no one would have eaten it. Even Cline stated that when he went to the house, "I smelled the poison. I smelled it twenty-five foot from the house." We retained an expert to conduct experiments, and it became clear that the gas rose from the food not long after the poison had been placed there. The person who served the food was the murderer. James and Annie Mae were miles away when Reese added the poison to the already heated food.

The state then presented the most untrustworthy testimony available. The "jailhouse confession" was set forth by three men, all facing long prison sentences for serious crimes; all said that James had confessed. Cline released them, and they later confessed that their testimony had been perjured at Cline's request.

Jon Nordheimer, a reporter for the *Miami Herald*, was interviewing Richardson during the time frame of the alleged confession. He told me that Richardson had consistently asserted that he was innocent. "He obviously thought that it was the most incredible thing in the world that anyone might think that he could have killed his own children." Nordheimer did not believe that James had confessed, and he did believe that Cline had lied.

I interviewed Cline, who said that James killed the children for the insurance money. "That was the first essential clue."

I pointed out that there was no policy.

Cline replied, "What do you expect Richardson to say? We believed the insurance agent. It was the insurance that led me to it at once. Insurance was the important question. That's why he did it, for the insurance money. That's how they are. Sure, Richardson denied it, but who would you believe? Purvis, an insurance salesman, or something like Richardson?"

I asked why, then, Purvis had not been called by the state to testify at the trial. Cline responded that he thought he had. However, the insurance agent had told Cline personally that there was no policy.

The next evidence, Cline said, was the fact that they did "a lot of investigating and found poison in the powder and the sugar. He wanted to kill his wife too." I said that only James used the powder, and Annie Mae never put sugar in her coffee, although James did. He looked at me, now recognizing that I knew something about the case. He said, "Well, he put it in there to throw suspicion off of himself."

He said that the poison gas smell was so strong "you couldn't stay in the house." I asked how, given those circumstances, the children could have eaten the food and how Bessie could have served it. He answered, "Sometimes people don't pay attention to what they smell."

He was generous enough to share his philosophy with me. "You got to understand these people." He was referring to people he almost always called "niggers." "Well, we don't have problems here, I mean with"—he paused—"the colored, that you have in the big cities. We have none at all."

I congratulated him and asked if he could share the Arcadia formula with me.

"We don't have these problems, and I don't think we will have. What we do have is control."

I interviewed Schaub, the prosecutor, at his office in the Manatee County Courthouse. His campaign literature on display there listed his conviction of James Richardson first as his most important victory and the reason to reelect him. He told me that Richardson was a despicable person who only cared about money. His proof: "He was unusual for a Negro. He didn't drink, didn't own an automobile." He added that Richardson fed his children only "grits three times a day." The state's evidence in the case said that "the meat" given to the children for breakfast had been poisoned.

I had been there less than five minutes, and Schaub had condemned Richardson for not drinking and lied about the food prepared for the children. The very modest income James and his wife earned for toiling in the fields precluded the possibility that they could afford an automobile.

When Schaub said that the motive was insurance, I asked why Purvis had not been called as a witness. He said, "I felt that this agent would not have testified that there was a policy. So, I didn't put him on." When I asked why no record had been made of Purvis's testimony at the preliminary hearing (the defense wanted the court reporter to remain, but Schaub, with the support of the judge, had told him to leave at once), Schaub answered, "I didn't want that testimony preserved."

I asked Schaub to think about the matter and tell me, "What was the strongest evidence against Richardson?"

He responded, "Only he could have done it. Or his wife. We had nothing to prove that she did it, so it had to be him."

I pointed out that Bessie Reese had served the food and asked if he ever considered that she could have done it.

Schaub said, "There was no motive for her and no inclination." I inquired first about the "inclination." Schaub then admitted that she had killed her second husband. When I asked about her first husband he said, "There was a story going around that she had poisoned him, but we never looked into it."

I then inquired about her lack of a motive. "Did her third husband leave with Richardson, fall in love with Richardson's cousin, and decide not to return to Bessie not long before the children were killed?"

He responded, "We heard about that. We never went into it, though."

I asked a question about his conclusive presumption. "Yet Mrs. Reese was never a suspect because she had no motive, no access to the food, and no inclination?"

Schaub said, "That's right. That is correct. I don't have much more time now, so we will have to conclude."

If you wonder how the jury could have convicted in the absence of any credible evidence against James, the answers are a biased and ignorant judge, reckless and deceitful prosecutors and law enforcement officers, and a racist jury. As the jurors began their deliberations, an alternate juror was excused. Grant Kessler had heard all of the evidence with his fellow jurors.

Kessler said, "It looks to me like the state didn't have much of a case." He said that he would have voted for a conviction anyway. "Someone had to do it, and he could have done it. All niggers lie anyway. You know how they are."

For a reason that eludes and confounds me, this has been the most difficult and consuming part of my memoirs to write, although the conclusion was the most gratifying of my professional life. Perhaps it is because I understood in depressing reflection that I had chosen to devote my life to work in a judicial system that is so given to bias that I was forced to question the basis of my commitment and wonder if I had wasted my life hopelessly seeking to drain an ocean of corruption one drop at a time.

In time the death sentence was reduced to a prison sentence well in excess of one hundred years. This was not due to my work but to a Supreme Court decision in another unrelated case that had a retroactive effect. We had dismantled every aspect of the case fabricated by the state, but there seemed to be no path through the judicial system for relief. Johnny Robinson and I had become good friends, and he continued to attend meetings of the parole board, hopeful when he entered the room and defeated as he left. I visited with James and noticed that he had two possessions in his cell: a Bible and *Arcadia*. He had learned to read, had earned a high school diploma, and had become an ordained minister.

His sermons were dedicated to preparing his flock for a satisfying life when they were released.

If you do drugs you are not free even if you are living outside of these walls. If you are an alcoholic you are a prisoner. If you continue to be illiterate you are confined. I hear the ocean in my mind but I know that I will never see it again. But even in my prison cell, where I will live until I die, I will be more free than you, if you allow yourself to be a victim of drugs or liquor or illiteracy. When I read I travel far places in my mind, I walk on the sandy beaches and I hear the ocean call to me.

As many as three hundred prisoners attended James's prison church. When he insisted that Jewish inmates who wished to join were welcome, he was opposed by some Christians with ancient and discredited stories.

You see what I mean. If you will let me teach you how to read then you can read the real facts for yourselves and not just listen to slander. God made all of his children. And he didn't do it so they could bear false witness against each other.

||||||

Twenty years after the children died, in 1987, Trish and I were married in New Orleans. Arrangements were made by Jim Garrison, then a judge on the Louisiana Circuit Court of Appeal, for the ceremony to take place with him in his courtroom. Then we walked to a magnificent dinner in a private room at Antoine's with our families and Jim.

Not long after we were married, we traveled to Florida to visit John Robinson and there learned that there had been a hopeful development regarding James Richardson. We were told that Bessie Reese, who was in a nursing home, had confessed to two nurses that she had murdered the Richardson children. I quickly made arrangements to met with them and learned that they had been warned not to talk to anyone about the statements that Reese had made to them. Knowing that their jobs were in jeopardy they signed affidavits detailing the confession. Trish and I knew that we needed to put an innovative and unprecedented plan in place to overcome the legal obstacles.

We agreed to start the process in Arcadia where it all began. My wife was young, beautiful, and in her mid-twenties. She remains young and beautiful but has left the twenties behind. I was concerned that the task ahead was too fraught with danger. She said quite solemnly that she was not afraid.

We rented a large meeting room in Arcadia; it was the auditorium of the then-abandoned school that had been occupied only by black students before integration was enforced. It is where the funeral for the Richardson children had been held. The highlight of the meeting would be a tape recording that James had made for me in prison asking the people of Arcadia to come forward and tell what they knew about the case.

We walked around town putting up posters, took out advertisements in the two local newspapers, visited the decent man who had been elected sheriff to replace Cline, and met with a black minister and his congregation. They agreed to distribute leaflets announcing the End the Silence meeting. The minister volunteered to chair the meeting, and Johnny, after some persuasion, agreed to attend.

The meeting with the new sheriff was both encouraging, indicating that some things change, and frightening, revealing that some things do not. He said he would assign his chief assistant to be present at the meeting. He also said that since the Klan was very active in the community, it was important for us to leave town before nightfall and return the next day for the meeting. I told him we had rented a motel room. He sighed and urged us to leave because he could not protect us. I looked at Trish. She said, "We're staying." The sheriff said that he would send a car around every hour or so.

Once in the motel room we took a mattress from one bed and placed it to cover the window. I thought, but did not say, We are probably the only two people within one hundred square miles of this room who don't have a weapon. Other than our concerns, the night passed uneventfully.

People filled the auditorium the next day for the first large integrated meeting in the city's history. The deputy assigned by the sheriff stood at the front of the room where all could see him as he scrutinized the audience. Five white men in their twenties or thirties dressed like cowboys—cattle rustling still led the major crime statistics for the county—walked in together and sat in the last row just off the center aisle. I thought if there was going to be any trouble it might originate there.

I played the tape of James. Some cried, some applauded, and many responded with information that was useful but not dispositive. I was still watching the five men in the back. When the meeting ended, four of them left, but one walked forward toward me. He said that he had something to tell me, but he wanted the sheriff's officer to be present.

The three of us met. He began, "If someone stole the official file in this case from the state's attorney's office, could he be charged with a crime?"

I asked, "Hypothetically, stole it when?"

He said, "Ten years ago."

I told him that I was certain that the person could not be indicted since the statute of limitations had expired, but if he was indicted I would represent him. The deputy sheriff nodded in agreement. Remus Griffin then gave us information that changed the world for us:

> I was dating a woman ten years ago. She was the secretary to John Treadwell, the local prosecutor with Schaub in the Richardson case. When your book, *Arcadia*, came out she read it. It was called "the book" here and was passed around in a brown paper bag.
>
> The next time she saw her boss, Treadwell, she asked if what the book said was true, if he had framed an innocent man. Treadwell was drinking pretty heavily then, starting early in the morning. He said, "We almost killed an innocent man; that's why I drink now." He nodded at a file cabinet and said, "The file's in there. I was supposed to burn it, but I just kept it, couldn't get rid of it."

When she told me that story I asked her for the office key and where the file was. I went there that night and stole the whole damn thing. I mean the man was still in prison. I've had it for ten years. Didn't know what to do with it.

I asked if he would give it to me. He said he would. The file detailed the anatomy of a frame-up. I began carefully reviewing the yellowing and fragile documents with Johnny, a friend for almost twenty years and the only counsel in the case.

Even before we started looking at the old documents, Johnny said that nothing in them could help. Then he said he wanted to burn the file. He asked, "What will my peers think about me if this case is reviewed?"

I was silent. I wondered if he had felt guilty all these years for having lost the case. It was true that he had had no real criminal defense law background and that he had specialized in domestic relations law in his short career. But he had made a valiant effort, along with a few mistakes, in a case in which a flawless Clarence Darrow might not have prevailed over the government's persistent misconduct and the court's blatant prejudice. The file answered every question and resolved every doubt. It had been created before there was a Florida sunshine law making such public documents available. The prosecutors had the absolute duty to produce the documents as exculpatory evidence, yet their very existence remained a tightly held secret for two decades until they were finally in my hands. The defense team never knew that documents that might have saved James at the outset even existed. However, they did exist, and I was reading them. The staples and paper clips were rusty and marked the pages with their age. I was careful to keep the hundreds of pages intact, knowing that a desperate Schaub might challenge their authenticity. He never disappointed me.

The only allegations by the state that could pass the laugh test as admissible evidence were statements by three convicts who said that James had confessed. The file contained "interviews" of the three men conducted by Cline before the trial. The sheriff who boasted that he had total "control" had been so arrogant that with a court reporter present taking down and preserving every word, he suborned perjury as he instructed each of the convicts, Ernell Washington, James Weaver, and James Cunningham, how to lie.

Each one had insisted at the outset that James had never confessed, that James said he could not believe that anyone would think he might kill his own children, and that he believed that Bessie Reese was the murderer. Cline was offering the three prisoners release from prison if they committed perjury at trial and threats about what would happen to them if they did not. If just those transcripts had been provided to the defense, even with that judge and even in Arcadia, the case might have been dismissed. I proposed to Johnny that he release the file to the press and demand that the governor appoint a special prosecutor. I said that I would assist him in drafting documents. He was adamant in his refusal. I did not understand then why, and even now in retrospect I have no idea why he opposed reopening the case. He had introduced me to the salient facts, welcomed me into his home to live while I investigated, and had provided leads for the inquiry. He knew that a possible, although unlikely, conclusion of those efforts might be a reopening of the case. The only explanation that he ever proffered to me was that he would be demeaned in the eyes of his colleagues and that anyway James might be released in four years on probation. It was the only argument we had ever had. I stressed his word "might," said the words "only four years," and added that even if his prison stay did end he would be released as a convicted murderer.

John left Daytona the next day on a previously scheduled trip. He said that he was not going to mention the file to James. I visited James in prison and gave him photocopied portions of the file. He began to cry while he read. I asked him why, and he shook his head sadly and said, "I thought they just made a mistake. They knew I was innocent, and they wanted me to die." I suggested that James ask Johnny to file a motion for a new trial. I called John and told him of my meeting. He was coldly furious.

Several days later James called me while I was in my home in Washington, DC, where I had lived since the mid-1970s. He was always very polite; he asked how I was and "Is your beautiful wife OK also?" He said that Johnny had visited him and told him to forget about a motion. James told me, "Mr. Robinson said he would not represent me in that and that even if I won they could try me again and I could be convicted and executed."

Before I could assure him that if the conviction was set aside for prosecutorial misconduct the case could not be retried, it became clear that the complexities of the law were not on his mind. "I told Mr. Robinson that I didn't care about that, that I wanted my name cleared, and that getting that was more important than my life." Then he said, "Would you be my lawyer and help me?"

I knew that if I agreed to represent James that it would undoubtedly end my friendship with Johnny. Yet for me there was no conflict. I said, "Yes, I will represent you." I called Johnny and told him my decision and implored him to be my cocounsel. He refused. He said he would not be part of any effort that sought a review.

I wrote a detailed letter to Robert Martinez, the rather conservative Republican governor of Florida, urgently requesting that a special prosecutor be appointed to review the case. I called Governor Martinez and asked for instructions regarding the delivery of the original file. He suggested that I leave it with the office of his counsel. We publicized that event by informing the media that I would hold a press conference on the steps of the state capitol in Tallahassee.

Trish and my good friend Steve Jaffe accompanied me to the office of counsel for the governor where I had intended to deliver the original file to a receptionist. Instead I was greeted by Peter Dunbar, the governor's counsel, who was waiting for me. I offered the file to him, but instead of merely accepting it he cordially invited us to join him in his office for a talk. Soon a cabinet member joined us as well. As I handed the file to Dunbar, Trish took a picture of the transfer. I wanted a record of the service of the documents. Dunbar asked Trish why she took the picture, and she said that she was so proud of everything her husband did she wanted photographs of each highlight.

By then Schaub had stated and reiterated his claim that there was no surviving original file and that I had manufactured one. Dunbar examined the documents with their old yellowing pages, rusted paper clips and staples, and the marks they had left on the pages. He then smelled it, explaining that he had recently gone through some of his own personal files that had been in a garage for several years and said that even the smell was original. "So much for Mr. Schaub's false claims," he said as he pronounced the file to be original. Schaub later agreed that the file was authentic even as he tried to explain away his misconduct.

On the steps of the capitol building I distributed copies of relevant portions of the approximately one thousand pages to the news media. The case became a major headline story for the newspapers in Florida and was featured on numerous radio and television news programs.

The governor did not respond. Since the matter was not, and could not, be part of a viable judicial proceeding at that time, there was no established legal forum to which I might appeal for a rapid resolution. There was, however, the ultimate appellate court in a democracy, the yearning for fairness among the American people.

Dick Gregory arrived and called Howard Manly at *Newsweek*. Howard had previously interviewed Greg; at that time Greg had told him that he only gave interviews to those who were part of "the movement."

"Are you part of the movement?" Gregory had asked.

"What is the movement?" Howard responded.

Greg offered this explanation. "It means that when I call you to tell you something is important, you come on over and start writing."

Howard had agreed then, and now, much later, the call came. The *Newsweek* article "From Tragedy to Travesty" told the story to the nation.[2]

Representatives of many television programs contacted me for interviews with James. The prison authorities, who had always been courteous to me, were now very gracious. They agreed that I could decide who would be allowed to interview James, and if I agreed to a television interview, the entire crew could be present in an accommodating area. I discussed each proposal with James. He always said, "You decide, Mr. Mark."

David Frost called. He asked for a substantial exclusive interview with James for his recently established American TV program, *Inside Edition*. David said that he was aware of the programs that asked Americans to turn in some wanted suspect. "I would like to see *Inside Edition* report on a man in prison who may be innocent." I respected David (now Sir David, having been knighted in 1993), but I explained that an exclusive interview would result in the rejection of other programs that wanted to cover the story. I said that my only concern must be what was best for James.

"Would a financial contribution to his defense fund help?" David asked.

I said that it would not. "What would help is that at the end of your program you advise the viewers that they may contact Governor Martinez to express their views, while a card gives his address." I said that I was not seeking an editorial role and that he was free to ask any question and draw any conclusion but that the audience should be informed that they could act.

David said that he did not believe that his employers would agree. We said a regretful good-bye. David called back two hours later and said it was a deal.

I discussed the concept with James, and he was pleased. The warden immediately made plans for David and his crew, and the program was soon aired. David had kept his word and had far exceeded our hopes. He conducted an interview that established the innocence of his guest and concluded with an impassioned plea to join in an effort to free James, urging viewers to write to Governor Martinez not tomorrow, not even later today, but at this moment.

More than eleven thousand letters arrived at the governor's office within days of the broadcast of *Inside Edition*. Of course, for the governor there were political considerations. The two governors who preceded him were Democrats. Many voters, including many African Americans, believed that Richardson was innocent and were not pleased with Martinez's refusal to respond.

The file had been delivered to the governor on October 19, 1988. With local counsel, I filed a petition to the Florida Supreme Court asking for a new trial, not expecting any favorable result. Schaub then filed a lawsuit against me and local counsel for $35 million for publicly speaking about his involvement in the fraudulent prosecution. I deposed Schaub, and his responses doomed his meritless case. Schaub's absurd action was later dismissed. His term soon expired, and he did not run for reelection that year or ever again.

Months later, toward the end of January 1989, Martinez had still not responded. I stated that I would begin a fast at his office in Tallahassee the next day and continue until action was taken; Reverend Jesse Jackson and other prominent leaders would join me there. Dick Gregory said he would begin his fast at the gates of the prison where James was incarcerated. Greg said that he would fast until the governor appointed a special prosecutor.

Dunbar called me. He requested that I call off the vigils. He said that they needed more time. I said that James had previously suffered a heart attack while in prison and later had undergone open heart surgery there. "I don't want a posthumous victory, Peter, a man's life may be at stake." He asked for a forty-eight-hour delay; we agreed upon twenty-four hours.

By then the prison authorities and the state officials had concluded that James might well be released and even that he was probably innocent. They permitted me to arrange press conferences with James at the prison with almost no advance notice. A reporter for the *Palm Beach Post* called and asked if she could interview James. She seemed sincere, knowledgeable, and bright. We set a date and met her at the prison. The three of us strolled out of the building to a picnic area inside the prison walls. She and James had a serious and moving discussion. She then said, "Mr. Richardson, when you are free, could I take you to lunch in Palm Beach?" James was speechless, almost unable to breathe normally. He looked at me to see if some sort of trick was being played or if a deadly trap was being constructed. Twenty years before, in Arcadia, had he made such a suggestion to a white woman he might have been lynched; certainly he would have been beaten and threatened with death. He stood up slowly, shook his head, and walked back to his cell.

The next day, Martinez appointed a special prosecutor. The media asked for my reaction to the person chosen to investigate. I had hoped for an independent retired federal judge with no present contact with prosecutors. I was concerned that the appointed attorney to speak with the authority of the state was an active-duty state's attorney, a colleague of Frank Schaub's. Since I knew nothing about her, I made no public comment except to wish her well in her important endeavor. Her name was Janet Reno, the Dade County prosecutor with jurisdiction over Miami.

The Florida Supreme Court had previously heard the argument but reached no decision. Finally it appointed a retired circuit judge, Clifton Kelly, to conduct a hearing to be held in Arcadia. Kelly decided to allow both Schaub and the prosecutor, Treadwell, to make long speeches.

Trish and I arrived with Steve Jaffe and Dick Gregory at the courthouse. National and international news media were present with five very large satellite trucks ready to broadcast the proceedings live. A large crowd surrounded the building; most of the group was young. Inside the courtroom James was waiting, guarded by local police and sheriff's deputies. Janet Reno and her two colleagues soon appeared, as did Schaub and Treadwell.

We heard loud chants from those outside who could not be accommodated by the limited number of seats for the public. I walked toward a window and opened it. The crowd had grown and many more were arriving. Hundreds of men and women, black and white, young and old, were insistently chanting, "Free James Richardson."

The judge arrived and called upon the prosecutors to speak. We heard the same discredited and blatantly false statements repeated. It was a scene from the movie *Judgment at Nuremburg* replayed, but Burt Lancaster was not there to call a halt to it. It must have been painful for James, but his expression was one of acceptance.

Then Judge Kelly called upon me. I thanked the court and acknowledged the members of the bar, looking toward Reno and her associates, who nodded in return; I could not even pretend to greet Schaub and Treadwell as colleagues. I looked at James, he smiled at me, and I began.

"A long and crooked path, Your Honor, has brought us together in Arcadia, more than twenty-one years after the tragedy that took the lives of seven children in this city.

"It is appropriate that this two-decade drama end in Arcadia, where it began, and end as well in a courtroom. It is the role of law, in our society, to make the crooked paths straight. And it is the responsibility of justice to confront and end injustice.

"We are here today seeking justice—not clemency, not mercy; we seek justice."

I reviewed the facts and said, "In almost four decades of practice at the bar, I have never seen the equal of the criminal conduct engaged in by Frank Schaub, John Treadwell, and Frank Cline."

The courtroom was silent during the hour that I spoke. I concluded with a plea to the judge as the chants "Free James Richardson" began to echo through the courtroom.

"Stand with us as we ask this court to strike down the judgment of conviction. Stand with us so that throughout Arcadia, throughout Florida, and throughout the nation, people may joyfully proclaim, 'Free at last. Thank God Almighty, he is free at last.'"

When I returned to my seat James stood and embraced me. I knew the most important statement was yet to come. On rare occasions, a defendant convicted and sentenced to death or a life prison term is released. It is almost unprecedented that such a result is brought about with the consent of the state. Here were the powers assembled in a small and troubled town, two longtime local prosecutors sticking to their horror stories, a retired local judge chosen by a court that had ruled that Richardson was guilty, and an active-duty prosecutor with the last word, both literally and figuratively, speaking for the state. And here we were, a black man convicted of murdering his own children and a white lawyer from New York. Many of the people of the little city seemed to be with us, but not one of them would have a vote.

I wondered what Janet Reno was thinking, why she had not instructed her staff to talk with James or with me as they had with the prosecution team. Was she about to support part of our position and wanted to be clear of remarks that she had leaned too heavily on the facts I presented and the emotion and eloquence of James? Or would she take the well-worn path with stepping stones that read, "No one is entitled to a perfect trial. Mistakes may be made since we are all human. The Supreme Court carefully reviewed the facts and determined that the guilt of the defendant was established beyond a reasonable doubt." I had heard those lines recited many times and prayed I would not hear them again, not today and not in this place. Not with James sitting alongside me trembling.

Reno said that I had made very serious statements about the manner of the trial, accusing the prosecution of the worst things that can be said about them as lawyers, accusing them of hiding and lying about the evidence that would have absolved James. I wondered if I had gone too far, if I had strained the credulity of State's Attorney Reno.

She kept us in suspense not at all. She said that the prosecutors had engaged in gross misconduct throughout the trial. She offered example after example of Schaub, Treadwell, and Cline coaching and even threatening witnesses, suppressing exculpatory evidence, suborning perjury, and utilizing perjured testimony at trial. She concluded, "In this case, it seems that Mr. Richardson is innocent, and had the case been fairly tried, he would have been acquitted." She looked directly at the judge and told him, "Justice was not served. James Richardson was deprived of a fair trial."

She paused for a moment and then said that I was correct and she joined in the motion to set aside the conviction. There was silence and then applause. When the word reached the street, people shouted for joy and openly sobbed. It was the second happiest moment in my professional life.

We awaited the judge's decision. He was back in chambers, evidently conferring with himself. He was there for what seemed to be a long time. One reporter said he was going to miss the crucial news hour. A wit said he had heard of a hung jury but never of a hung judge.

Eventually the judge took the bench. His remarks were very brief. "I hereby vacate the judgment of conviction. Mr. Richardson, you are free to go."

James and I held each other, tears in our eyes. This was the happiest moment in my professional life. I told James that he was free. He nodded but could not grasp the concept.

I said, "You can go anywhere." I told him that we had a place in Daytona where he could spend the night in his own room. He looked bewildered. I asked, "Are you ready to go?"

He said, "What do you mean?" At that point the sheriff approached me.

He quietly said, "Mark, I just have to take James back to our office to process him out, give him his belongings. It will only take about fifteen minutes."

James looked at me with resignation. He knew he was not free. He was ready to go with the sheriff. I explained that I would see him shortly, and we could leave town.

He said, "Whatever you say." After twenty-one years in prison he could not readily accept his new status. Before he left he asked me one question. Looking at Janet Reno, he said, "Could I just thank the lady?"

The scene outside of the courtroom was joyful and chaotic. I said just a few words to the assembled cameras and reporters, mainly that

James would meet them the next day at the Hilton in Daytona and that now James and a few friends were going out for dinner. Then Trish, Greg, Steve, Remus, and I began the short walk to the sheriff's office to meet James. It was 1989, and hundreds of people followed us chanting, "Richardson, Richardson, Richardson." It was the first integrated march in the history of Arcadia, perhaps thirty years too late for the civil rights movement, but a start for Arcadia.

I entered the office and saw James, who had picked up his small bag containing all of his worldly goods, including his Bible, and thanked the sheriff and his deputies for their kindness. They shook hands with me and with James, and we knew we would not meet them again.

Then I said to James, "The magic words for today are *sound bite.*"

That phrase, quickly shortened to "MWT," originated some weeks earlier. I had asked James what he would like for dinner once he was free. He said he could not think ahead that far and that he had survived by not getting his hopes up. That way he would not be disappointed. "Even when I thought I would die in the electric chair I was thinking, well at least I will be going home to my children." I paused and then returned to the subject. He said, "I don't know what they have to eat out in the free world." I suggested that I would take him to a supermarket where he could see what was available and then to a restaurant in the area that prepared that food.

He seemed bewildered and asked, "What is a supermarket?"

I said, "The magic word for today is *supermarket,*" which I then described.

Knowing that he had a great deal of catching up to do, we had the magic word for today exchange every time I saw him. "A sound bite in this case means that when we leave here you will be surrounded by many reporters, photographers, and television crews who want to talk to you. I will tell them to meet you in Daytona tomorrow. And you will deliver a thirty-second speech—a sound bite."

"What should I say?" he asked.

I said, "Anything you want."

We left the office together. James spoke. "I want to thank the people of Arcadia for coming together, black and white, to save me. I am so grateful. But I know that there are still problems here. It would be good, very good, if you could stay together, change things here, and make this place a better place for everyone. Thank you." I looked at my watch. It took just thirty seconds.

The trip from Arcadia to Daytona Beach that evening was ethereal. We stopped at a gas station, and the car was immediately surrounded by cheering people who wanted to see James and shake his hand. We pulled into a buffet-type restaurant on the way after we hurriedly left Arcadia due to the sheriff's reminder that it would be better to be on the highway while it was still light. An unmarked sheriff's car accompanied us part of the way. In the restaurant a minister came to our table to express his love and happiness. He left to make a call. Soon one of the two nurses who had cared for Bessie Reese arrived. She had signed an affidavit for me stating that Reese had confessed several times to being the murderer and exonerating James, an affidavit I had given to the governor and to Janet Reno. She had played an important part in obtaining the victory. She rushed in crying and embraced me. James was eating. I told him who she was and what she had done. He slowly put down his silverware, stood, looked into her eyes, and then held her in his arms, trying to thank her, but both of them were crying so vigorously that words could not convey the feelings that were exchanged. Crowds surrounded James asking for his autograph.

We arrived at the small condominium at Daytona Beach Shores. We were tired but too exhilarated to sleep. The telephone never stopped ringing, and I recall that I never stopped smiling.

We were up to greet the dawn, the first day of freedom. James opened the sliding doors that overlooked the ocean twelve floors below. "I knew it. I remembered that it would sound like this," he said. Within minutes, just after the sun rose, James and I walked on the beach. We saw people on the balconies that had usually been deserted at that hour. They stood and waved to James. Most of what they shouted was lost in the wind but "Welcome," "We love you," and "Congratulations" seemed to predominate. He was smiling. He stopped to pick up sand and let it run through his fingers. He said, "Mr. Mark, I am free."

I said, as I had said a hundred times before, "Mark. My name is Mark. There is no Mister in it. OK, Mr. James?"

He laughed, lost in thought, and said "All right, Mister—, I mean all right, Mark. Mark, I am free."

Janet Reno called to say that if there was to be a civil suit against the state, she wished to be our first witness. Four years later I heard that she was being considered for attorney general of the United States. I wrote to President Clinton saying that it would be a pleasant change to have as the highest law enforcement official a lawyer who actually believed in the rule of law. When she became attorney general she called to thank me for my support and reminded me of the promise she had made. "Of course, that was before I became the attorney general. I just want you to know that nothing has changed. I still wish to be the first witness for James Richardson."

A fine law firm in Florida instituted a lawsuit for James. The federal judge ruled that no matter how outrageous or even criminal were the acts of the prosecutors, they were cloaked in absolute immunity. The case was dismissed. The case against the sheriff's office has been settled.

Attorney General Reno publicly stated that she would follow the law in all respects although she opposed capital punishment. The reason for her rejection of executions, she said, was James Joseph Richardson. An innocent man might have died in spite of reviews by all relevant courts since some of the evidence had been distorted beyond recognition by the prosecutors and other evidence hidden from the court, the jury, the defense, and ultimately the appellate courts.

The *New York Times* on April 29, 1989, published an editorial entitled "Why Execution Is Dead Wrong." It began, "How many James Richardsons does it take to change an attitude? It is a deadly serious question." It concluded, referring to James and another man condemned to death due to prosecutorial misconduct, that these cases "vividly show humans and their governments are fallible and corruptible. Prudent humility dictates that fallible people refrain from inflicting irreversible punishments." After James read Reno's words and the editorial, he said to me, "Maybe my suffering was part of God's plan so that other people might be saved."

The Winter Soldier Investigation 13

IIIIIIIIIIIIIIIIIIIIIIIIIIIIIIIIIIIIIIIIIIIIIIIIIIIIIIIIIIIIIIIIIIIIIIIIIIIIIIIIIIIIIIIIIIIII

I n 1970 Jane Fonda was in New York filming *Klute*, in which she played the role of a call girl. Donald Sutherland was Klute, a detective, and Alan Pakula directed the work. Henry Fonda owned a beautiful townhouse in Manhattan. It was staffed with a butler and maid. Although Henry was not living in the home during the filming, he refused to allow Jane to stay there since she had taken a strong position against the war. He also publicly expressed his dislike for me when giving interviews, a view that he had never offered to me when we talked. He was furious at me, he told interviewers, since I had led his daughter to oppose the war and since I had introduced her to the GI coffeehouse movement. GIs who opposed the war in Vietnam met together in coffeehouses off the military installations where they were stationed to discuss their options. In fact, Jane had openly opposed the war before we met and had spent time with the originator of the coffeehouse movement before that.

Donald, a brilliant phrasemaker with a unique mind, quipped over dinner one night that Henry had moved from the grapes of wrath to the raisins of petulance. I do not believe that Jane's father supported the war; rather, he was disturbed by what he saw as an

213

obsession that was making his daughter notorious in an industry with little patience for such behavior.

The studio arranged for an apartment for Jane in Manhattan, and she invited me to stay there. I went with Jane to her father's New York home to assist her in collecting some of her belongings. I thought that Jane seemed very sad, not depressed, but consumed in thought about being removed from her father's home because she could not look away from real life as she pursued her golden career. Being an actress, she made a valiant effort to conceal her feelings, but I had never seen her so moved. I thought then that I had been blessed with parents, not famous and not powerful, but two people who loved their children unconditionally and who supported me and my older brother and little sister in every effort we made, even those they might not have fully adopted.

Jane's Manhattan apartment, with me in temporary residence, became a meeting ground for former and active GIs, journalists, Dick Gregory, members of the Black Panther Party, and those I had worked with in New York over the years in civil rights, civil liberty, and political campaigns. In a sense Henry had created a political salon. All of them, of course, wanted to meet Jane.

On one occasion Huey Newton, the leader of the Black Panther Party, called. He was staying at a nearby fashionable hotel that, he said, was exhibiting racism toward him and his guests. I suggested that I visit the Howard Johnson hotel on the west side of downtown Manhattan; it was a place I knew to be generally available and almost always anonymous. I drove to the hotel and rented several rooms in my name, and Huey and his friends followed. Of course, the caravan of taxicabs with the lead one carrying Huey and the others filled with other well-known suspects did attract some notice.

The entire matter was not without repercussions, however. Much later, when I visited Angela Davis in her jail cell in Los Angeles, I asked her if she had ever discovered the method used by the police in locating and arresting her; she had not. All she knew is that she and her associate were staying at a nondescript Howard Johnson's in

New York and when they went into the lobby for breakfast several officers, of the many who were gathered there, recognized her. That was the morning after Huey, his entourage, and I had inadvertently led the police to the hotel. Angela, who was never convicted of anything, took my news with an amused smile. I remember her seated on a cot in a double jail cell filled with boxes that served as bookshelves for scores of her books as she responded to my apology. "I would forgive you if there was anything to forgive you about."

The informal meetings at Jane's had results that could not have been predicted, including the inception of the Winter Soldier Investigation, one of the most effective dramas in the march to end the war in Vietnam. Al Hubbard, a veteran of the war, visited Jane's apartment with an invitation. His organization, the Vietnam Veterans Against the War (VVAW), was planning an eighty-six-mile march from New Jersey to Valley Forge. They named it Operation RAW for "Rapid American Withdrawal." Military precision had been employed in organizing a series of events culminating in a rally at Valley Forge. Jane, Donald Sutherland, and I were invited to speak at the rally. The group decided they would "invade" towns along the march and, using actors, carry out supposedly brutal acts upon the "unsuspecting" inhabitants in much the same way our forces had acted against Vietnamese civilians. I agreed, as well, to join the three-day march and observe the event. The honorary commander was Army Brigadier General Hugh B. Hester, retired. The sponsors were Senator George McGovern, Senator Edmund Muskie, Representative John Conyers, Paul O'Dwyer, and me.

The former GIs, more than two hundred of them, began their "sieges" dressed in fatigues as they had been in combat. They carried replicas of weapons, some with bayonets affixed; their faces were painted, their expressions grim and serious. They shouted orders to one another as they approached unsuspecting and otherwise peaceful little American towns or villages on the march. They screamed at the villagers, prodded them with rifle barrels, conducted sweeps, and took and interrogated prisoners. They ordered civilians to fall to the ground and remain silent and struck those who did not respond quickly enough. The victims of the apparent brutality were guerrilla theater actors who had been stationed in public areas to play the role of local civilians. Men and women a short distance beyond the battle scene stared in confusion and horror at the violence that had suddenly erupted. Children screamed, and some wept and held onto their mothers or fathers.

No one dared to confront the squad of fully equipped and armed soldiers who appeared to have gone mad. For reasons that they could not begin to comprehend, their neighborhood had been invaded and turned into a war zone. Their neighbors were being brutalized and threatened with death. Suddenly the carnage ended as the interlopers marched out of the town on the way to continue the drama in the other small towns in New Jersey and Pennsylvania.

A few civilians handed out leaflets to the stunned observers explaining that the soldiers had acted in their presence as they had in Vietnam, except that here no one had been killed or injured.

That night we set up bivouac in a field. For many of the GIs the graphic reminder of where they had been and what they had done before coming home was unbearable. They had set up guard posts so that soldiers could sleep in peace. But there was no peace; there was little sleep. A shrill and terrified shout—"Incoming!"—caused an immediate response. Many jumped to their feet, grabbing their toy weapons. Others screamed "Gooks!" as they swept the area silently with useless, ersatz, noisemaking automatic weapons. The crisis eventually passed, and the gentle hum of insects lulled a few of us until the cries of anger and fear again erupted through the night.

For three days these brave young people sought to exorcise their demons during the day and wept through the nights. It culminated at Valley Forge, where hundreds of veterans gathered to promise that they would someday tell the truth to the American people about a war that had become a war crime.

Operation RAW was a remarkable and unprecedented effort. Those who experienced the drama will never forget it, yet relatively few Americans even knew it had taken place. If the veterans were going to speak to America, a very different approach was required, one that permitted the passion of the GIs to reach the heartland of our country.

A couple of civilians suggested that there be a mock war crimes trial. I knew there could be no credible trial, mock or otherwise, without defendants represented by their chosen counsel, a judge, an impartial jury, and rules of evidence that in large measure restricted hearsay and other nonadmissible evidence. All of that was lacking here. In addition, the dual engines of due process require that statements of all witnesses be given under penalty of perjury and be subject to cross-examination. Those prerequisites would not be present in a mock trial.

At a meeting I arranged with Al Hubbard and other VVAW leaders, I proposed that we hold hearings, not a trial, so that the GIs could tell America what they had seen and what they had done. I recalled Tom Paine's words that "the summer soldier and the sunshine patriot will, in this crisis, shrink from the service of his country." Inspired by the recent march to Valley Forge, where our new nation had survived a terrible winter, I suggested it be called the "Winter Soldier Investigation" (WSI) because no summer soldier could face that task.

A public investigation with former GIs speaking to the American people was, I proffered, the most direct and honest approach. And, I urged, it should not conclude with an "indictment." In time, hopefully, that would be provided by the American people.

The VVAW asserted, I believe correctly, that the hearings would have credibility if only those who had served in Vietnam made decisions about the authenticity of those willing to testify. The civilians—I put myself in that category although I too was a veteran, but of an earlier war—and the veterans working with the WSI all agreed that the Vietnam veterans should be in charge.

The VVAW established a six-person steering committee comprising three national officers and three rank-and-file members representing the chapters that were rapidly growing. I knew Al Hubbard and Tim Butz, two of the steering committee members. In the days ahead William F. Crandell, who had commanded a rifle platoon in Vietnam and was a rank-and-file member of the committee, became an essential leader. He was thoughtful and open to suggestions, and he had a sense of humor. Many years later Bill wrote *What Did America Learn from the Winter Soldier Investigation?* I believe it to be both the consummate short history of the WSI and an important assessment of its impact and promise.[1]

The goal was to have representatives of every US military outfit that had fought in Vietnam appear. The former GIs—officers, non-commissioned officers, enlisted men and women—organized themselves and their brothers and sisters in the service with remarkable skill and commitment. Jane and Donald and I raised funds and tried to secure some national interest in the project. The selection process of determining who would speak at the hearing was a fascinating operation. The former GIs sought corroboration for all forthcoming statements, and searching questions were asked and the answers duly noted.[2]

The Pentagon and the Nixon administration responded. Nixon's "plumbers," led by Charles Colson, reviewed the records of each veteran. A then-secret memorandum written by Colson, entitled "Plan to Counteract Viet Nam Veterans Against the War," stated, "The men that participated in the pseudo-atrocity hearings in Detroit will be checked to ascertain if they are genuine combat veterans."[3] The FBI then began surveillance of the VVAW members, those who had fought and some who were wounded in the service of their country, as suspects in a dissident organization.

Part of the Pentagon's effort to silence the voices of the veterans included an effort to defame me and prevent the circulation of my book *Conversations with Americans*, which I had recently written about war crimes in Vietnam.[4] That book, not surprisingly, had some difficulty in finding a publisher. Scott Meredith, America's most innovative and effective literary agent, agreed to try to secure a publisher before he read it. A few days after I delivered the unfinished manuscript to Scott, he called to ask me to visit him in his office immediately. He said he had read the manuscript the previous night and was horrified and educated by the words of the veterans. His son, he said, might soon be drafted, and since he did not want him to undergo a similar experience, he would use all of his influence to get the book published at once.

Scott sent the manuscript to more than twenty publishers, and while they had some interest in the manuscript, most expressed concern bordering on alarm. They thought the book might have an adverse effect on the publisher and probably could not be released in America.

Scott said his visit to Simon and Schuster was memorable. While the firm agreed to publish the book, its counsel was a strong supporter of General Westmoreland, and he argued against its publication, suggesting instead that the Department of Justice be contacted and given the manuscript so that I might be indicted for treason.

In the introduction to *Conversations* I pointed out that a number of fictitious names were used, since the veterans were concerned about reprisals. I had, however, shown the editors at Simon and Schuster all of the original statements with the full name and rank of each witness, including those for whom I had used fictitious names. I also played some of the tape recordings for the editors.

In the introduction I stated, "The transcripts in which each person is identified have been delivered to a prominent New York attorney who was formerly counsel for the United States Department of Justice. Should the responsible agencies of government wish to investigate the charges contained in the following statements, the relevant information is accessible to them."

I asserted in the book's introduction:

If you convince your soldiers that the enemy is less than human, comparable to baggage at best, a child assassin at worst, and then inform them that their mission is to score high in the body-count exercise, you cannot feign surprise when you discover what the war has become.

If Americans know less than all there is to know about the terrible cost the war is imposing upon the civilian population of South Vietnam, they know next to nothing of the real cost America is paying for its adventure. The real price is in the sacrifice of an entire generation.

Simon and Schuster did eventually publish the book, and I went on an extensive tour discussing the book with the media in all the major cities in the United States. The book was published on November 16, 1970, but not reviewed by the *New York Times* until December 27. It was then reviewed by Neil Sheehan. In essence, he said that a number of witnesses cited in the book were not former members of the military and that I had fabricated some of the interviews. Sheehan had accepted the false statements provided to him by the Pentagon and had apparently conducted no independent research. Sheehan did not consult the former Department of Justice attorney referred to in the introduction who would have provided the real names for those who used pseudonyms.

Immediately after Sheehan's review, counsel for Simon and Schuster demanded in writing that I return the advance for the book and pay them damages for harm to their reputation. The publisher also withdrew the book from bookstores throughout the country and violated its contract with me by refusing to publish a paperback version. The government had used the same methodology in this matter that it had perfected over the years in responding to inconvenient facts. It created a false legend, offered it to a journalist for a credible news outlet, and when it was published quoted the media as corroboration for its views.

Sheehan made a public relations tour to promote his book review. Yet he refused to answer any of my telephone calls to him or my letters to discuss his work. One radio station informed me that he was going to be present for a national program and asked if I would join.

I agreed at once, and the reporter said he would not tell Sheehan I would be there, for fear that Sheehan would cancel.

When I met Sheehan for the first time on that radio program I asked him if he had ever, in three years of coverage of the war in Vietnam, reported a single event revealing any act of misconduct by any member of the US military. He said that he had not. When I asked why his coverage was lacking in that regard, he responded that he knew of no misconduct by any American military personnel. When I asked about the war crimes at My Lai, he stated that they were just rumors.

I spent the next months traveling around the country securing statements from those individuals who Sheehan claimed did not exist. One former US Marine who fell into that category was employed by the governor of a major eastern state as his veterans' adviser. He was not in the capitol that day because he was at Camp Pendleton, a Marine Corps base in California, on behalf of the governor. He insisted to me, when we met for lunch, that he did exist and provided all sorts of documents regarding his service for his country and later for his state.

At the conclusion of my work, I met with Scott to demonstrate, through scores of documents, that Sheehan's review was demonstrably inaccurate. Scott arranged for the two of us to meet with the leadership of Simon and Schuster after we had sent all the documents to them. The publisher apologized profusely for having relied upon Sheehan, who they then believed had made a number of serious false statements.

Simon and Schuster sent a letter to me withdrawing their request for the repayment of the advance, apologized again for having withdrawn the book from circulation, and discussed the possibility of reissuing the book in a paperback edition, a suggestion I declined to pursue. Above all, Simon and Schuster paid to me a substantial sum in damages for their precipitous action for which they then admitted they had no rational or legal basis.

As for the pending WSI hearings, when I tried to visualize them, I wondered how survivors of the massacres and victims of other war crimes would view our plan. Would they be the silent, tragic fig-ures, or would they wish to be heard as well? Could we give them a voice? After conferring with my colleagues I visited Paris where I met with representatives of the National Liberation Front of South Vietnam (NLF). Their "embassy" was a lovely townhouse. My hosts were referred to as journalists by the French government, since the French did not have formal relations with the NLF. My hosts were sophisticated, well educated, and aware of the antiwar movement in the United States. After explaining some of the details of the pro-posed Winter Soldier Investigation, I made a request that Vietnam-ese survivors of war crimes attend the hearings. They listened closely, occasionally jotting down a note, and then politely but incredulously inquired if I believed that the US government would allow witnesses from Vietnam to enter America. I replied that I had not fully dis-closed the details of the plan.

The hearings would be held in Detroit, near the Canadian border and just a short ride from Windsor, Canada. A Canadian television station, CKLW-TV, had agreed to have three camera crews pres-ent in Cleary Auditorium in Windsor where the Vietnamese would speak. The station would broadcast their words, via closed circuit, to the hundreds of veterans and visitors in Detroit. The Windsor sta-tion was also negotiating with the Canadian Broadcasting Company for a program to be broadcast throughout Canada.

My hosts were impressed and said that the concept presented many difficulties, since the witnesses were in South Vietnam and the war was raging. It also presented, they said, an unusual opportunity. They asked if I could return the next day.

The next day was a working session without the formality of the day before. We discussed dates, events, geography. It was a hopeful start; they thought that they might be able to arrange for survivors to make the long trip north, by foot through jungles and by bicycles where there were roads, and then fly to Europe before the trip to Canada. They discussed the obstacles and proposed solutions in a very methodical and businesslike manner. Yet for me, an American discussing massacres with representatives of the victims, there was a sense of shame and horror for which I was unprepared.

Some GIs had agreed to speak of a slaughter of approximately four hundred unarmed civilians, some of whom had been sexually abused, tortured, and maimed at My Lai, an event partially known in the United States since November 1969 when Seymour Hersh wrote of it in the *New York Times*. My Lai and My Khe, I was patiently told in Paris by a Vietnamese scholar referring to his journal, were villages of Song My, a province in which a number of massacres of many people had taken place. He politely inquired if I could fix a date so that they might know to which one I referred.

The Winter Soldier Investigation was held at the Howard Johnson Motor Inn in Detroit from January 31, 1971, until February 2, 1971. One hundred five Vietnam veterans appeared at panels to provide information about war crimes they had seen or committed. The panels were arranged by unit so that the words of the veterans were available to corroborate one another. Bill Crandell later wrote, "The testimony was chilling. Veteran after veteran described the training and orders that led to the murder of civilians. Several vets admitted that they had committed torture and killed prisoners, had seen acts of rape and arson, all stemming from policies of their commanders."

The Pentagon sought to impugn the integrity of the veterans by stating, for example, that Michael A. Hunter, an important witness, had never served in the US Army. That false allegation was published by the *Detroit News*. Hunter was a Vietnam veteran who had been awarded a Silver Star, two Bronze Stars, the Air Medal, and two Purple Hearts, as he had been wounded twice. Documents proving that Hunter was in Vietnam were presented to a camera crew from CBS, and photographs of those documents were later broadcast throughout the nation. Hunter's father, a colonel in the US Army, was astonished by the false charges against his son.

Hunter's testimony was chilling, and one can understand why the government did not want it to be shared with the American people: "I took part with the First Air Cavalry and witnessed American military personnel carve symbols on the chests of the enemy dead and also cut off their heads. Their heads were impaled on sticks and placed on the trails. . . . The First Air Cavalry also killed villagers, burned their villages, and destroyed their livestock. . . . The standing orders for our outfit were to take no prisoners, which meant to kill those who were attempting to surrender."

The *Detroit Free Press* conducted its own inquiry into the statements of war crimes that the veterans were offering. Their investigative reporters could find no indication that the participants were not who they said they were, had not been where they said they had been, or that their testimony was fraudulent.[5]

Two stunning events provided information that had not been previously known regarding the purpose and result of American foreign policy. Dr. Bert Pfeiffer of the University of Montana offered a groundbreaking analysis regarding the toxic effects of Agent Orange upon civilians, the ecology, and ultimately the veterans themselves. That statement was largely ignored by the media for a substantial time.

The second revelation was that during 1969 General Creighton Abrams approved the illegal entry of the US military into Laos. A number of American GIs were killed and others wounded during that operation. Abrams had ordered a news blackout to prevent the American people from learning about the illegal incursion, named Dewey Canyon by the military. In fact, all the American dead were officially listed as being killed in Quang Tri Province, South Vietnam, and no reference was made to Laos.

At the Winter Soldier Investigation, two veterans spoke about their participation in the search-and-destroy missions in Laos. The Pentagon insisted that there had been no American presence in Laos, thereby implying that the Vietnam veterans had been making false statements. A *Detroit Free Press* reporter located and interviewed two former servicemen who had not heard of the Winter Soldier Investigation. They both corroborated the testimony, saying that they "did indeed" enter Laos and engage in combat there. The government continued to deny that there was a Dewey Canyon operation. However, when the Pentagon disclosed the name of the then-current search-and-destroy mission in Laos as "Dewey Canyon II," the matter was settled.

On Sunday, January 31, veterans from the First Marine Division, Third Marine Division, and First Air Cavalry Division reported upon crimes committed by those units. On Monday, February 1, the veterans were from the Fifth Special Forces and the 101st Airborne Division. On Tuesday, February 2, those who served in Vietnam with Lieutenant Calley's American Division, the Twenty-Fifth Infantry Division, the First Infantry Division, the Fourth Infantry Division, and the Ninth Infantry Division offered their testimony. The *Detroit Free Press* continued its close scrutiny and found there to be no valid complaint about the authenticity of the witnesses.

Among the veterans who addressed the purpose of the hearings was Donald Dzagulones, who stated, "We gathered not to sensationalize our service but to decry the travesty that was Lt. William Calley's trial for the My Lai massacre. The US had established the principle with the Nuremberg trials of the Nazis. Following those principles, we held that if Calley was responsible, so were his superiors up the chain of command—even to the president. The causes of My Lai and the brutality of the Vietnam War were rooted in the policies of our government as executed by our military commanders."

Sergeant George E. Smith, a former prisoner of war held by the NLF, spoke of the fair treatment he received while in captivity. When he was released, he spoke out against the war. He immediately faced court-martial charges. The charges were later dismissed due to insufficient evidence.

Excerpts from the transcripts follow.

Scott Camil: "My testimony involves the burning of villages with civilians in them, the cutting off of ears, cutting off of heads, torturing of prisoners, calling in of artillery on villages for games, corpsmen killing wounded prisoners."

Robert Stephen Craig: "My testimony covers the maltreatment of prisoners, the suspects, actually, and a convoy running down an old woman for no reason at all."

Mike McCusker: "I will testify in detail about the systematic killing of residents of two villages by members of the First Marine Division."

Joe Bangert: "My testimony is about the disembowelment and skinning of Vietnamese women in Quan Tri and the killing of women, children, and men in helicopter assaults."

James Duffy: "I will testify about the dropping of gas into villages 'just for kicks' and the practice of giving hydraulic fluid to village children to drink with the logic that 'the only good gook is a dead gook.'"

Steve Rose: "I will testify about seeing a wounded civilian thrown out of a helicopter and witnessing enemy ears being prepared for shipment to the United States."

Bill Hatton: "I will testify about the stoning to death of the Vietnamese child by twenty marines and the distribution of 'cookies' filled with heat tabs thrown to Vietnamese children as 'candy.'"

Rusty Sachs: "My testimony concerns the leveling of villages for no valid reason, throwing Viet Cong suspects from the aircraft after binding them and gagging them with copper wire."

After each veteran briefly summarized his testimony, the panel leader then asked each of them to provide details. Members of the press and the audience were then invited to ask questions.

Nixon's secret group could not prevent the hearings from taking place but was able to persuade the Canadian government to state that the Vietnamese who had traveled from villages in South Vietnam to Europe would not be permitted to enter Canada.

After the hearings were completed, a young decorated lieutenant in the Naval Reserve who had been in Detroit appeared before a committee of the US Senate. John Kerry, now a senator, said, "We who have come here to Washington have come here because we feel we have to be winter soldiers now. We could come back to this country; we could be quiet; we could hold our silence; we could not tell what went on in Vietnam; but we feel because of what threatens this country, the fact that crimes threaten it, not Reds, and not Redcoats, but crimes which we are committing that threaten it, that we have to speak out."

The impact of these courageous GIs coming home to tell the truth to the American people was not immediate. The media at first relied upon Pentagon denials that surfaced through government media assets. The Colson operation was also effective, through its intelligence assets in the media, in preventing the important story from circulating widely.

Senator Mark Hatfield entered a transcript of testimony by the GIs into the Congressional Record. Senator J. William Fulbright, chairman of the US Senate Committee on Foreign Relations, convened hearings in April and May 1973, based upon the statements of the GIs made during the Winter Soldier Investigation. In time, the facts about the effects of Agent Orange, the illegal incursion into Laos, and the crimes committed against the civilians of Vietnam were understood and became part of the people's successful efforts to end that war. In 1972, the documentary film *Winter Soldier* was released. And in 2006, for the first time, a declassified document revealed that a massacre described in Detroit more than thirty-five years earlier was confirmed by the US Army.

Mountain Home

||||||||||||||||||||||||||||||||||||||||||||||

During the war in Vietnam, the emissaries from our country were poisoning the land and the water while indiscriminately killing civilians and warriors alike with Agent Orange and napalm. They were dropping more explosives upon a relatively small third-world country than were used by all the combatants during World War II.

In our country, the call to end the war was growing stronger. I had previously met Bob Rix, likely the most informed counselor on GI rights in the country, in 1970 when Jane Fonda and I had discussed the need to create a national office where GIs facing reprisals for opposition to the war could obtain support. At that time I introduced Jane to Don Duncan, a highly decorated former Green Beret and the author of a book about the early days of American participation in Vietnam. We decided to establish the GI Office in Washington, DC. Any GI who was experiencing legal problems with the military authorities for having exercised his or her First Amendment rights was guaranteed free legal assistance. Bob, then the director of the Washington Area Military Law Panel, joined the GI Office collective when it was organized. Jane and I publicized the office and raised the funds that it required; Don moved from Los Angeles to DC to run it.

In the springtime of 1971 I was living in Washington, awaiting the beauty of the cherry blossom display. Rallies for peace were being organized throughout the nation, with possibly the largest and most impressive one scheduled for San Francisco. I was invited to speak there and accepted. However, a few days later the mail brought a letter from Jon Robertson of Boise, Idaho. The stationary disclosed that he and his father carved briar pipes that were, they claimed, the finest in the world. I doubted that; I had been a pipe aficionado and collector for many years, starting with ones given to me by my father. Later I was to learn that my doubts were misplaced; they were the best pipes I had seen.

Jon was planning a two-day weekend meeting in Boise during April 1971 to oppose the war at which, he hoped, the governor of Idaho and I would speak, and Phil Ochs, an outstanding musician and composer, would entertain. The conference, to be held in a downtown park, was called a "Festival for Life." There was a conflict; I was looking forward to the meeting in San Francisco, a place where I had several friends and now the opportunity to address tens of thousands of supporters. Idaho, though, was part of Nixon's beloved "heartland" and a place where the antiwar movement had not yet developed. I agreed to call the West Coast organizers to see if I could be spared.

The response, "We have too many speakers now, Mark. It's fine, just fine, if you can't come—and good luck in Boise," lacked tact, if not clarity. I embarked upon a journey that would take me through Boise to Mountain Home, Idaho, my next home. I was the only featured speaker at the outdoor amphitheater in the Julia Davis Park in Boise; the governor had taken a poll and decided that he was needed elsewhere. Phil's songs, including "I Ain't Marching Any More," had become an intrinsic part of the movement for peace. The audience had been very responsive to his songs and to the demand that we halt the war against the people of Vietnam. I spoke of the GI Movement, the actions of active duty members of the military taking organized action against the war. I spoke of coffeehouses that had been established near some military installations, but off base, as a place where those against the war could meet in safety. Several young men and a young woman standing some distance from the podium and slightly apart from the group caught my attention. They were dressed in civilian clothes, but their haircuts and demeanor told me they were very likely members of the armed service. I had not known that there was a military installation in the area.

After the formal part of the proceedings concluded, I talked with many of those present. I walked toward the folks I had noticed earlier. As we introduced ourselves I learned that they were stationed at the Mountain Home Air Force Base, approximately forty miles away. They said that they were very interested in learning how GIs could organize in opposition to the war and wondered if I could stay to assist them. They said there were others who also were interested, and we agreed to meet at the same location the following morning.

The war against Vietnam had largely turned from a grunt operation, an infantry-based battle, to an air war as our determined military leaders proclaimed that "we will bomb them back to the Stone Age," a period in which the leaders apparently found comfort. I was concerned that our movement had failed to keep up with the Pentagon's most recent strategic adjustment. While there were GI coffeehouses and projects at or near army, navy, and marine corps camps, none existed near air force bases. That night I thought that the absence of a GI project at any US Air Force base might soon be remedied. It was an important development, and if the men and women at Mountain Home were serious and dedicated, I would change my plans and stay for a few days.

Sunday morning was bright with promise and sunshine. The GIs had made the trip to Boise, a town so bereft of trees that it made you wonder what the French were thinking when they named it (*boise* is French for "wooded") or if at that time forests had loomed about. There were enlisted men and an enlisted woman, noncommissioned officers and a first lieutenant. Several others had present duties at the base and were not available for this meeting but were committed to participate in future discussions. They seemed interested and eager to do something. They were also more than a little concerned about the possible consequences of trying to bring about change while serving in the US Air Force. They knew the wide-ranging authority of the military and, therefore, doubted that they had the power to make a significant contribution. They expressed the ideas and concerns I had heard so many times before among honorable army, navy, and marine corps GIs stationed at installations in the United States and in Europe.

It is important to understand that the GIs I met with did not present a blank slate; they were not unthinking young men and women who had not seriously contemplated their status. For many of them escape was found through the abuse of drugs, for others through individual, quietly performed acts of sabotage. What they sought, although not all were aware of it, was a means of working together, setting specific objectives to bring the war and their involvement in it to an end, informing their naive fellow citizens that war crimes were being committed in their name, and accomplishing those goals while reducing the risks they were facing daily.

We talked for hours about how each person has intrinsic power and how one person acting alone can make an important difference. After an open and comprehensive meeting the next morning, I began to understand the depth of their conviction and the level of their opposition to the war. We spoke about the risks involved. I would try to contact civilians in the area who might help. I would be available by telephone for legal advice. It was an important decision for each of them to make and one that should not be taken too quickly or without regard for possible consequences, perhaps including company punishment or court-martial proceedings.

We all, especially the GIs, knew of the risks involved. When isolated in Mountain Home we, civilians and GIs alike, were subject to insults and beatings. One GI, a rather rotund young man of Asian descent who appeared to be defenseless, was surrounded by a few men who had straggled out of a bar. They were about to attack him when he warned them that he was a student of karate. They laughed and struck out at him. A moment later the landscape was decorated by the fallen and writhing bodies of the injured. The GI walked away.

We also knew the reprehensible record of the oppression of those who had made similar efforts before. The first GI coffeehouse, the UFO, was opened in South Carolina. GIs from nearby Fort Jackson were arrested and some sent to Vietnam. Unable to destroy the UFO by arresting GIs and sending them to Vietnam, the authorities charged three civilian operators with operating a public nuisance. They were convicted and sentenced to six years in prison. In Texas, Pfc. Bruce Peterson, the editor of a GI newspaper, was arrested for alleged possession of such a minute amount of marijuana that it was "destroyed" while being tested. He was sentenced to eight years in a federal penitentiary. Two years later the conviction was set aside.

During February 1970 a GI coffeehouse near Fort Dix was bombed, and three GIs and one civilian were injured. A marine corps coffeehouse at Camp Pendleton was occupied when someone fired a machine gun at it, wounding a marine.

Organizing a group, meeting with others to talk about the war, providing a place for veterans to discuss the war with recent recruits, and providing counseling were acts not prohibited by the Uniform Code of Military Justice. Unlawful acts that might jeopardize the GIs were to be avoided.

Observing these brave men and women relate to one another without regard for rank or gender or ego, willing to take well-calculated risks because they believed that people of principle in their place could do no less, made it easy and quite natural for us to decide to put aside all other considerations and join with them, for however long it might take. I called again on Carolyn Mugar, a talented organizer and dear friend, and asked if she would join me for a brief stay. It soon became clear that we were going to have to remain much longer than we had expected. We rented a nondescript little house in Mountain Home for lodging and a place to meet with the

GIs, almost all of whom lived on the base ten miles away. We stayed for more than two years.

It was agreed that the GIs would make the decisions and that Carolyn and I and the other civilians who might volunteer later would offer advice and counsel when requested. In addition, we would undertake tasks that members of the service could not perform. They called me Mark, sometimes Dad, which I believe was said facetiously, and sometimes the Organizer, a title that Carolyn soon was awarded.

The first issue was to find a name for our project and another for its newspaper. In a moment of alacrity that feat was accomplished by the GIs who suggested we name our project the Covered Wagon. Almost everyone cheered and laughed at the audacious suggestion. I liked it because it called to an earlier time in this area and because, while it had an American feeling, the Basque shepherds still used sized-down covered wagons in their daily work in the desert that surrounded Mountain Home and the base. Politely suppressed laughter made it clear that I was missing something, probably everything.

A GI, patiently but unable to repress some mirth, explained that they had all attended security briefings at the base. If someone suspected sabotage or a breech in security, he was instructed to wave his arms frantically above his head three times and call out "Helping hand" (until that moment, a classified code phrase to be used only as a cry for help). However, if it was established that sabotage was actually occurring, the GIs were instructed to keep waving and shout out "Covered wagon" to summon help. "Then let's call our newspaper *Helping Hand*," another participant suggested.

And so it began. Within days, work on the newspaper, our first endeavor, was under way with a homemade light box permanently ensconced on our kitchen table. We agreed that there would be a different editor for each issue. The GIs who were contributing to *Helping Hand* thought it prudent not to sign their work. There was one dissenter from that collective wisdom. Airman John O'Connor said he wanted to sign his article, and he did. By the time the second issue was being prepared, John's courage proved to be contagious; each participant decided that his or her name should be published.

The Covered Wagon earned the trust of its members. It was the only democracy functioning within miles. A general membership meeting took place every week for years. Each meeting was chaired by a different GI, from the lowest-ranking airman one week to a captain or first lieutenant the next and a member of the Women's Air Force (WAF) the next. Everyone present was entitled to speak, to make motions, and to vote. There was no fee to join. Membership was completely unrestricted. If you were present for a meeting, you were a member. Members included GIs, their wives or husbands, high school students from the community, farm workers, career officers who dropped in out of curiosity, construction workers from a road-building project, and a local amiable alcoholic from the next-door bar. Once the Mountain Home chief of police, a rather testy and hostile public servant, visited. He was invited to stay, to speak, and to vote. He looked around for a few minutes and then left silently. As he reached the door he turned, looked at me, and nodded affirmatively.

There were no rules except that drugs were prohibited. GIs never wore their uniforms, and the word *sir* never passed anyone's lips. That was not due to any regulation, just the fact of liberation.

Helping Hand evolved into an excellent journal that was widely read at the base, in Mountain Home, in Boise, and at GI coffeehouses and similar projects throughout the world. Our style basically precluded the over-the-top rhetoric found in other GI newspapers. "If we are going to control our own destiny, let's just do it, not talk about it," a GI offered at an editorial meeting. It was just a suggestion; it became our modus operandi.

The newspaper presented two challenges: write it and distribute it. The first assignment was accomplished with ease. Many who had never written before proved to be communicators with substantial talent. It contained articles by GIs returning from Vietnam, discussions about life on the base, photographs, poetry, and even sarcastic awards for particularly offensive conduct practiced by officers in command. Its theme was clear: end the war and bring our brothers and sisters home. The first issue was published by fourteen airmen and women, twelve sergeants, two lieutenants, two captains, and two civilian supporters.

Each issue of *Helping Hand* was eagerly awaited by the GIs on the base and equally feared by the command. During my last lawful visit to the base I met with Colonel Gilbert Hereth, the base commander for most of the three years that the Covered Wagon was an active force. I asked for permission to distribute the newspaper on base. He did not want a confrontation; neither did he want the paper on his base. He might not approve of its articles, he suggested. I said that I was certain that he would not approve of all of the articles, "but then the First Amendment does not come into operation only with publications that you approve, sir." I did point out that the base's news rack presently featured magazines with content, including pornography, that I presumed reflected neither the taste nor the political view of the colonel. The commander considered. He waffled. I gave him a complimentary copy of the first issue. He thanked me. He said that he and his staff would have to review the publication and let me know. That might take two weeks. "In the interim, since it is not banned now, are we free to distribute it, that is, at least until there is a decision to the contrary by the command?" Reluctantly and thoughtfully he agreed, wheeled around, and left even before I could offer a handshake or perhaps a salute.

Minutes later I entered the base to distribute the *Helping Hand*. I was arrested by the military police, escorted off the base, and banned from the base for life. During that process I requested that the officers contact Colonel Hereth for clarification. They responded that their orders had come directly from him.

That evening we began to formulate plans for surreptitious distribution on the base and public distribution everywhere else. Most citizens abhor the concept of censorship but generally are not aware of its draconian existence because the information has been suppressed without their knowledge. We were determined to get the information about the war and the opposition by our GIs out for all to read. On Sunday, June 13, 1971, we paid a friendly visit to our colleagues in the press at the editorial offices of the *Idaho Statesman*, the leading daily newspaper in the area. Twenty of us, almost all GIs, many carrying guitars, banjos, flutes, or violins, entered the newsroom and announced that the grand opening of the Covered Wagon would take place the following day. The message was delivered in lyrics with a musical background. The reporters were delighted. The next day the newspaper reported that the GIs were set to "free the 5,000," referring to the airmen at Mountain Home, and to oppose the war. The weekly *Intermountain Observer* reported that while "coffee, tea and sympathy for the airmen who oppose the war are to be guiding themes for a theatre-and-newspaper enterprise, the main thrust of Covered Wagon is against the Vietnam war, against militarism, and toward helping the airman who has problems on or off the base."

Our living room and kitchen were bursting with GIs and friends, including Karma, a frightened and abused dog we had just rescued from an impatient local dog pound, and Crispin, a collie puppy. The Covered Wagon needed a new and larger home. I had heard that the old and abandoned Mountain Home Theater on Main Street was available. I rented it for fifty dollars a month.

Airman Dave Harp was a very talented artist who thought that Picasso's *Guernica* would be an appropriate decoration for our theater. I thought he was going to buy a small print. With the help of other GIs he created a massive mural covering the entire length of one wall in just a few weeks.

The grand opening of the new space for the Covered Wagon featured a discussion led by attorney Bob Rix. Bob remained at the Covered Wagon for a week, leading training sessions every evening. His detailed explanation of the Uniform Code of Military Justice and of additional military regulations and recent cases provided enough information for GIs to feel confident that they knew the limits of the rules and that they could remain within the letter of military law and still advocate GI rights and organize against the war. One of the airmen said the regulations used against them were now a tool to deploy.

We continued to develop furtive tactics for distributing our message on base. Stacks of the newspapers appeared quietly in clubs, barracks, officers' quarters, mess halls, movie theaters, and anywhere the GIs might gather. Many GIs hitchhiked ten miles from the base to the Wagon to pick up a copy and take a few spare ones for their friends. As counsel, I had advised the GIs not to engage in open and public distribution on the base, since they likely would be prosecuted. My suggestion was not always respected. In fact, within forty-eight hours of the publication of the first issue, more than two thousand copies of *Helping Hand* were distributed to GIs.

Distribution was primarily executed by our civilian guests, who entered the base and handed out the *Helping Hand* to groups of airmen eager to accept the publication. Each civilian was apprehended, escorted from the base, and banned for life. But we had many visitors, and almost all joined the honor roll of being banned for exercising First Amendment rights. Dr. Benjamin Spock, then seventy years old, was thrown off the base, as were Dick Gregory, Ben Vereen, and Jane Fonda.

George Smith, whom I met during the Winter Soldier Investigation, came to visit us. He had been sent to Vietnam as a sergeant in the Green Berets. He was captured in South Vietnam and held as a POW from 1963 until 1965. George spoke at the Wagon to a large audience and shared dinner at our house with more than fifteen veterans of Vietnam, many of whom were not members of the Covered Wagon. They all seemed to share as well similar views about the ongoing war. All opposed it; some were passionate in their criticism, others less vehement.

George then decided to visit the base so that he could distribute a letter he had written to his fellow airmen. That letter had been years in the making. At the same time he sought to distribute the latest issue of *Helping Hand*. His letter recounted his two years as a POW. He had been held with other American POWs in a remote area of

South Vietnam under the cover of the natural triple canopy. He and his fellow American prisoners, he said, were adequately fed and not mistreated. None were tortured, except for the fact of confinement. His life had been threatened on numerous occasions, but those inadvertent threats came from the US Air Force. When jets dropped bombs, napalm, Agent Orange, or other explosives and chemicals near the prison camp, the American prisoners prayed that they would be spared. "The only threat to our life came from our own air force," George said. "And I promised my fellow prisoners that if I ever got home while the war was still being fought I would ask the air force to stop the bombing."

George entered the Mountain Air Force Base to honor his commitment to those still in prison camps in Vietnam. Colonel Hereth immediately ordered that he be arrested and copies of his letters confiscated. He was physically removed from the base and then banned for life. George said he had last been arrested by the National Liberation Front of South Vietnam and then it was not for seeking to exercise his First Amendment rights but for waging war against them in their country.

George spoke at colleges in Idaho, was interviewed by a major network television station in Boise, and appeared on an ultra-conservative talk radio program. When asked if he agreed that he had been brainwashed, since he did not accept the military's view of life in the POW camp, he said, "Oh, yes. I was brainwashed when I was being trained by our Special Forces and convinced that we were going off to fight for the liberation of a country where the people would welcome us as liberators."

The members of the Wagon paid for George's travel expenses and arranged his schedule for talks throughout the state. At the regular weekly meeting following the visit, members said that they were gratified that a dissenting view had been so well presented to the GIs and other residents of the state. They reminded the most recent members that our mission was to tell the American people the truth about the war.

We believed that our newspaper was likely going to become a primary organizing mechanism, and we were committed to making it an effective document. It was the size and shape of a small magazine, generally between sixteen and thirty-two pages, and professionally printed. Its circulation varied depending upon our creativity and the effectiveness of the command to suppress it. Often more than twenty-five hundred copies were printed and distributed. Above all, it was reliable. It was published every month. It lacked the revolutionary rhetoric that other GI newspapers engaged in, although copies of those papers were available in the Covered Wagon library, since we saw opposition to the war and protection of the rights of GIs as our goals.

Those who had just come back from Vietnam vowed to bring the war home to the American military by recounting to their brothers and sisters in uniform the exact nature of the war. Their newspaper was their voice. They were determined to work with GIs at other bases and camps throughout the United States and in Europe and even in Vietnam. They also sought to reach out to civilians in Mountain Home, Boise, and elsewhere.

At the base there were problems even closer to home. Some of the GIs were scheduled to ship out almost immediately for Vietnam. Some had apparently been chosen for deployment due to their work at the Covered Wagon. They had talked at the Wagon to airmen who had just returned, and many made the decision that they would refuse the orders for assignment in Vietnam. They would neither be involved in massacres nor help to increase the totals for the daily body count, a count that included civilians, children, and other victims along with combatants, a count that Walter Cronkite continued to read to a naive America as he assured us each night that all was going well.

They did not want to die in a country that did not want them to be there and for a cause they rejected. They were willing to face long prison terms in a federal penitentiary; they were no longer willing to participate in an unjust war.

I had learned a great deal about the law regarding conscientious objectors (COs) and counseling from the sessions with Bob Rix, and I had studied the Uniform Code of Military Justice. I concluded there might be no need for any GI to defy orders and face a certain court-martial. If the GI had a sincere conscientious objection to war, he could not be required to fight.

Everyone in the air force was a volunteer, rather than a draftee, making the case exponentially more difficult but not impossible. The government's reasoning was not hard to predict. If they joined willingly, signing a four-year contract while the war was being waged, how could they possibly now claim that they are conscientious objectors? Therefore, their applications should be summarily rejected.

A response that they joined under duress, since they knew that they were going to be drafted by the army if they did not, while truthful in most cases, would in all likelihood not prevail. Less improbable but also vulnerable to attack was "I have decided now that I oppose all war. That was not my thinking when I enlisted. It is now my sincere belief based upon what I have learned about war after I entered the service and, in fact, in large measure due to what I have learned about war from my returning comrades."

That concept did not enjoy the approval of the military and outraged the generals who issued rulings. It nevertheless was the law, and we determined to make a stand, citing our rights under the applicable military law passed by the Congress.

I began the counseling service even before our doors were open. The first client was Jimmy Schaffer, who attended his first Covered Wagon meeting after taking LSD. He was the first of our group to decide that sobriety was required if he was to become an activist in a movement for peace. He applied for CO status, received an honorable discharge, and then moved to Mountain Home to study the Uniform Code of Military Justice. After weeks of research, study, and work as an apprentice, he became the best CO counselor I have ever known. Soon he replaced me as the organization's primary CO counselor. Later he began to teach others his new trade and wrote a book on the subject that reached GIs at numerous military bases.

Captain Gary Aker was a lawyer who was a member of the judge advocate's office at the base. He believed in the concept of military justice until he saw how it was applied. Soon he became the attorney for the Wagon and wrote articles about military injustice for the *Helping Hand*. Gary was granted an honorable discharge.

During the decade preceding the establishment of the Covered Wagon, the armed forces, led by the Joint Chiefs of Staff, had made it clear that conscientious objection claims were nuisances best dealt with by immediate rejection and threats. During that ten-year period approximately twenty-five hundred members of the military serving in all branches of the service, stationed both in the United States and throughout the rest of the world, had applied for discharge as conscientious objectors. Eighty percent of those applications were denied out of hand. Those who lost and were forced to remain in the military often suffered serious consequences. On the average only fifty applications were granted per year.

During the first year after the Covered Wagon was founded, sixty-eight GIs stationed at Mountain Home were counseled, applied for conscientious objector discharge, and obtained a final ruling. Every application where the service member had secured counseling at the Wagon was granted, and all received honorable discharges. The base was small and in population represented less than two-tenths of 1 percent of the armed forces personnel. Yet in one year alone it obtained more CO discharges than the national annual average for the entire military during the previous ten years. Thirty additional applications were pending as the Covered Wagon celebrated its first anniversary. They too were ultimately successful.

In addition, many other enlisted personnel were discharged for having worked effectively, and legally, in opposition to the war. A number of officers were asked to resign due to their work with the Covered Wagon. Other officers resigned without being requested to do so. While the military may have rationalized that at least they were getting rid of troublemakers, each honorable discharge for opposition to the war was a victory for the GIs at the base and an inspiration to GIs throughout the world who learned about the phenomenon.

Many of those who were discharged stayed in Mountain Home to continue the work of the Wagon. Others went home to work for peace in their own communities. They recounted that their time at the Covered Wagon was a turning point in their lives and that lessons learned there in cooperation with their comrades remained with them.[1]

Carolyn, gentle, energetic, and tireless, became a central, likely the central, figure at the Wagon. Her special impact upon issues related to women was important in meetings held with those women who were either married to, or friends of, GIs or were themselves members of the WAF.

Women in the military, including those stationed in Mountain Home, found that too often their leaders considered them to be fringe benefits for both married and unmarried male officers and high-ranking noncommissioned officers at the base. While women were not subject to the draft in the United States, other considerations often made service in the military appear to be a viable escape.

Why did women join? Some were genuinely very patriotic. They responded to military commercials and advertising promising them a dignified life in the service of their country. Others, due to gender discrimination, found paths to employment that they wished to pursue as civilians closed to them. Others were persuaded by the opportunity to further their education after service, especially since some parents and other advisers sought to discourage them from hopes of higher education, stating that it would be a waste, since they were going to get married and have children anyway.

When they entered the service, they found that they had left a civilian society of de facto discrimination only to encounter a military that enforced discrimination against them in a more orderly and rigorous fashion. Many, though certainly not all, came to believe that their leaders were less interested in providing a dignified life for them and more interested in relieving raging hormones for the men, isolated from other women.

One of the dirty little secrets about the life of women in the US Air Force was the official position of the government regarding abortions. All members of the WAF were required to attend mandatory sex education briefings. At Mountain Home the lectures and directives were presented by the psychiatrist, Dr. Estes, and the chaplain, who in civilian life openly and publicly opposed abortions and demanded that they be considered illegal. Four members of the WAF wrote an article that was published by *Helping Hand*. They stated that the psychiatrist "consistently referred to the women present as sex objects and more than once referred to the fact that WAF are there for GI morale." Both officers also stressed the fact that "free abortions are available at Travis Air Force Base," as was free transportation and arrangements ensuring that the parents of the woman would never learn of the abortion.

The women's reaction to the reality of military life, to the reports from those returning from combat, to the shared good times at the Covered Wagon was more pronounced than that of their male counterparts. Penny Rand was the first WAF to join and help organize our work. She became a symbol of independence and courage for other women in the air force. She sought and received an honorable discharge. In fact almost 10 percent of the members of the Women's Air Force present at the Mountain Home Air Force Base when the Wagon opened its doors had left the air force in a little over one year.

The air force had also been having problems with black airmen who were treated with less respect and given fewer opportunities than their white counterparts. Instead of addressing their concerns, the military decided to segregate and isolate them. Mountain Home provided an ideal air force Siberia. The black members of the military were for the most part frustrated and angry, and many viewed the white GIs as elite and privileged. Of course, we sought to reach out to them; the fact that some members of the Wagon betrayed racist attitudes was not helpful in that endeavor, and the military exploited this unfortunate situation to disrupt our unity. A magic moment was required to keep our group from fracturing.

Dick Gregory arrived. Some think of Greg as a brilliant standup comedian. He is that. Some consider him to be an outstanding author, a naturalist, a protector of the environment, a nutritionist. Those too are all true. And none of it matters when judged against his life's contribution as a tireless and courageous activist for the rights of the voiceless.

We had outlined an ambitious program for Greg. Since he was performing without a fee, as did all those who visited us, and was paying for all of his own expenses, a commitment that some without resources could not make, our demands were just short of outrageous. Fly from New England to Boise, be driven forty miles to Mountain Home, immediately meet with the members of the Wagon who were available that afternoon, distribute our newspaper on the base, an exercise that would end in his arrest and release, perform at the Covered Wagon during the early evening, be rushed back to Boise to perform at a late show at Boise State College to raise funds for the Wagon, and then get a few hours' sleep at an airport motel before catching the early morning plane home. When I met him at the airport and told him of the plans, he said, "Fine, let's get started."

The commander, guarding against an alliance of black and white air force personnel, restricted the black airmen to the base during the early evening hours so that they could not attend the Gregory appearance. It was late in the evening when I called the Wagon from the college as Greg's performance was ending. "A lot of the black guys are here. They just left the base, and they hope to meet Mr. Gregory. What should I tell them?"

I told Greg what I had learned. "Well, doctor, we had better get into that car for another ride across the desert. We don't want to keep them waiting any longer." Dick Gregory sat on the stage and talked with humor through the night to the fifteen black servicemen. We drove him to Boise in time to make his flight.

||||||

I met Sergeant Steve Hawkins when he returned from Vietnam decades ago. I will not forget him. How could I? He carried his violin and his classical music with him to Vietnam where, for one year, he loaded bombs for the air force. When he came to Mountain Home he played for us. He was, at first, unable to forgive himself for having participated in the war. He dedicated his remaining days in the air force to organizing for the Covered Wagon. When his four-year term was almost completed he would not accept the honorable discharge that the military was about to award him. Instead he demanded that he be discharged as a CO. He changed the beneficiary for his military life insurance policy to the Covered Wagon. When he did leave us, it was to become one of the leaders of the Vietnam Veterans Against the War, then based in Chicago.

Airman Tom Tierney decided that he would shut down the base. He never discussed the idea with his buddies. One night he rode his bicycle onto the flight line to prevent bombers from landing and F-4s from taking off. Huge floodlights scanned the area as the base froze into absolute inaction. In panic, jeeps and other vehicles were dispatched. Ten minutes later Tom was in custody. Since the military announced that it would court-martial Tom, we were preparing a defense based upon the assertion that he sought to prevent a major crime, the continuing war, by committing the smaller offense of trespassing. The base leadership was not eager for a show trial; instead, they quietly discharged Tom. He went home to Denver to work at his bicycle shop, to organize for the VVAW, and to assist active-duty GIs at Lowry Air Force Base.

One evening a twenty-eight-year-old avionics maintenance officer at the base, Captain Larrie Knudsen, told his wife that he heard some of his colleagues talking about the Covered Wagon. He said that he was going to look into that group because he wanted to keep his friends from getting involved, since that would jeopardize their military careers. When he returned home that night, after an evening of talk and singing, he reported that he had liked the people there and that they made sense. When asked by his incredulous wife if he was thinking of joining, he answered sheepishly, "I'm now the librarian."

Larrie was the great-grandson of H. M. Knudsen, the cofounder of Morrison-Knudsen (M-K), which was located in Boise and likely the largest war profiteer in Idaho and one of the largest in the United States. When it became known that M-K was constructing the notorious "tiger cages," torture cells for political prisoners in Vietnam, the US Senate began an investigation.

Larrie was the featured speaker at a rally held by the Wagon outside of the M-K headquarters. As a bugle played, he raised pennants on the large M-K flagpoles. They called for the end to the war. Then he lowered them to half-mast. "We do this," he said, "to honor those on both sides who have died in this unjust war."

On August 5, 1971, members of the Covered Wagon, civilians and active-duty GIs, staged a commando raid upon the six-story M-K headquarters. We entered the front door either alone or in the company of one other. We each walked to a washroom on an assigned floor. At exactly 2:12 PM we emerged and handed out letters to each employee. By 2:20 we were all out of the building. The letters, entitled "Memorandum of Conscience," stated that M-K is a war profiteer and directly engaged in genocide. All of the construction of prison facilities, tiger cages, and other instruments of torture and detention in South Vietnam was being carried out by the M-K monopoly. It concluded:

> We appeal to you directly because you are directly involved in genocide, as are we, through our membership in the United States Air Force. Only by direct action against the war and against the institutions that make war and profit from it can we escape responsibility for the crimes that are committed daily in our name.

The public events were spectacular and helped develop the support for our work that would become significant when the military and hostile civilians in the area worked their mischief. Country Joe McDonald, who had founded the band Country Joe and the Fish in Berkeley during 1965, came to perform his songs at the Covered Wagon. Months later Joe returned to again volunteer for another gig. One afternoon I walked out behind the Wagon and saw Jimmy Schaffer and other GI musicians deeply involved in a creative session with Country Joe playing along with them. Jimmy told me that was his favorite memory of the Wagon. One GI later recalled, "We drove to the lake and went swimming. When I got to the raft I saw Donald Sutherland; he was standing on the raft and reciting Shakespeare for about fifteen minutes."

We organized a "March Against Genocide" that was covered by both the *New York Times* and the *Los Angeles Times*. The conception and organization came from the GIs. We decided to march from Mountain Home to a federal building in Boise through forty miles of desert to remember Hiroshima and Nagasaki. Carolyn was there, running back and forth as the photographer, and I marched along, really limped at the end, as a very proud member of the Covered Wagon. We marched under large silk banners, made from parachutes (I had no idea where they came from), that said BRING OUR BROTHERS HOME and WE ARE TAKING THE GI OUT OF G ENOC I DE."

Perhaps the most spectacular events were the shows starring Donald Sutherland, Jane Fonda, Barbara Dane, Dick Gregory, Ben Vereen, Country Joe, and many others. Two performances on Sunday afternoon at the Wagon filled the house, and two appearances at the liberal arts auditorium at Boise State College were sold out. General admission was $2.50; GIs and students were asked to contribute a dollar if they could. All proceeds went to the Wagon.

Before the first show at the Wagon began, I suggested that the Covered Wagon Musicians, renamed the Sgt. Rock Band for the event, open with a couple of songs they had written. The director of the show was not pleased, saying that "amateurs" should not be involved. The GIs were hurt. They looked to me. I said, "If you want to play, play. You know all about empowerment, and you know how good you are." The program opened with the band, and all of the professionals, especially Donald and Joe, said that they were the highlight of the day. Later, in their tour across America, the band played with Pete Seeger and Holly Near, sometimes performing for audiences of thousands.

A terrible memory for us was the night that arsonists set fire to the theater. Everything burned to the ground as a number of leading citizens cheered. The *Guernica* mural was gone as were the musical instruments, the counseling books, and the pending CO applications. The local police department was disinterested in exploring the facts and the culprits were not apprehended or even seriously sought.

After the Wagon was destroyed, the people's troubadour, Barbara Dane, visited us to remind us that the phoenix rose from the ashes. Barbara was a well-known singer who had abandoned her traditional career to devote her energy and talent to those seeking peace and justice.

Carolyn arranged for the purchase of an abandoned migrant-worker camp as our new home. It was not a theater, but it had one very large room in a large house and a motel-like cottage on the property. We moved in. I gave up the lease on the Mountain Home house and settled into the small structure. With a lot of help from our friends, the Wagon continued with its mission—to grow and inspire and outrage.

Wounded Knee

||||||||||||||||||||||||||||||||||||||||||||||||||

15

I t was winter when the "occupation" of Wounded Knee began in 1973. Indians had moved in substantial numbers to Wounded Knee on the Pine Ridge reservation. Russell Means, Gladys Bissonette, and Ellen Moves Camp, all leaders of the liberation movement, were longtime residents of the reservation and invited others in the American Indian Movement (AIM) and elsewhere to join them. They chose the site of the last Indian massacre, committed a century earlier, since they believed that the spirit of those who had died there would protect them. Their mission was to expose the terror that was visited upon them daily.

The "siege" of Wounded Knee by US Marshals, the US Army, and the Guardians of Our Oglala Nation—a private police force organized by Richard Wilson universally known as the GOON Squad on the reservation—began hours after those who protested conditions on the reservation had arrived at the village for an open public meeting. The authorities set up roadblocks, cordoned off the town, and arrested those they could locate. The government sent fifty US Marshals to surround Wounded Knee. The government forces were equipped with automatic weapons, including .50-caliber machine guns, grenades, and grenade launchers, and were augmented by snipers, armored personnel carriers, and helicopters. The siege lasted for seventy-one days.

Steve Hawkins called me one afternoon from the Chicago office of the Vietnam Veterans Against the War. "Mark, we sent a few guys down to Wounded Knee, South Dakota, to see if we could donate some food to the Indians. They just disappeared. They are all veterans. They knew there would be a checkpoint and they were planning to stop there and ask for permission to leave the food there for the Indians. We haven't heard from them and we wonder if they were arrested. Could you find them and bail them out?"

A couple of veterans at the Covered Wagon drove me from Mountain Home to Boise. I told them I would be back in a day or two and then flew to Rapid City armed only with the names of the missing VVAW members. I located them in the local jail; their only crime had been to drive to the FBI and US Marshal roadblock with some canned food in their vehicle and ask the agents if they could deliver the food to the Indians. They were immediately dragged out of the car, handcuffed, and thrown into an FBI vehicle.

One federal judge, Andrew W. Bogue, who occupied the upper floor of a working bank, finally granted my application for bail. My job was done, and I began to check airline schedules for my trip home. My clients were pleased, but almost a dozen other men had joined them, all with the same story, all asking for me to arrange their bail. I took their names and rushed back to the bank. Judge Bogue grumbled but he did grant my requests. The jail was filling up and the authorities were running out of space.

In those early days in Rapid City I had not yet met a single leader of the American Indian Movement, most of whom were in Wounded Knee, and I had no clear idea why they were there. I did feel that the government had no moral or legal right to attempt to starve them to death by surrounding them with agents who regularly fired into the village with bullets and noxious gas and to imprison those good citizens who only asked if they could bring food to the small community.

By then there were scores of people similarly arrested and placed in the Rapid City jail, and many more were apparently on their way. It was clear that substantial additional legal professionals were needed. During that time tribal leaders and other supporters on the reservation asked me to look into the violations of law that were occurring each day. I became the person in charge of the investigation into conditions on the reservation, and I was permitted to visit the village to meet with prospective clients.

While interviewing hundreds of residents on the Pine Ridge and, when possible, transcribing or recording their statements, I learned that fear was a quality that was almost always present. The GOON Squad, headed by Wilson, had intimidated, beaten, fired at, and killed innocent civilians. I also learned that the US government, the entity charged with the responsibility for maintaining the peace and enforcing the law, consistently demonstrated either its lack of concern or support for the terror.

The murder rate on Pine Ridge between March 1, 1973, and March 1, 1976, was 170 per 100,000. In 1974 Detroit was considered "the murder capital of the United States" with a rate of 20.2 per 100,000. The national average was 9.7 per 100,000. Many of the murders on the reservation remain unsolved, and fifty of those who died violently were Wilson's political opponents.

Our efforts to assemble a legal team in South Dakota started with an informal association with Ramon Robideau, a politically moderate local Native American lawyer, and progressed when a young lawyer, Larry Leventhal, came from Minnesota to join us. Larry had received a call from Clyde Bellecourt, one of the AIM leaders at Wounded Knee. My calls to old colleagues at the National Lawyers Guild were answered with astonishing speed. Len Cavise and Roger Finzel left their practices in Washington, DC, and many followed. Some of the guild members volunteered for two weeks, a genuine sacrifice for young attorneys, since most paid their own travel expenses and received no fee. A surprising number of other trial lawyers, including Roger, have never left the cause of Indian rights and remain at the forefront of struggles in South Dakota, Nebraska, New Mexico, and elsewhere, now three and a half decades later.

The name I suggested for our legal assistance fund was the Wounded Knee Legal Defense/Offense Committee (WKLD/OC). It did not really scan, but the name had staying power. Eventually the little firm that started in a Rapid City motel room became a force for civil rights and liberation with approximately two hundred lawyers, numerous amateur paralegals, investigators in training, and newly minted researchers, all of whom played important roles in defending the almost eight hundred cases of Indians who were prosecuted and of which 90 percent were won.[1]

When it became clear that my trip to Rapid City was not a temporary move and that I would be there for a considerable period of time, I asked Carolyn Mugar to join in the effort. The motel room was replaced by a suite of rooms, which soon also became inadequate. We then rented a house in Rapid City. Not long after we had settled into our new accommodations, I noticed some concerted activity at a building not far from our office. It was a residence for students that was owned by a university and available, between terms, for rental by tourists and others. Some of these newly arrived guests sat in unmarked vehicles not far from our place recording the license plates of those who visited us. I noticed that another "tourist" was in an upper bedroom window with binoculars trained upon our house. This activity made me a bit suspicious of the identity and motivation of our neighbors. The fact that they were all men wearing suits over white shirts and conservative ties—the FBI-required dress code under Hoover—merited closer examination. I asked Carolyn to bring her camera and join me. Several others came along.

So that it could not be asserted later that we were trespassing, I walked up to the desk clerk and inquired about vacancies. The place had been fully rented, I was told. I inquired about vacancies for the following weeks. Several of the new tenants arrived and panicked as Carolyn took pictures of them. One shouted into his telephone,

"Now they're shooting." I quickly suggested that we were only shooting film. The lobby crowded quickly. One agent pushed Carolyn and attempted to take the camera from her. Another pushed one of our investigators when he stood in front of her.

I called the local Rapid City Police Department and a squad car arrived within minutes. I pointed out the man who had assaulted Carolyn and asked that he be arrested. With a confidence verging on arrogance, several of the men called the ranking police officer to one side of the lobby for a confidential talk. They showed their identification and the officer walked across the room and said to me, "They are FBI agents." I said where they worked was irrelevant and pointed out that we had filed an oral complaint for criminal conduct and would sign a written complaint at headquarters. The officer rather apologetically took the FBI agent into custody and drove to police headquarters. We all followed in a minor caravan of cars. Scores of FBI agents and their supervisors were already in place when we arrived. They shouted obscenities in menacing tones; they wore handguns that they took no precaution to hide.

When the accused agent approached the steps to the building, he again attacked Carolyn, reaching for her camera and knocking her down. She waved away questions about any injury and closely examined the camera to see if it had been damaged.

In the face of the blatant and public violation, the police were constrained to charge the FBI agent with assault. The request for remand or a substantial bond was denied since the agent was only charged with misdemeanor simple assault. The bureau's Washington office sent him back to San Francisco on the next available flight and we never saw him again. The FBI agents expeditiously, effectively, and permanently abandoned their nearby rented premises, and we later devised and printed "wanted" posters describing the FBI fugitive and offering a prize for his capture.

||||||

There was a break in the day-to-day work in Rapid City and on the reservation, and one of the volunteers said she knew of an incredibly scenic place not too far from Denver. We could camp out, she suggested. I told her that I preferred the Hilton to a pup tent, having last slept in the woods during a bivouac when I was an eighteen-year-old GI involved in basic training during World War II. But after she was able to convince me, we loaded my car with provisions, stopped at a surplus military outlet, and drove about four hundred miles. It was dusk when we started to assemble the tent. Then she suddenly and quietly pointed to a place near the tree line. There were two men with rifles or shotguns moving slowly and furtively toward us. We were silent. I moved into the trees to get a better look while becoming almost invisible to them. I saw Ronald A. Williams, an anxious and eager FBI agent with a cowboy mentality that had been blatantly obvious in Rapid City. I did not recognize the man with him. Likely, I thought, another agent.

There may have been an innocent explanation, perhaps a bizarre coincidence, but we were isolated and they were hundreds of miles from their base. I decided not to inquire. Quietly and swiftly we struck the tent and threw it and the other provisions into the car. Without putting on the lights or starting the engine I put the car in neutral and released the brake. We rolled down the hill for several hundred yards and then fired up the engine and roared out of there.[2]

||||||

The siege ended with an agreement between the American Indian Movement and the government. It was followed by the indictment of seven Indian men. Two of the men, Dennis Banks and Russell Means, were charged under identical indictments as the leaders of the uprising on the Pine Ridge Reservation. The government contended that Indians with guns, Indians who didn't belong there, unlawfully held the hamlet of Wounded Knee for seventy-one days and that in doing so they committed a number of ordinary crimes such as larceny, burglary, and arson. In addition, the indictment charged that the Indians shot at federal law enforcement personnel and wounded an FBI agent and a US Marshal. The government contended that Dennis Banks and Russell Means were the leaders of the "takeover" and that because those who committed the various crimes were agents of the two defendants, Banks and Means were guilty of conspiracy and of any crime that allegedly took place during that time frame.

Attorney Bill Kunstler arrived from New York and agreed to represent Russell Means. Russell also asked me to represent him. Dennis Banks had local counsel. I explained to Russell that even though Bill and I both represented him, only one of us could make opening and closing statements on his behalf and only one of us could conduct cross-examination of a government witness. Russell's suggestion was that I become lead counsel for Dennis. Dennis agreed.

Our defense would be that the Treaty of 1868 between the US government and the Sioux nations is a valid and viable document that precludes agents of the government from entering the western portion of South Dakota where Wounded Knee is situated and that, therefore, the government lacked jurisdiction. The defense also contended that the liberation of Wounded Knee was justified. The conditions on the reservation—75 percent of the people unemployed, the highest rates of alcoholism, suicide, and infant mortality in the United States, the terror imposed by the government-supported vigilante organization, the government-sponsored exploitation of Indian land for the benefit of a handful of white ranchers—were all part of the continuing governmental policy of genocide against the Indian people. We also knew that the evidence would show that the liberation was not accomplished by outside agitators as the government had contended but was ordained by the traditional Oglala leaders, the elderly chiefs, headmen, and medicine men, and by the men, women, and children who lived on Pine Ridge.

During the period between the siege of Wounded Knee and the commencement of the trial in Saint Paul on January 7, 1974, I traveled nearly daily to the Pine Ridge Reservation gathering evidence and interviewing witnesses. Pedro Bissonette was the vice president of the Oglala Sioux Civil Rights Organization, a group protesting against the excesses of tribal government and the terror of the GOON Squad. Pedro was a source of crucial information we were seeking to document. He was to be an important witness at a forthcoming trial. Pedro was also very likely the finest boxer to come from South Dakota for many years. He was born on the reservation and had lived there almost all of his life.

On the evening of October 17, 1973, I received a telephone call from a nurse I knew at the Pine Ridge Hospital. She said, "Mark, they killed Pedro and they are planning to take his body away so that no record can be made of his wounds." She told me the body was in the morgue at the hospital. She let me in a side door of the hospital and led me to the morgue. The records showed that Pedro arrived at the hospital at 10:10 that evening and then was pronounced dead. The police reports stated that Pedro had been shot one time by a GOON Squad leader, Joe Clifford, at 9:00 PM, just a very short distance away from the hospital. My examination discovered that Pedro had been left in the road for more than an hour to bleed to death. The pool of blood was still there as witnesses came forward to provide testimony.

I examined Pedro's body at the morgue. He had been badly beaten before he had been shot. There were seven bullet holes in his chest in a small pattern, apparently from a .38-caliber weapon. It seemed that he had been shot at very close range. There was a grazing wound to his neck and three bullet holes in one hand. There were burns on his face, similar to those left by tear gas fired from a short distance. I photographed the wounds and the records, spoke into the tape recorder, and jotted down notes.

The nurse and I agreed that we would not disclose my presence until my evidence was no longer on the reservation and was safely secured. I assured her that I would not reveal her name, a promise I kept in spite of official demands. I hid the camera in the trunk of my car, placed the film in my pocket, hid the tape under a seat in the car and the legal pad under another one.

As soon as I left the reservation I stopped at a service station and called Leonard Cavise. Len called William Clayton, the US attorney who later prosecuted the case against Dennis and Russell.

Clayton agreed that the body would not be removed from Pine Ridge. However, the body was almost immediately sent to Nebraska, where an autopsy was performed, and the false statements in the police report, a single shot and no other visible signs, were confirmed. The government did not know that we had evidence to the contrary; it did know, however, that it had the power to make the facts irrelevant. The government placed Pedro's body in a coffin so irrevocably sealed that it could not be opened. Pedro was buried and we demanded a grand jury inquiry.

I met with two of Pedro's closest friends, Poker Joe Merrival and Joe Pourier. In the weeks that followed, the three of us investigated the facts surrounding Pedro's death, arranging for the testimony of twenty witnesses before a grand jury that was meeting in Sioux Falls, South Dakota. One afternoon as we waited in the corridor of the federal courthouse in Sioux Falls for our turn to testify, Joe Pourier, who had become a close friend, turned to me and said that he had been silent too long. Joe was the local manager and installer of the Bison State Telephone Company that serviced the Pine Ridge reservation. He told me that, upon orders of the US Marshals and the FBI, he had installed a telephone tap at FBI Roadblock One. The tap was on the Wounded Knee telephone used by the occupants of the Trading Post during the siege and allowed the government to illegally monitor conversations between attorneys and clients. We had irrefutable proof that the government had engaged in illegal actions.

As I traveled back and forth to the reservation, I started drafting a motion in my head, stopping on occasion to jot down an idea on a legal pad, which would recount the psychological state of the reservation inhabitants in defense of the charges. The home that the witness and his or her family would return to after testifying was a place of substantial danger so long as Wilson and his large squad of terrorists were permitted to commit crimes with immunity. Thus the charges must be dismissed because justice could never be obtained even if the trial was held in a different venue. I named it "The Reign of Terror Motion." It would be formally considered only by the judge, but I knew that the media would be at the trial, and knowledgeable and jaded reporters might dismiss just another motion among many to be filed and not read it. I thought that its title might attract their attention.

After meetings with Russell and Dennis and consulting with other counsel, I prepared a motion for a change of venue to move the case to an area where the jury pool was not as tainted and prejudiced against Native Americans. I discussed it with Fred Nichol, the senior federal judge for the South Dakota District, who had assigned the trial of the case to himself. I was pleased that Bogue, who had demonstrated his prejudice against Indians in general and our clients in particular, was not going to try the case, but I was concerned that a South Dakota jury would sit in judgment.

Motions to change venue are routinely denied. Judge Nichol, a South Dakota resident for many years, a former member of the South Dakota House of Representatives, and a former assistant US attorney for the District of South Dakota, considered the motion and granted it. The case was to be tried in Saint Paul, Minnesota, a very cold but fair environment. It was our first decisive victory in the case.

The nine-month trial began in Saint Paul, Minnesota, in thirty-below bone-chilling, snowy winds. Five solid weeks were devoted to selecting an impartial jury of nonpeers, twelve jurors and four alternates, none of whom was Indian. Dennis and Russell each were charged with violating eleven laws, and each faced almost one hundred years in jail on the government's theory that as leaders they were responsible for every crime allegedly committed during the siege. Before the trial began Judge Nichol dismissed one count, and after the trial commenced, before the case was submitted to the jury, he disposed of five additional counts.

When the trial of *US v. Banks and Means* was under way, I made the information about the wiretap known to Judge Nichol in chambers. Joseph Trimbach, the special agent in charge of the FBI for the tristate area, denied that there had been any wiretapping, legal or illegal, and denied that he had ever authorized or sought a wiretap. He specifically denied, under oath, that he had ever in his lifetime even seen an application for a wiretap.

The trial was interrupted for a hearing conducted in the absence of the jury. The hearing lasted longer than most trials, a period of more than five weeks. Judge Nichol said his faith in the FBI was badly shaken during the hearing and, in his opinion, the FBI had illegally tapped the Wounded Knee telephone and that Trimbach had made false statements.

Although Judge Nichol declined to dismiss the case at that point, as a result of the wiretap and other governmental misconduct, he wrote in his opinion that "the government should be forewarned that this Court will continue to be acutely aware of its compliance, or lack thereof, with this Court's discovery order and with the rules of law."

The government presented evidence to show that two federal agents had been wounded, one seriously, that food and other articles had been taken from the Trading Post while Russ and Dennis were in the immediate vicinity, and that both of the defendants played a leading role in organizing life in Wounded Knee, and in the negotiations with the government, soon after the "occupation" of Wounded Knee began. They presented evidence to show that the defendants and others were armed and that some of the weapons they were seen with looked very much like weapons that had been in the Trading Post.

The prosecutor presented videotapes and written documents in which Russ and Dennis said that they would die if necessary for the rights of the Oglala people, so that their present and future children might live in freedom. Yet it appeared to the defense that the failure of the evidence to tie either defendant to any alleged crime and the growing understanding in the jury of the reasons for Wounded Knee might preclude a conviction. It was during the government's case, as a result of the cross-examination of the prosecution witnesses, that the jury was to develop its first insight into life on the reservation as even prosecution witnesses described the uninhabitable living conditions at Wounded Knee.

Marlon Brando came to town to support our clients and the cause of Native Americans. He asked me what he could do to assist. I suggested that he come to a court session and then address the media outside of the courthouse.

He said, really almost quietly mumbled, "What should I say?"

"Marlon, you know all about the struggle of the Indian people; just express your feelings."

He asked, "Would you write a speech for me? I need a written speech." That night after the court session I wrote a several-page speech that I handed to him the next morning. He entered the courtroom, walked over to Russell and Dennis and embraced each of them, then sat in the spectator section. All eyes were focused on Marlon—the jurors', the journalists', and the judge's.

In court, Marlon methodically studied my proposed speech. At the end of the day, we left the courthouse together. Many reporters, photographers, television crews, and radio reporters holding tape recorders were set up in front of the steps. Marlon spoke in a persuasive stentorian voice as he pleaded for the rights of an oppressed people, all the while holding my speech, then tightly rolled up, in one hand. He did not utilize a sentence or thought from it.

It was said that Marlon never appeared on television for an extended interview. I suggested that he appear on the *Today* show together with Russell and Dennis during our one weekday off. The producers accepted at once. At two o'clock in the morning Marlon called and asked me to come to his hotel at once. There was, he said, a major problem, an emergency. Marlon was alone in the huge suite. He said, "Mark, did you see *Tango*?" He was referring to a recent film, *Last Tango in Paris*, directed by Bernardo Bertolucci and starring Marlon. The film opened in New York in 1972, and both men were nominated for Academy Awards. I said I had seen it.

"What did you think of it?" he asked.

I told him that I did not much care for it, but that when he was on the screen I was always mesmerized by his performance for reasons that I could not identify and that was so even when he appeared in a poor film.

He sighed and said, "All acting is shit. There is nothing to it, no skill, nothing. I can't even memorize lines anymore. And the reviewers are either con artists or just really dumb."

Marlon continued, "The leading film critic for a newsmagazine said that when I looked toward heaven at one point, it was an inspired conceptual statement or vision on my part." He shook his head sadly, looked at me and smiled, and said, "Mark, my next lines had been written on a piece of cardboard taped to the ceiling."

Finally, I asked if there was some other urgent reason that he wanted to talk with me at that hour. He thought about the question for a moment and said, "Yes, the *Today* show."

Marlon, speaking very slowly and haltingly, said that I could speak faster than he did. He suggested, therefore, that I should appear on the *Today* show instead of him. Of course I pointed out that the invitation was offered to him, and that if he declined none of us, including Russell and Dennis, would be on the program. Then he suggested that the two of us should appear without the defendants. That was not a viable plan, since our concept was to have Russell and Dennis speak to America. He agreed and asked me to write an opening statement and a few other comments he could use, as he would not know what to say. I agreed because it was very late, I had a trial to attend to in a few hours, and it probably would take less time to write what he asked me to than to continue the discussion. I knew that he would not use what I wrote, but that he would speak extemporaneously and that he would be brilliant. I started a file entitled "Speeches Written by Me for Marlon and Never Given."

||||||

The defense began with two authors, one Indian, one white, who testified about the treaty and the understanding of Indian people regarding the treaty. Dee Brown, author of *Bury My Heart at Wounded Knee*, and Vine Deloria Jr., author of *Custer Died for Your Sins*, explained that treaties were sacred documents to Indian people and that they were formalized with religious pipe ceremonies.

Frank Kills Enemy, an elderly leader from the reservation, testified that his grandfather had signed the Treaty of 1868. He spoke in Lakota and testified with the assistance of Oscar Bear Runner, an Oglala Sioux from Pine Ridge. Kills Enemy spoke movingly of the faith that the people had in the treaty and the suffering of the people since the Indian Reorganization Act of 1934.

Three witnesses testified about the white ranchers who were upset because Indians were escaping from the reservation, including testimony about a civilian roadblock established by them to prevent residents from leaving. One described an elaborate conspiracy to "get a plane and drop dynamite on the people in Wounded Knee unless the government cleaned them out."

During the trial we obtained an FBI radio log that stated that the current prosecutor, R. D. Hurd, met with the leader of the ranchers who were conspiring to commit murder. At a hearing during the trial, we called Hurd as a witness. He admitted that the log was accurate and that the white ranchers had disclosed their plans to him. Hurd admitted during his testimony that neither he nor the FBI had investigated the matter or considered prosecuting the ranchers.

Agnes Lamont was the next-to-last defense witness. She testified that her son had been killed at Wounded Knee by the federal police.

The last witness for the defense was Gladys Bissonette, a fifty-five-year-old Indian woman who had been born on the reservation and had lived there her entire life. I had met Gladys in Wounded Knee a year and a half before. We became good friends, although it was not until we met to talk about her testimony, two weeks before she appeared in court, that I fully appreciated the depth and the breadth of her knowledge and participation in the historic events of 1973.

She testified for two days, and on more than one occasion spectators, lawyers, and jurors wept openly as she described the suffering and struggle of the Indian people. In six decades of trial work I have never met a witness quite like Gladys Bissonette. She took her oath to tell the truth upon a pipe that she carried into the courtroom and explained that it had been her grandfather's sacred pipe.

Bissonette was in Wounded Knee for the full seventy-one days of the occupation. She was a negotiator for the occupants and many times met with representatives of the Department of Justice, Department of the Interior, and US Marshals Service in a tipi that had been set up in the demilitarized zone.

She was present at the meeting when the decision was made to go to Wounded Knee. She testified that there were about six hundred people at the meeting, from every district on the reservation. There was a vote on the proposal that the Oglala people should ask the American Indian Movement to come to the reservation to help in the struggle. The resolution passed unanimously. Gladys explained that before such an important action could be taken the advice of the chiefs, headmen, and medicine men was required. Nine of the elderly leaders, some in their eighties, some in their nineties, met in a small room to deliberate. Almost one hour passed and then the traditional leaders appeared before the people. Speaking in Lakota, the ancient language of their ancestors, each chief, each headman, each medicine man said that the American Indian Movement should come to the Pine Ridge Reservation to join in the struggle. The leaders asked Russell Means, an Oglala Sioux and the only AIM member present, for help.

I asked her opinion, as an Oglala Sioux who had lived her whole life on the reservation and as a traditional Indian, whether she believed that Russell Means had any choice other than to respond to the request that had been made to him.

She replied, "Russell did not have a choice. He had no alternative but to listen to the chiefs. He is a traditional Indian. Even if he knew he might suffer or die he had no choice. This is the way of the Indian's life." And with that answer the question of unwanted outside agitators was disposed of forever in the minds of the jurors.

Bissonette testified about a gas attack upon the residents of the village that was launched early in March by the federal forces and how the wind was coming from the southwest and headed right for the village. She testified: "We had many children in the village and old people too. So I started praying. My prayers are usually heard at noon. So I started praying to the Four Winds, the Great Spirit, and Mother Earth to give us some help that this gas may not come into the village." She paused for a minute and then said, "And the wind changed that quick and took it back toward the FBI." Some of the jurors, on the edge of their chairs, burst into applause.

Bissonette testified about the period toward the end of the siege when the fire into the village from the surrounding federal positions became increasingly heavy. Automatic and semiautomatic weapon fire continually raked the village while the marshals and FBI agents fired thousands of flares toward the village to start grass fires and burn down dwellings and churches. On one of those days, Frank Clearwater, a forty-four-year-old Indian who had hitchhiked from North Carolina with his wife, Morning Star, was shot through the head while he rested in a church from his long journey. He was taken to a hospital in Rapid City, South Dakota, during a lull in the firing. Arrangements were made with the federal government for his wife to join him in the hospital, but when she tried to leave she was arrested and thrown into the Pine Ridge jail. Frank Clearwater died alone the next day. A little later Gladys's nephew, Buddy Lamont, born on the reservation, which he left only to serve in the US Army, was killed by the federal police during a firefight.

There was a very long moment of stillness when Gladys finished testifying. There was no sound and no movement in the courtroom. And then Russell Means rose and said, "Your Honor, we believe that the story has been told. We stand on our treaty rights. The defense rests."

At meetings with Russell and Dennis and all counsel we discussed the question of whether either of them would testify. We thought we had won the case through cross-examination of government witnesses, and discretion would advise that taking the stand might pose an unnecessary risk. After Gladys testified, it was clear that no additional evidence was required.

There was a recess for several days so that the government could prepare its rebuttal to our case. In an astounding move, the prosecutor placed Louis Moves Camp on the stand. Louis said that he had been in Wounded Knee from the first day, and that he had remained there for sixty-four of the seventy-one days, leaving on May 1. If his testimony was to be believed, Russ and Dennis were guilty of all the charges.

Moves Camp claimed that although he had been charged with five felony counts that were then pending against him in South Dakota and he faced more than one hundred years in prison, the government had offered him no deal in exchange for his testimony. The prosecutor and the witness agreed that he was not being paid for his testimony (except the ordinary witness fee of thirty-six dollars per day for the time that he was under subpoena). The witness said that he was not even concerned about the South Dakota felony cases because he was certain to win them. Moves Camp testified with conviction to events that took place in Wounded Knee, in his presence, during the latter part of March and throughout April.

During Louis's testimony Carolyn Mugar and I traveled every evening to Wisconsin, piecing together the story. We learned that rape charges were about to be filed against Moves Camp, but the FBI agents persuaded local officials not to do so since Moves Camp was a necessary witness in another trial.

I discovered that Moves Camp had stayed with the agents at an exclusive dude ranch in Hudson, Wisconsin, and that on the night of August 16, he went on a barhopping tour with FBI Special Agents Price and Williams in River Falls, Wisconsin. Williams was the activist agent who tried to pay me a visit in Colorado. Louis ended up with a high school girl, and the next morning he told his FBI friends a rather bizarre story of his sexual exploits with her. Their amusement was somewhat shattered when a River Falls police sergeant called Price to inform him that the young woman was in the police station charging their star witness with two counts of forcible rape and five counts of forcible perversion. Price called Louis, who was in the next room, and told him what the police said but assured him that he would not be prosecuted. After the FBI intervention, no complaint was filed against Moves Camp.

Then we discovered that Moves Camp and the FBI had made contact on August 5, 1974, and that from August 7 for a period of approximately three weeks, when he began to testify, he had been in the constant company of those two FBI agents.

When the components all fell into place I informed the court of what I had learned. We wanted the jury to know the full story about the government's star witness. The judge held a lengthy hearing out of the presence of the jury.

However, prosecutor Hurd represented to the court that the only criminal charge even considered against Louis in Wisconsin was "a possible charge of public intoxication." Before it was over, we were able to prove that Hurd knew about the rape allegation before we did, having been informed of it by the assistant special agent in charge of the tristate area, Phillip Enlow, on the very day that it occurred.

Moves Camp, who testified that he was in Wounded Knee during late March and April, actually arrived in California on March 17, 1973, and remained there for many weeks. We proved it through the testimony of the president of a local cable television company in Monterey, who brought program logs with him to show that Moves Camp was interviewed twice by his organization during that period. We proved it through the testimony of Jay West, a former Bureau of Indian Affairs police officer, at whose home Moves Camp stayed while he was in San Jose. We proved it through the documentary evidence of college newspapers that published pictures of Moves Camp as he spoke at West Coast colleges during the time that he swore he was in Wounded Knee.

We proved that he was concerned about going to jail for the five felony counts through the testimony of his wife and her mother and father. He had told them all that there was no way out for him, that the Indians he had assaulted knew him and could identify him, and that the federal judge who would try his case, Andrew Bogue, was a bigot who hated Indians in general and AIM members in particular. "I just have to find some way out," he told them.

We proved that he had been paid $2,074.50 for three days of testimony and that the Department of Justice arranged that extraordinary payment when assured by their representative at the trial, Earl Kaplan, that Moves Camp's testimony would "insure conviction." We proved that Hurd knew about that extraordinary payment when he insisted to the judge that the star witness was just being paid thirty-six dollars per day for three days of testimony.

At the hearing, I cross-examined the FBI agents who were with Moves Camp during the period when he had committed the rape. My questions came in a staccato manner, increasing in speed and volume. One agent, although trained in the art of courtroom tactics, instead of answering deliberately, matched my tempo.

"And after he told you what he had done with the high school student and that the prosecutor was about to charge him with rape, what did you tell Moves Camp?"

The agent quickly responded, "I said, 'Don't worry, Louis,'" and added that he was going out to talk with the prosecutor.

I paused and then said, "You said, 'Don't worry, Louis.'"

The agent realized the problem and began to deny that he had just said what he had just said. We had the record read back. The judge agreed that he had heard enough.

We argued that since Moves Camp knew that the FBI wanted him to testify falsely and that the FBI had exercised control over his future, that evidence should be presented to the jurors. The judge agreed with us. The entire Moves Camp story was presented to the astonished jury. All that remained were closing arguments and the wait for a jury verdict.

Lawyers tend to believe that closing arguments are often decisive, and they spend a great deal of time preparing for that moment when they, not the client, not the judge, and not even the witnesses, are center stage. It has never been clear to me that the final direct talk to the jury generally is dispositive. Since there is a fiction that the defendant in a criminal case is presumed innocent, a concept often not shared by the jurors, the prosecution makes the first closing argument, and then after the defense has closed, the prosecutor makes a second closing statement to which the defense may not reply.

Hurd spoke first, pointing out that the defendants were criminals and that evidence offered by the defendants about problems on the reservation was not relevant. Bill Kunstler and I had discussed our proposed statements. Bill wanted to make a standard closing in which he marshaled the evidence offered by the government and the defendants and evaluated it. He asked to make the final closing remarks. Since we had all, defendants and counsel, agreed to a joint defense, in a real sense we each spoke for both defendants. I accepted Bill's suggestion and he made an excellent and persuasive speech to the jury. He dealt with the evidence in some detail.

I decided to devote my remarks to two themes: the government was indifferent to crimes committed on the reservation in its name (corruption in advance of the occupation) and that the government was deceptive to the judge, the defendants, and the jury (corruption during the trial). The first thesis was offered in the nature of a self-defense theory, although admittedly it was not a perfect fit. The second argument tested the credibility of the government's witnesses and prosecutors.

Lawyers often rely upon media-assisted arguments, flashing images upon a screen and using PowerPoint presentations. The show may be slightly entertaining, but after a long trial, its shelf life is limited. I prefer a simpler approach. I requested, as aids, a blackboard and a piece of chalk. The message is less transitory; it is present during the entire closing and often much longer.

I wrote, as the jury watched, DON'T WORRY, LOUIS, the statement made by the FBI agent during the trial, and I DON'T CARE IF THE CONDITIONS ON THE PINE RIDGE INDIAN RESERVATION ARE GOOD OR BAD.

R. D. HURD. Hurd had uttered those exact words in his remarks to the jury. I talked about the terror on the reservation and the assaults upon those who were targeted by the GOON Squad.

I told the jurors how the Louis Moves Camp episode was a microcosm of the entire case. The government coerced Moves Camp into making false statements, knowing that, as he testified, each statement was untrue. The FBI agent said "Don't worry, Louis," and the rape case disappeared. The government, including the Department of Justice, the US attorney's office, the FBI agents and supervisors, endorsed that effort. Yet Moves Camp was the only witness the government presented who connected Dennis and Russell to any criminal conduct.

The jurors listened; some shook their heads in sorrow, I thought, about the acts of their government. Some appeared to be angry. I hoped that anger was directed to the prosecution. When Hurd rose to speak he was confronted by an issue he had not contemplated. Behind him and facing the jurors remained the large blackboard with its message. He looked at it, looked at the jurors who studied him, and wondered what he would do.

Erasing the words in the presence of the jury was not an appealing option; it would have emphasized the words and his attempt to evade them. Instead, he chose to uncomfortably deliver his final plea, including his assurance that the government did care, in front of his own words to the contrary.

On Thursday, September 12, following two full days of closing argument by the defense and government attorneys, the court charged the twelve jurors—nine women, three men; eleven white Americans and one Latino American—dismissed the four alternate jurors—three white women and one white man—and the jury retired to deliberate.

The press reported that the alternates were strongly committed to finding our clients innocent and noted the almost instant friendship that developed among the alternate jurors, the defense team, and the defendants. It appeared to them that a guilty verdict was highly unlikely and that each defendant would be acquitted on all counts. Thursday afternoon and evening passed without definitive word from the jury.

On Friday morning the judge called the lawyers for both sides to his chambers to announce that one of the jurors had become ill. A government doctor and her own family doctor had examined her and a twenty-four-hour recess was suggested before a valid prognosis could be made. Hurd almost immediately claimed that the ill juror, Therese Cherrier, was his hold card, his strongest juror for conviction. I then talked with the alternate jurors, as the judge had permitted, who said they very much doubted the accuracy of Hurd's statement.

During the long trial, we observed the jurors as they observed us. I noticed that Cherrier seemed focused and serious, and while other jurors laughed on occasion, she remained stoic. I had no idea what her demeanor meant for our clients. If Cherrier could not resume deliberations, any alternate juror could not be recalled. The court would be required to declare a mistrial and a new trial date would be set unless we could conjure up another approach. I suggested that we consent to a jury of eleven. While a jury of twelve is required by law, the Federal Rules of Criminal Procedure permit a lesser number of jurors, if both the defense and prosecution agree, and if the judge concurs. Hurd told the press that he probably would not stipulate to an eleven-person jury, pointing out that in the absence of a joint stipulation the judge would be constrained to declare a mistrial and that he, the prosecutor, could then try the defendants again.

One fact emerged with some clarity during the long period spent waiting for medical bulletins. The US government, which had relentlessly prosecuted Banks and Means for more than three-quarters of a year at an exorbitant cost, did not want this jury to render a verdict. The judge called us all into chambers early Monday morning to read the latest and the last medical bulletin. The doctor's report stated that while Cherrier said that she would crawl back to the courtroom on her hands and knees before she would agree to being excused, he had concluded that she would not be able to return to jury duty "at that time or at any time in the near future." The judge had no choice under those circumstances. He excused her.

In chambers, strongly supported by Russell and Dennis, we asked that the jury of eleven be permitted to meet and consider a verdict. Judge Nichol "importuned" the government to stipulate to the reduced jury. Hurd said that he needed to contact the attorney general. The court adjourned for the day.

Long after I had gone to bed that night the ringing telephone woke me. It was Denny Casano, a reporter for the *Minneapolis Star Tribune*. He said, "I've got to see you now. I can come over to your hotel. OK?" I got dressed and met him in the lobby of the Commodore Hotel.

I suggested a drink; he said he had "been pretending to drink all evening and I think I would like one now." I had no idea what he was talking about. He said, "I have a story to tell you, and I think that when I finish you will agree that it was worth getting up for in the middle of the night."

He told me he had been at the Smuggler's Inn, an upscale lounge near the courthouse, and had spent many hours there with Hurd, who was drinking when he was not talking. Denny went on for a considerable period of time, but Hurd's themes were constant and consistent: they had lost, the government would not allow a jury verdict, they hated defense counsel, the judge, and the jury. Much of the language was obscene.

I asked if the matter was off the record, and he replied that Hurd never uttered that phrase. I said that I meant if his revelations to me were off the record. He said, "Mark, this is too serious for that. I'm a journalist, but first I am an American citizen. Use it all any way you want." He quickly wrote out in longhand a specific and detailed account of his meeting with Hurd and then signed it under penalty of perjury.

Later that morning in chambers, Hurd said that the government would not agree to a jury of eleven. The judge then pleaded with Hurd to change his position. When he refused, I told the court what Hurd said the night before in some exquisite detail. Judge Nichol was perplexed and his facial expression betrayed that feeling as he studied me. He knew I would not seek to mislead him, much less fabricate such an elaborate story, but he could not believe that Hurd had made such outrageous statements to a reporter.

Any question about Hurd's several-hour tantrum the night before was resolved when I handed Judge Nichol the sworn statement signed by Denny and informed the court that Denny was in the courtroom, waiting to testify about the meeting and answer any questions the court or prosecutors might ask.

We had devised a new strategy overnight for the situation. During the course of the trial we had filed and refiled an amended Reign of Terror Motion for a dismissal. We decided to again renew that effort with a newly amended thirty-four-page document entitled "Motion for a Judgment of Acquittal," with supporting affidavits that detailed all of the government's considerable misconduct since the court's last ruling on the motion, including its refusal to agree to a jury of eleven. We argued that while the government was permitted to exercise its option to accept or reject a numerically smaller jury, it did not have the right to do so for the wrong reason. Here, the government's purpose was painfully apparent.

Judge Nichol paused for a moment, looked intently at the representative of the Department of Justice, and said with a studied calmness that was a thin disguise for his anger that he would announce his decision for us and for the remaining jurors in open court at three o'clock that afternoon.

And so it was in the final moment that Dennis Banks and Russell Means, described by the US attorney as hoodlums with contempt for the rule of law, showed more faith in the workings of the judicial process and the jury system than did the Department of Justice.

We all reassembled that afternoon to hear the judge rule that the government was guilty of misconduct, had in fact struck foul blows in several areas, in addition to the misconduct complained of in the previous motion. "You will recall I said that I was at the brink of dismissal. I think it's only fair to say, and you will see the reasons why very shortly, I am now over the brink."

In granting the motion to dismiss all of the charges against both of the defendants, the judge focused primarily upon what he referred to as "the Louis Moves Camp matter," saying "that is a most serious, most serious misconduct on the part of the government."

Newsweek summarized the ruling:

While the prosecution sat ashen-faced before him, Judge Nichol unleashed a blistering hour-long denunciation of what he considered government irresponsibility throughout the trial. He charged that the FBI had "stooped to a new low" by withholding some documents and doctoring other evidence.[3]

I asked Judge Nichol if I might speak with the jurors and he agreed that it was a good idea. I often spoke with jurors after a trial in order to learn of their perceptions and thus improve my craft. In this case, while that remained a motivation, I primarily wanted to ask them if they had any thoughts about the historic implications of the case.

Maureen Coonan, Dick Garcia, and Fran Aiken, three of the jurors, told us that the jury had voted unanimously on Thursday to acquit both defendants of the charge that constituted the heart of the government's case, the charge of conspiracy. They all agreed that Therese Cherrier had been the strongest advocate for a verdict of not guilty on that and every other count.

I then met with a large group of the jurors at the Commodore. Ten of the sixteen jurors and alternate jurors were present. Together we formed a group and called it Jurors and Others for Reconciliation, likely setting a quasi-judicial precedent. The group drafted a letter to be presented to the attorney general of the United States calling upon the government to dismiss all Wounded Knee and other federal cases pending against Indian people and supporters. They asked the government to use its good offices to secure the dismissal of similar state charges and to initiate an era of reconciliation regard-ing treaties.

Later, I visited Cherrier in a Saint Paul hospital. She asked if she could be the first to sign the letter to the attorney general, "since the prosecutor slandered me by asserting that I would be a convicting juror." She was in a hospital bed, her left arm paralyzed, unable to focus her eyes well enough to read. I read the letter to her. Slowly and laboriously she sat up and painstakingly signed the letter and then fell back onto her pillow.

"Russell and Dennis were right," she said. "People say that they're angry. Of course they are. They have a lot to be angry about. I want you to apologize to them for me. I'm afraid that because I got sick they won't have a jury verdict of not guilty, which they deserve. Tell them that when I get out of here I want to do whatever I can to help the Indians. I learned a lot during the trial."

The former jurors, by then committed activists, arranged for a meeting with the office of the attorney general in Washington, DC. The American Lutheran Church Convention passed a resolution supporting the request of the Jurors and Others for Reconciliation and donated five thousand dollars to the group to cover expenses for their planned trip to Washington, DC. The meeting took place with a number of the jurors and more than forty church leaders from the National Council of Churches, the Lutheran Church of America, and representatives of the National Student Association, National Edu-cation Association, American Civil Liberties Union, and others. The attorney general and his associates were not persuaded. In almost every case, the unfair prosecutions relentlessly continued. The jurors, however, continued to find the defendants not guilty.

O Canada

16

||||||||||||||||||||||||

F red Branfman called me in the mid-1970s. He had been to Laos in 1969, where he collected pictures drawn by children that he later had published. The drawings were of large airplanes dropping bombs on little children and their families and little children looking upward with fear. Many pictures, all with one basic theme: the aircraft were ours; the deaths and injuries were theirs. The scenes provided an opportunity for Americans to understand how powerless, terror-stricken children viewed all that they knew of our great country. Fred had testified before a special session of the US Senate Committee on Refugees and later published books and articles about the US bombing of the Plain of Jars in Laos. He also, in time, helped run Jerry Brown's California political efforts and Gary Hart's aborted appearance on the national scene.

Fred said that there was someone, a young man, who wanted to get some advice and legal help from me. I asked for his name and some information about the subject and told Fred to have him call me that morning. He said that the matter could not be discussed on the telephone and that it would be better if I met the client at a neutral place. Had I not been acquainted with Fred's background, I might have thought he was being a bit more dramatic than necessary.

I agreed to meet the young man at the American Café on Massachusetts Avenue in northeast Washington, DC, just a short walk from my home and office.

That brief call from a friend about a prospective client set in motion a series of events that would occupy me for months while placing my colleagues and clients in grave jeopardy and causing some very anxious moments for me as well. The facts of our furtive adventures would remain secret for decades. In retrospect, I believe that my actions, which could be fairly characterized as reckless, were justified by the circumstances, although some lawyers in large insurance firms would doubtless disagree.

Early that afternoon a young, slim Asian man approached me outside of the restaurant. We walked; he wanted to talk outside, although he was shivering. He was not dressed for the winter, not even for what passes for winter in Washington. We exchanged names and handshakes, and he talked.

The context is of some relevance. The war in Vietnam was raging. Colonel Nguyen Cao Ky, the military and political leader of South Vietnam, our ally, was also a pilot and ran the air force. It was decided by those prescient military scholars, led by General Westmoreland, that we, or at least he, could see the light at the end of the tunnel, that victory beckoned, and that the war, the longest one we had ever been engaged in, was certain to end soon and in a blaze of glory.

The path to victory, they reasoned, required the bombing of civilians in Vietnam, destroying the Ho Chi Minh Trail, terrorizing the enemy and those who might be sympathetic to them or even unacceptably neutral. That task was to be carried out by the air force of South Vietnam under the orders of Ky. There was not much risk for the pilots. The enemy their leaders chose was unarmed in many cases and, in others, underarmed at best.

At that moment my new client, Tran, who was a member of Colonel Ky's air force, was temporarily on assignment in Texas where he received training as a bomber pilot. He was not alone. "About 10 percent of the entire air force of Vietnam is there being trained in

Texas," he told me. As we walked from the US Supreme Court gardens into the large park behind the Capitol, he said that he did not want to kill his countrymen, that he was not afraid of war, his mission was after all not very dangerous, but that bombing his defenseless neighbors was something he could not do.

I asked how I could help and why he had come to see me. He said that he wanted to apply for sanctuary in the United States, and he hoped that I could do that for him there in Washington. I asked what would happen if we applied for asylum and his request was denied. He said that he would be sent home and executed as a lesson to others, since many of his friends felt the way he did, and if he could leave, others, perhaps many others, would follow.

I assured him that the war was fueled by the United States and that I was reasonably certain that there was no hope that the present US government, totally committed to prosecuting the war, would offer any assistance to one of Colonel Ky's defecting warriors. Ky, I explained, was chosen, and fully supported, by the United States. Tran was dejected; his eyes glistened with tears as his only plan for escaping from a terrible dilemma had suddenly become inoperable.

We walked in silence toward the Lincoln Memorial. I could not provide him with the assistance he requested. I considered various options and then guardedly, and with substantial reservations, told him that I had an idea I wanted to pursue; I would return to my office, do some research, and meet him later that day. Much later, when we became friends, he told me that he had thought I might be going to the authorities to have him arrested. I then confessed that I too had been concerned that I was being set up by those same authorities. Nevertheless, we each had decided to set our doubts aside and to trust the other. I walked to the Library of Congress, the first law library in the United States, and began to examine statutes, case law, and policies of foreign countries.

When we met again, I told him that I believed that the Canadian government would likely grant asylum to him if he made that request from inside the borders of that country. "Could you take me to Canada?" he asked. I expected that question, for I had little doubt that he would be unable to arrange to enter Canada legally, and I knew he did not have the requisite knowledge or contacts to enter any other way. I knew that I could not try to assign this risky venture to anyone else and that the fewer people involved, the safer the mission would be. I agreed to help.

He asked if I could make arrangements for next week, since he wanted to go back to Texas and meet with two other pilots who shared his view. I gave him the number of a pay telephone not far from my office—this was long before the advent of cell phones—and we arranged a schedule for calls.

While he met with his comrades I began to set up an underground railroad from the nation's capital to a secure refuge in Canada, knowing that we would be required to enter Canada under cover of darkness and not at a designated entry place. Carolyn Mugar, of course, was the first person I talked to, since I was familiar with her selfless commitment to important causes and her discretion. She also had a sturdy Volvo station wagon, and we had miles to go. Some of the details are not important here and might cause difficulty for some if discussed, but it is appropriate to say that the response of those we asked for help on this dubious journey was immediate and generous, reminding me again of the compassion of the American people.

Tran returned from Texas with two young men. Carolyn and I were sartorially prepared for our guests. We had shopped at thrift shops and had assembled many warm, if incongruous, outfits. The five of us began our trip north. There was a night's stay at a women's collective where we received advice about another place to spend another night, hearty food, and a memorable breakfast the next morning with pancakes served with maple syrup that the collective members had obtained from trees made available by a friendly farmer. We studied maps and made plans for the crossing.

When we approached the border, the three men and I left the vehicle. Carolyn drove to a checkpoint, entered Canada legally without incident, and then drove to a predetermined place to wait for us.

The four of us walked into a field of rather deep snow to the amazement of my associates. We moved forward cautiously, staying low all the time and seeking cover behind the branches of bare bushes and of larger tree trunks. A partially frozen stream was ahead. We managed to cross it but did not escape its penetrating and stinging assault.

Hundreds of yards later as we neared what we believed was the Canadian border, we saw two people clad warmly and wearing substantial fur hats. They were accompanied by two German shepherds. I thought that it was likely that they were guards. We took out packages of ground beef wrapped in plastic to throw to the dogs if they attacked. I knew that it was not much of a plan, but it seemed to be all we could do as we were not armed and we would not have harmed the dogs even if we were able to. I crawled closer through the snow, all thoughts of comfort banished by the fear of arrest. I knew that little or nothing would happen to me but that my colleagues might be arrested and sent back to Vietnam to await Colonel Ky's justice. After a long wait we concluded that the "border guards" were a man and woman taking their dogs for a winter walk.

We waited until they left the area and then crossed into what we hoped, if we had read the map correctly, would be another country. In the darkness of a forest we were able to locate what looked to be a car parked on a small road. As we cautiously drew closer we recognized the most welcome sight of a blue Volvo, and we knew at last that we had entered Canada. Carolyn drove us to a nearby Canadian city where other Vietnamese who resided in Canada were assembled. Newspapers were spread on the floor and soon were covered with bowls of wonderful food.

Carolyn and I drove back to Washington. Our venture had been successfully concluded. Three men who wanted freedom had found it, and many others on the ground in Vietnam would be spared. Our work had been completed, and I knew that an element of luck, perhaps stars and planets in the right order or border guards not eager to spend too much time outdoors away from a comforting wood stove, had likely helped. I also decided to embark upon more lawyerly-like challenges in the future. And I was tired, chilled, and eagerly looking forward to the next weekend of good food, companionship, and a football game.

The next morning I received a telephone call from Texas. Two more pilots wanted to visit Canada. Our next weekend was devoted to repeating the trip. The calls from Texas continued, and three more pilots made the trip the next weekend, and still others the next and the next for a very long time. Each trip ended in the same house and another feast. Soon there was no room for all of us, and the earlier arrivals stayed at their newly leased apartments. Requests for asylum were granted, and the immigrants attended school or found jobs.

At the air force base in Texas there was official panic. Their pilots were missing. Had they defected? Had they been kidnapped? Were antiwar American activists involved? Investigations began and became more intense. How could this more than embarrassing phenomenon be explained to Ky and the other leaders of South Vietnam who had entrusted their most skilled warriors to a secure military base in the United States?

At the base, pay telephone booths were guarded. Passes were scrutinized and restricted. Guards were required not just to stop unauthorized people from entering but primarily to keep authorized people from leaving. The calls from the base to the pay phone on Pennsylvania Avenue continued and then were replaced by calls from outside the base made by trusted American friends to whom messages had been smuggled. When the gates were closed in Texas, the pilots scaled fences or, in one instance, tunneled under them. The underground railroad continued and grew.

When the war ended, a large number of young men, all trained pilots, were temporary residents of Canada. When US troops withdrew, several of my fellow travelers called to thank us "for saving our souls and for saving the lives of our neighbors." Before the conversation became too maudlin, one of them suggested that the real reason I spent my weekends in furtive travel was that I valued the gustatory experience so highly. While he was, I believe, being humorous, the comment was not without some basis. A few weeks later a small lacquered box made in Vietnam arrived in the mail with a thank you note.

Years later I met a person with contacts to the Royal Canadian Mounted Police. He told me that an intelligence unit of the RCMP had suspected that I was involved in what the organization called the mysterious appearance of Asian pilots in the south of Canada. They concluded, he said, that it was a meritorious cause and decided to look away as it continued. I could never verify that account; in fact I was reluctant to even try. In any event, it is clear that the Canadian authorities noticed that many recent arrivals, all young Vietnamese men, had sought asylum in growing numbers. Thank you, O Canada, for loving your neighbors and supporting their hopes, not their fears.

Memphis, America

17

|||||||||||||||||||||||||||||||||||||||||||||||||||||||||||

The weapon of assassination created the politics of the United States from November 1963, when President Kennedy was killed, through February 1965, when Malcolm X was murdered, and into the year of 1968 with the assassination of Dr. King, followed closely by the murder of Robert Kennedy. In four and a half years, four major American leaders had been shot down. The nation had lost four icons, each at a crucial time in history. Many Americans, including those who had not known any of the murdered men, felt diminished and experienced pain and a sense of loss. I knew John and Malcolm, Martin and Bobby. I had worked with three of them and was discussing an alliance with the fourth in the days before he was murdered. We were all of the same generation; both Martin and Malcolm were two years younger than me.

On April 4, 1968, Dr. Martin Luther King was assassinated in Memphis. I had known Dr. King and had worked with him as a soldier in his army of justice, and few events in my life moved or horrified me as did that murder. This courageous man, who had not yet celebrated his fortieth birthday, was the greatest civil rights protagonist in the history of the country and the nation's most inspiring speaker. In an outstanding display of mental gymnastics, Hoover and his FBI almost immediately decided that James Earl Ray was the assassin. Ray, a fugitive who had earlier escaped from prison, was not inclined to surrender for numerous unrelated reasons. He left the country and was arrested in England by agents of Scotland Yard. He could not be extradited to the United States for the murder unless the US government offered evidence of his complicity at a hearing in Bow Street Magistrate's Court in London. The FBI and other federal agencies, as well as the Memphis police, had conducted intensive investigations in an effort to discover some evidence that Ray was guilty.

The shot that killed Dr. King, it was said, was fired from a window in a communal bathroom of a boarding house. Charlie Stephens and his wife, Grace, lived in the boarding house. At the time of the assassination Charlie, leaving his required glasses in the room with Grace, left to visit the bathroom in the hallway of the rooming house, one of the consequences of continual wine drinking, but the door was locked, and no one replied to his knocking and shouting. He searched for another bathroom but then walked down the stairs and was in the process of urinating in the backyard when a shot, which he later stated he did not remember hearing, was fired.

Charlie had left the door to the room open, and Grace, who was sitting in her bed reading a book, heard the shot and then saw a man walk past her door and down the steps. He was carrying something in his hand. The FBI and the local prosecutors asserted the shot had been fired from the window in that bathroom. The local police and the FBI agents knew she had seen the killer, and they demanded that she sign an affidavit stating that she had seen James Earl Ray.

Grace told reporters and police officers what she had observed and described the man she saw. Later, when the police showed her pictures of Ray she asked about his height, weight, and age. She stated that she was certain that Ray was not the man she had seen. Grace was offered a reward of $100,000 by FBI agents and local police officers if she would agree to sign an affidavit stating that Ray was the man she saw. She declined, stating that she would not lie, and was threatened with incarceration by the agents. Without that sworn statement Ray could not be extradited to the United States.

After the shot had been fired, Charlie had entered the room filled with strangers and demanded to know what was happening. It was then that he was told that a shot may have been fired from the building and about the reward. Later Charlie Stephens, who had observed nothing incriminating and little else that day because he was an alcoholic who was drunk at that time, told the police he would sign a statement saying the man was Ray.

The extradition hearing took place on June 24, almost three months after Dr. King had been killed, and Ray was returned to the United States based upon the Stephens affidavit. At trial Ray was represented by local counsel in Memphis and later by a well-known attorney who failed to adequately represent him. He was coerced into accepting a guilty plea and was sentenced to prison for life. Many black leaders stated from the outset that they did not believe that James Earl Ray, charged with the murder, acted alone or acted at all. Some years after the assassination, Reverend Ralph Abernathy, Martin's closest friend and colleague in the struggle, asked me to investigate the matter. He was joined in that request by others. Reverend Jim Lawson offered to help if I decided to look into it, and he encouraged me. Dick Gregory knew of the potential cost and never suggested that I accept that challenge. He made it clear, however, that he would stand with me and work with me if I decided to proceed. I decided to investigate the assassination and later ended up becoming Ray's attorney in an attempt to obtain a trial for him based upon his coerced plea.

I made the trip to Memphis. I was not the first to conduct an inquiry and to raise serious questions about the prosecution's case, as I had been after the assassination of President Kennedy. This was not, as that had been, an enthusiastic and naive charge into the morass of clues, false clues, and government cover-up in a headlong search for the essential truth. This time I knew that my quest might be costly. I also knew that I had no choice, since I had been chosen by those I respected highly, although I confess that on occasion I wondered where all of the powerful and well-placed lawyers, members of Congress, and journalists were and why they had not taken on the matter as a serious and full-time commitment.

The French have a phrase for a reporter who is committed to learning and telling the truth: *journaliste engagé*. It translates into "an engaged journalist." An "engaged" American journalist in Memphis (while we don't have the phrase, we have a number of people who nicely fit the description) told me that he and others had interviewed Grace soon after the assassination in the rooming house from which the state claimed Ray had fired the shot that killed Dr. King. The reporter also told me that Grace suddenly disappeared a short period thereafter.

Then an attorney provided the essential clue to her location. She had heard that Grace had secretly, and in violation of all of the applicable laws of Tennessee, been placed in a mental institution nearly ten years earlier. The asylum was in Bolivar, seventy miles from Memphis.

Within hours I was on my way to meet her. Sammye Cook, a woman who believed in justice, volunteered to drive me to the state complex. An investigator went with us. I asked Sammye to remain in the automobile and to keep the engine running. Instead, she walked alongside of us when we entered the asylum.

My plan was to find Grace and interview her. In the time before it was feared that terrorists lurked in the most unlikely places, it was possible to enter most institutions by merely acting as if you had been there before. I walked in the front door, took the first left, and, when I saw a reception area, avoided that cubicle by making a sharp right. I greeted the first person who looked as if he might be an inmate: he was shabbily dressed and less aggressive looking than the guards. I asked if he could tell me where to find Grace.

I followed his directions to a room where I saw a scene that would have appalled Dickens. It was a large and crowded dormitory serving as a warehouse for poorly dressed and severely drugged people of various ages.

We found Grace and introduced ourselves. I showed her a tape recorder and asked if she had any objection to my recording the interview.

"I don't mind at all if it makes it easier for you," she answered.

"Do you remember April 4, 1968?" I said.

"Yes," she answered. "Sure. Very well."

Here are some of the relevant portions of the interview that I conducted with Grace Stephens during my first meeting with her in November 1977.

Lane: What happened that day?

Stephens: I was lying in bed reading. Then my husband came in and said that he couldn't get into the bathroom. He had to go around to the other side to use the other bathroom. So he went off. I don't remember exactly how long he was gone. Then I heard this shot.

Lane: You heard a shot?

Stephens: Yes. I recognized it as a shot. My father was a great hunter. He taught us all about guns. In fact, two of my husbands collected guns.

Lane: After you heard the shot, what happened?

Stephens: In a few minutes the bathroom door opened. I could see that. My door was partially opened, and I was propped up in bed, as I said, reading.

Lane: You could see out into the corridor?

Stephens: Yes, and the bathroom door was right next to us.

Lane: Did you see anyone come out of the bathroom?

Stephens: Yes. I saw this man come out. He had something in his hand, but I couldn't see what it was because he was carrying it next to the railing.

Lane: Since then have you seen pictures of James Earl Ray?

Stephens: I've seen pictures of James Earl Ray, but I never saw that man in person.

Lane: Was the man who you saw come out of the bathroom James Earl Ray?

Stephens: No it wasn't James Earl Ray I saw. It didn't look anything at all like him.

Lane: Did anyone from the police talk to you afterward?

Stephens: Yes. We had police, reporters, and more reporters. It was a mess. There was a picture that looked like the man I had seen. I pointed it out [to the police], but they never did pay any attention.

Lane: You have seen pictures of James Earl Ray?

Stephens: Yes, since then.

Lane: Is there any doubt in your mind that the man you saw was not James Earl Ray?

Stephens: There's no doubt in my mind. That wasn't James Earl Ray. It was an entirely different man. He was older, had dark hair; he was a brunet.

Lane: Do you remember what he was wearing?

Stephens: A windbreaker. I called it a hunting coat then. And under the coat he had on a checkered shirt, a loud, checkered shirt. The coat was open.

Lane: Did your husband Charlie ever see that man?

Stephens: I don't think he did. He couldn't see without his glasses, anyway. He didn't have his glasses on; they were on the bed, in the room.

While I was talking with Grace, two state employees, one of them the person in charge of the building, suddenly approached me.

"You cannot talk to Grace," one of them said.

They were joined by several other guards who ordered Grace to leave and then demanded that I surrender the tape recording to them. They said the rule at the institution was that no one was permitted to talk with Grace. The switchboard operator told me that a note posted at her desk stated that Grace was not allowed to have any visitors or receive any telephone calls unless the institution's administrator gave special permission. That rule applied only to Grace. I sought to explain the relevant law to them; they appeared to be unable to grasp it or, more likely, were not interested.

When one of the men stepped toward me to take the tape recorder, I quickly moved around him and ran to the car that we had left in front of the building. As we began to drive away, the guards rallied. Two of them stood in front of the car to prevent us from leaving. I asked Sammye to proceed, believing that there were limits to the sacrifices that the underpaid state employees were willing to make. At the last moment they jumped away, and we drove through the gate.

We had gone a short distance when we heard sirens and saw what looked like two fast-moving state police cars with lights flashing closing in on us. I took the tape from the recorder and placed it under my seat and then inserted a blank cassette. Sammye asked if I planned to give them the tape recorder. I said that I would give them nothing unless they pointed guns at me.

We pulled over as the police cars drove us off the road onto the shoulder. The men who approached us wore badges that raised a question in my mind. They demanded that I give them the recording after I refused to drive back to the institution to talk with the director. No weapons were visible. I asked if they worked for the Tennessee State Police or the director of the mental institution. They admitted that although they wore police uniforms and drove vehicles that resembled state police cars, that they were basically the institution's security guards.

"So," I said, "you guys have no jurisdiction here."

As we began to drive onto the highway, one of them shouted, "You have not heard the end of this."

I agreed. By prearrangement we drove directly to a friendly radio station and broadcast the entire interview to the residents of the city of Memphis.

While these events occurred more than thirty years ago, I had by then practiced law long enough to know that in highly political matters the courthouse, although a necessary venue, was not the sole path to justice, since justice was a commodity often in short supply there. The thoughts of Grace Stephens had been freed, but Grace, an innocent and truthful witness to history, remained in captivity.

I visited the Memphis branch of the American Civil Liberties Union. The local officers, no doubt still traumatized and fearful of the events that shook that city a decade earlier, declined to help, stating that they did not have adequate funds to retain counsel for the simple habeas corpus application to the court. I asked how much that would cost, and the answer was $450. I wrote a check to the ACLU for $500 and specified that it be used to retain counsel for Grace. Later, attorneys for the local ACLU decided that the matter of Grace Stephens was "just not a good First Amendment case."

In a brief meeting with the organization's officials I confessed that I had not been clear enough. Grace, I informed them, was pleased to be so well cared for; she particularly admired the institution's gourmet cuisine and her stimulating interactions with the residents of the nearby communities. However, she wanted a vacation from her resort to march with the Nazis in Skokie, Illinois—a reference to the ACLU's defense of the Nazis' right to march in a largely Jewish suburb of Chicago. I asked if we now had a good First Amendment case. In spite of this respectful and tactful approach, the ACLU refused to provide counsel. They also never returned my earmarked donation.[1]

I then turned to Lucius E. Burch Jr., a famous liberal Memphis attorney with a large law firm, who had represented Dr. King and Jim Lawson. His office was impressive, and the firm occupied a grand building in a location so situated that it would have tempted Donald Trump's acquisitive instincts. Burch was descended from a couple of former presidents, Polk and Jackson—not Washington and Lincoln, but chief executives nevertheless.

He was gracious, welcomed me to Memphis, and, had it been later in the afternoon, would have, I suspect, offered me a glass of bourbon. When he asked why I wanted to see him, I began to discuss the incarceration of Grace Stephens.

He abruptly interrupted and very firmly said, "The King assassination is over. It has been solved. If that is what you want to talk about, this meeting is concluded."

I said that Grace was certainly innocent, and he broke in again to say, "I don't care about that; the case is closed and so is this conversation."

I tried one more time, asking if he was satisfied that the matter was settled even if Ray was not guilty.

He said simply, "Yes." He then paused and said, "Please leave my office now."

It was later that I learned that this liberal lion had been appointed by W. Preston Battle, the judge who presided over the judicial fiasco in which Ray was constrained to plead guilty, to chair the judge's Amicus Curiae Committee for the purpose of convincing Ray that he had no alternative to the plan that he plead guilty and to try to prevent any discussion of the facts about the murder of Dr. King.

I called Reverend James Lawson, who by then had moved from Memphis to become the minister of the Holman United Methodist Church in Los Angeles.[2] I was confident that Jim, a good friend with an unsurpassed commitment to justice, would act where others remained fearful. He was surprised to learn of the Burch encounter and the timidity of the ACLU. He had only one question: "Mark, what can I do to help?" I told him that I believed that if he could organize the Memphis clergy to demand fair treatment for Grace, together with local counsel, I could appeal to the court for her release. He wondered for a moment if he could do that from California. He decided that he could be more effective if he returned to Memphis. Soon he was on his way.

I rented a large meeting room at the Holiday Inn in Rivermont, where Dr. King had originally planned to stay in April 1968. It was crowded with black and white Protestant ministers of varying political persuasions along with the leading Catholic clergy and prominent rabbis. Jim spoke eloquently of the need to redress a terrible wrong as he described the unearned suffering of Grace Stephens. I was asked by a minister what we wished for them to do; they required no additional facts, just a plan for action. I said that if Dr. King had been wounded, not killed, one could imagine him walking to Bolivar and remaining at the gates of that institution until Grace was released. And, I added, all of us in this room would have walked with him.

Assassinations are often effective. Following the counterproductive riots marked by mass acts of arson fueled by frustration and outrage, the movement too was wounded, lacking leadership and inspiration. We were not going to walk to Bolivar, but we could, if we were audacious and bold enough, make an effective effort. The clergy responded by agreeing to sign a public demand for the end to the unfair incarceration and to appear on radio and television programs to publicize their concerns. They then dedicated sermons on Sunday mornings or Friday evenings or Saturday mornings to that cause.

The campaign, organized by Jim, was successful in large measure not just in response to his words but out of respect for his many deeds in the years he labored in the South, including the period when he led a church in Memphis.

A hearing in Memphis was set, and it was both short and well attended by the press since Grace's words and the reaction to her imprisonment had been well publicized. The judge ordered her release from the asylum, directed that she be sent to a halfway house, and appointed a local lawyer to act as her guardian.

Grace Stephens was transferred to confinement in a house in Memphis where she received no medical attention, no matter how urgent, and was not permitted to leave without being accompanied by a "keeper." Her court-appointed guardian was content to allow her to remain there indefinitely. He never communicated with her; he neither visited her nor placed a call to find out about her physical or mental condition. While her incarceration was in a less harsh environment than before, she was sane and had committed no crime, and she should have been free. Her confinement and the appointment of a tame lawyer not interested in his client's welfare were part of the state's effort to prevent her from speaking publicly. Not long thereafter, Grace asked for my help, and I returned to Memphis from Venice, California, where I was staying.

With the assistance of friends in Memphis, I located the address and telephone number of the home where Grace was being kept. I called and asked for Grace. As soon as she said hello, I identified myself and asked if anyone else was present, cautioning her not to mention my name.

She replied, "Why Cousin William, it's so good of you to call." I asked if anyone was on the phone with us or just in the room with her. She said, "Oh yes, it is a nice room, and I always have company." I asked if she wanted to leave town. "Why, that would be so nice, really wonderful. I would like to see you very soon." As an aside to someone in the room she said, "It's my cousin. He may come to visit me here sometime next week." I told her not to pack, just to take a few things that were important to her and step out onto the porch in exactly thirty minutes. I told her that when she saw a blue, fairly new four-door Chevrolet parked in front of the house, she should walk out quickly but not run.

I drove the car to the home; Grace walked down the stairs and entered the car. Two people in the house rushed out to the porch, and one of them shouted, "Where are you going, Grace? You can't leave."

I drove three blocks to an assigned spot and traded cars with another friend who provided an ancient, white, two-door Ford. I drove quickly, but within the speed limit, to the airport. Later, police reports mentioned the blue Chevrolet, which another friend was driving in an opposite direction. I had already contacted a lawyer to represent that driver should he be stopped and questioned. No matter how eager the police might be to find Grace, none of the parties had done anything illegal, except the judge who had ordered her confinement and the local police and FBI agents who had kidnapped her and delivered her to a mental asylum.

At the airport I bought two tickets—only first class was available—for the trip to Dallas. From there, we would change planes for Los Angeles. As we were about to leave the desk area to board the plane, a television crew of two men arrived. They had been monitoring the police radio band and, unlike the Memphis Police Department, had figured out that we probably were leaving town. I knew the interviewer and asked him to promise not to air the scene until the plane had left. He said he could not make that promise. At that point I picked up his camera and made a proposal. "If you promise not to air anything until we leave, I will permit you to film Grace on the plane and I will also not smash your camera right now." He asked if I knew how much that piece of equipment cost. I answered that I did not, but I was counting on the fact that he did. He said that he knew I was not serious and that I would not damage the equipment. He also said that since he did not want to add to Grace's suffering, he would delay the release of the story for thirty minutes.

The television camera was carried onto the plane by one man while the interviewer carried the bright lights. The scene immediately brought the captain out of the cockpit. He was both curious and aggressive. He saw a woman in a shaggy old brown dress. She had no teeth and not a lot of hair, and she looked as if she had been drugged daily for ten years, which she had been. She was sitting in first class and being interviewed by a well-known Memphis on-air personality.

"What's going on?" he almost shouted.

I answered, "This is Ms. Charlene Daniels, the heir to the Jack Daniels fortune."[3]

Grace looked around at the other passengers and said, "And when we are airborne all the drinks are on me."

Our change of planes in Dallas was routine, but when we arrived in Los Angeles in the middle of the night, FBI agents were present to meet us. A few friends in L.A., organized by Donald Freed and Steve Jaffe, about two hundred of them, surrounded Grace and ushered her to a waiting car, much to the exasperation of the frustrated agents.

Later, the court-appointed lawyer in Memphis filed a motion charging me with wrongdoing of some unspecified sort. I called the judge and asked for the hearing date. He said, "Well, Mark, this is a simple matter, not extraditable. There is no need for you to come all the way back to Memphis. Don't bother with this." I said I was returning for the hearing and that his court-appointed lawyer was to be my first witness. He said, "I just wish you would forget the whole thing." I insisted, and finally a date was set to hear the original motion and my countermotion charging local counsel with neglect of his client and ward's rights and for acting in an unethical manner that required the bar association to examine his privilege to remain as a Tennessee lawyer.

The hearing was well attended by the media, and I challenged local counsel to tell me what he had done for his ward. Did he know of her serious medical issues? Had he arranged for her to see a doctor? Had he arranged for her to see a dentist? Had he attempted to establish her rights to Social Security payments? Had he even talked with her once or visited the home to which she was confined? Each question was answered in the negative.

Before we went any further, the judge dismissed the motion that had been filed against me and suggested that we just forget the whole thing. As we left, the chastened lawyer said to me, "You don't like me very much, do you?" I was about to reply as Bogart, playing Rick, did to Peter Lorre: "If I thought about you at all, I probably wouldn't." However, a consideration for decorum and civility prevailed. Also I was on my way to the Rendezvous Restaurant for wonderful ribs, and therefore uncharacteristically charitable.

During my investigation I sought to have a House Select Committee on Assassinations of the US Congress conduct an investigation and issue a finding. The committee concluded that it was likely that Dr. King was killed as the result of a conspiracy. James Earl Ray never received a trial and died in prison.

Jonestown

18

I met Jim Jones and his congregation of followers for the first time on September 15, 1978. I was invited to address the residents of Jonestown on the subject of the life and death of Dr. King. I stayed a short time, and I met many men, women, and children who even now, more than three decades later, are unforgettable. I had never heard of Jones or Jonestown until shortly before then. Two months later, Jones died, as did many of the more than nine hundred residents of Jonestown, Guyana.

When I returned to Jonestown, I shared with Congressman Leo Ryan of California both an airplane ride to a small airport at Port Kaituma and then a trip by truck to the gates of Jonestown, and I was there on November 18, 1978, when the massacre took place. I was a witness to the mass murder; I was one of the very few survivors, and to this day I am unable to determine the reasons that the tragedy took place. Ryan became the first congressman ever killed in the line of duty. That day represented the greatest single loss of American civilians in a nonnatural disaster until September 11, 2001. Of course, I am aware of many bizarre and complex factors that preceded the murders, and I will share them with you.[1]

||||||

Jones left a student pastorship in the Sommerset Southside Methodist Church because African Americans were not allowed in the congregation, and formed the Peoples Temple Full Gospel Church in
Indianapolis in 1956. In 1960, Jones was appointed the director of
human rights by the mayor of Indianapolis. Jones often stated that he
was responsible for helping integrate that city and published articles
confirming that he played a major role in integrating churches, restaurants, an amusement park, a Methodist hospital, and the police
department. He and his wife adopted orphans from war-ravaged
Korea, and in 1961 they became the first white couple in the state to
adopt an African American child.

Later, Jones and his Peoples Temple moved to California. In 1975,
the contributions of funds and door-to-door canvassing by members
of his flock may have been decisive in electing George Moscone
mayor of San Francisco. The newly elected mayor appointed Jones
to a lofty position, chairman of the San Francisco Housing Authority
Commission. At a dinner honoring Jones, California Democrat Willie Brown served as the master of ceremonies; present were activist
and politician Harvey Milk, who had spoken at the temple; Governor
Jerry Brown; and Mervyn Dymally, another prominent California
Democrat. Jones met with First Lady Rosalynn Carter many times,
and in 1976 he met with Walter Mondale during his presidential
campaign. Mondale also endorsed the work of the temple. While
Jones was not shy about his contacts and some critics believed that he
was given to exaggeration, these connections were confirmed almost
word for word in numerous articles.

The Jones public persona was well established when Jones moved
his temple and followers to a remote jungle compound in Jonestown,
Guyana. White doctors, lawyers, and teachers formed a cadre in
Jonestown, where most of the residents were African American and
many were women and children. This is not to say that Jones was a
self-aware hypocrite, for it seemed that he truly loved his followers just
as he truly loved to have them obey him without question no matter
how outrageous were his actions.[2] This bizarre contradiction was not

unique; some of our nation's leaders and founders were willing to give their lives in the fight for individual liberties while they owned and would not release men, women, and children who were their slaves.

I was living in Venice, California, in 1978, completing a screen-play with my friend Donald Freed, a writer and teacher. Freed knew Charles Garry, the lawyer who had for years been the only attor-ney representing Jim Jones and his Peoples Temple. Garry arranged for Freed to meet representatives of the temple in his San Francisco office. Freed was so impressed with Garry's enthusiastic endorsement of Jones and his work and so intrigued about Jonestown, described as a paradise by Garry, that he accepted an invitation to visit the group in Guyana to determine if he would write the history of the settlement.

Donald Freed did not discover heaven in the large clearing in the jungle, but he was greatly impressed with much that he observed. "I began to see one tableau, one vista after another, of highly intel-ligent, highly organized social engineering which would have been impressive in New York City or San Francisco, but in the middle of the jungle, was remarkable." Freed visited the machine shop, which he described as "a combination of apprenticeship and teaching and work going on in an environment of well-cared-for machinery and tools. Creativity and technology seemed to be working hand in hand." Donald also told me that Jim Jones wanted me to visit the community and deliver a lecture about Martin Luther King. Donald urged me to accept the invitation. To the public, Jones was a socialist warrior for the oppressed.

A few days later, in September 1978, I received a telephone call from a temple representative based in San Francisco. She formally invited me to Jonestown and stated that, since their organization had no funds, they could not pay a fee for a lecture or for my time but would be able to cover minimum transportation costs, meaning a dis-counted economy flight. At first, I thought I would be unable to go, as I was scheduled to represent James Earl Ray in front of the House Select Committee on Assassinations. Ray's appearance was canceled, and at the very last minute I agreed to go to Guyana.

What Garry did not tell Donald and I later uncovered was that Jones had required each temple member to write a statement regarding misconduct, often sexual, and confess to any indiscretion or crime that seemed within the realm of possibility. Garry's last major clients were Jim Jones and his organization. For many years he had served as the group's attorney and the keeper of its secrets as well as its extortionate files. Later many of the members said they had fabricated the stories to satisfy Jones. Whether the confessions were true or false, they were used by Jones and Garry to prevent members from leaving the group or complaining about any actual misconduct.[3]

The enforcer for the organization was Timothy Stoen, a local assistant prosecutor. Stoen and his wife, Grace, were members of the church. Jones repeatedly reminded members of his flock, with Stoen present, that if they made any complaint to the police, his second in command, Tim Stoen, would know about it at once, and he would take appropriate steps. Those arrangements were secret and shared only with group members. Much later, I discovered that the temple had assets in the millions of dollars, much of it allegedly smuggled across borders by its leadership.

What Garry also did not tell Donald was that he had "encouraged them [the Peoples Temple officials] to get weapons" and that he had personally "set up the security systems" for Jim Jones. According to a Peoples Temple official, Garry's advice had apparently been accepted, since the area was patrolled by guards who had access to between two hundred and three hundred rifles and twenty-five pistols.[4]

||||||

When I met Jim Jones in Guyana he seemed quite aged, far beyond his years, and appeared to be sedated or on some kind of medication. He had about him an air of desperation and defeat. That evening, following dinner in the central meeting place called the Jim Jones Pavilion, the community was assembled to watch a film. On the screen, a young, good-looking, charismatic man was speaking in an eloquent and moving fashion about the problems of poor people.

I turned to one of the cadre and asked who he was. She laughed as if I had made a joke. It was only then that I realized that it was Jim Jones on the screen, although he bore no resemblance to the man seated a few feet from me.

While I was there for the purpose of giving a talk about Dr. King and not investigating conditions, I was astonished by what had been accomplished in an area that had been an impassable jungle a few years earlier. There was a school, a medical clinic, a brick factory, and dormitory-style housing for all. I also noticed there were classes where people of all ages were learning to read and speak the Russian language.

When I was alone with Jones and his staff, I asked about that apparent anomaly. Jones said that because of the efforts to destroy him and his community they were making arrangements to move to the Soviet Union. The idea that Soviet officials who stated that religion is the opiate of the masses would be willing to accept a large religious-based organization seemed an unlikely prospect to me. However, Jones said that he had many conversations with Soviet officials. He added that musicians, singers, dancers, and a basketball team from Jonestown had already visited Russia and were warmly welcomed. He spoke quietly and seemed sincere. I listened without comment but decided that I would be obligated to hear the Soviet view before I could accept the reality of the proposal. I asked if there was going to be a Jonestown in the Soviet Union. Jones said that was not the plan and that it was decided that the members would live in various cities and be employed in occupations of their choice.

The Cold War was raging, and obviously the defection of almost one thousand Americans, most of them African Americans, from the United States to the Soviet Union to seek freedom would have constituted a major public relations defeat for the United States. However, I was not sanguine that the program was likely to succeed. On my way home from Jonestown, I visited the Soviet Embassy in Georgetown, the capital of Guyana, and was assured that the Russians had agreed to the proposal. Later I learned that on October 2,

1978, Feodor Timofeyev, representing the Soviet Embassy in Guyana, visited Jonestown, remained for two days, and gave a rousing speech of support for the people there. During that month, temple members met almost every week with Timofeyev as they planned the potential exodus to the Soviet Union.

Jones and his advisers told me that they had little time within which to affect the transfer, since Timothy Stoen, no longer the enforcer for Jones, had left the temple and vowed to destroy it. He was seeking to arrange for an armed invasion of the community, stating that he wanted to retrieve his son John.[5] Stoen told the State Department that he was going to retrieve John from Jonestown by force if necessary by assembling an invasion team. Stoen drafted and published many allegations about abuse in Jonestown, some of which he claimed to have witnessed himself. Those allegations about his former clients may have been truthful or exaggerated, but Stoen had never opposed those actions at the time they had supposedly occurred. Stoen and his organization met with Congressman Ryan and convinced him to conduct an investigation of the Jonestown community. In fact, Stoen accompanied the Ryan delegation but remained in Georgetown while Ryan went on to Jonestown.

Before embarking on the trip to Guyana, Ryan was briefed by the State Department and intelligence agencies. The CIA was not enamored of him, since he had sponsored an act critical of the CIA.[6] Richard Dwyer, officially designated as deputy chief of mission of the US Embassy to Guyana, was the CIA officer in charge of the embassy.

For reasons not known to me, Dwyer was complicit with Jones in his efforts to control the Jonestown community. Over a substantial period of time, numerous complaints had been made to US government officials by people residing in the United States about the treatment of their relatives in Jonestown. They had complained that their parents or children were denied the right to leave and to return to the United States. They asked that their family members be interviewed in Jonestown by a representative of the US government to determine the facts.

When, through channels, the requests reached Dwyer, he adopted a procedure that he employed in every instance. First, well in advance of the proposed interview, he notified the leadership at Jonestown of the names of those he intended to meet. This gave the Jonestown authorities ample time to meet with and advise those to be questioned as to what their responses should be. In addition, Dwyer always permitted security guards from Jonestown to be present during the interviews. Dwyer had made it plain that those interviewed, regardless of their complaints, would not be leaving with him that day. No one ever stated a desire to leave because the circumstances had been contrived by Dwyer to remove that option.

When Ryan was briefed by the State Department and intelligence organizations before his visit to Jonestown, he informed them of his proposed modus operandi. He said he would be interviewing several people whose names he would not provide until moments before the questions began. He said he intended to question them in privacy with only members of his own staff present. Jonestown security and Jones himself were to be excluded. Ryan was assured by the officials of the United States that those methods had always been employed in the past and approved of by Jones. Of course, those assurances were false, and Ryan's reliance upon those assurances was the crucial factor that led to the violence that followed.

Jones had agreed that Ryan and his staff could conduct an inquiry in Jonestown. James Schollaert, an attorney on the staff of the International Relations Committee of the House of Representatives, called me on behalf of Ryan. He told me that the entire delegation would consist of two congressmen, Ryan and Representative Edward Derwinski, and each would have present with him one staff member. He agreed that no representatives of the news media would be present.

At that point, I received a telephone call from a representative of the Peoples Temple in San Francisco. She implored me to be present with Ryan in Jonestown. She said Jones trusted me, and she hoped that if any dispute took place, I might be able to play a calming role.

Within a few days, I received a telephone call from Don Harris of NBC television. We had worked together for a series that NBC-TV produced about the assassination of Dr. King.[7] Harris said, "Are we going to do another one together? Are you in this one, too?" I asked him what he was referring to, and he said, "Jonestown. I'm flying in there with Ryan; I thought you knew." I told him about Schollaert's representations to me, and he said, "Listen, Mark, I'm going in with a television crew, and there are a lot of other reporters going too. They are not leveling with you."

Harris told me a member of the Peoples Temple, Tim Carter, had attended meetings led by Stoen in which Stoen asserted that he had "masterminded" the congressional trip and that he had arranged for members of the media to accompany Ryan into Jonestown. Stoen said that his plan was to provoke Jones into an irrational response. I had told Jones that I thought that Stoen might be exaggerating. However, Stoen was right and I was wrong. He was an essential part of the planning of the trip, and Ryan and his staff met with him about their plans while they embarked upon a program to deceive Jim Jones, through me, about the reality of the trip. The effect of their scheme considerably lessened my influence with Jones and thereby reduced my ability to calm matters in Jonestown on November 18. It also convinced Jones that the government and Stoen were working together to destroy him.

When Ryan arrived, he was accompanied by reporters from throughout the country. I believe that they expected to be denied entrance, since they had deliberately violated the commitments they had made regarding the visit. If Jones refused to allow them to enter the community, there would have been a major national news story filmed at the Jonestown entrance, much of it televised, about the refusal of Jones to allow a congressional delegation representing relatives of those in Jonestown to visit. In that period, just before the temple's planned trip to the Soviet Union was about to take place, many Americans would have heard of Jonestown for the first time and likely would have been convinced that it was an evil and secretive place with Americans being held prisoner by a madman. Such coverage certainly would have lessened the impact of Jones's followers deciding for themselves to "choose freedom" in the Soviet Union. Such a confrontation was clearly predictable; the result was not. Finally, Jones agreed to allow the delegation to enter, expecting that there would be no individual interviews with residents, since no names had been submitted to him in advance.

The first evening went far more smoothly than could have been expected in spite of the fear and trepidation clearly evidenced by Jones and his staff. It included a dinner and a variety show in the Jim Jones Pavilion. It also included an enthusiastic speech by Ryan, who stated that he was favorably impressed by what he had seen.

However, later, when Ryan and his staff submitted the names of those they wished to meet with privately, there was a stunned silence from the leadership. Harriet Tropp, one of the Jonestown leaders, said to me that she was alarmed, since someone might decide to leave. I asked what was wrong with that. The place had no television access, fast-food restaurants were not available, the days were long, and the work was hard on the agricultural commune, and if a few people wished to leave, I could not see why that would cause a problem.

She responded, "Are you insane? You just don't understand the situation."

I thought she might have expressed her view with greater tact, but her analysis, particularly about my lack of understanding, was accurate. Jones was profoundly possessive, and even one defection would be more than he could handle.

I met privately with Ryan for a while. He said that the Jonestown community was a remarkable achievement and the only thing wrong with it was that Jones was there and in control. Don Harris asked if I could arrange an interview with Jones. I asked him whether he would agree not to be nasty or accusatory but to be fair even if he did not like Jones and found his answers to be preposterous.

Don, trying to figure out the roles inside Jonestown, then asked, "Who are the guys in the white hats, Mark?"

I said, "I'm not sure there are any."

He said, "Wow. You are the most committed advocate I have ever met. I can't believe you gave that answer."

I told him that I considered him to be a friend who asked a serious question and that I felt it wise to confidentially tell him about my reservations. I was hoping for a somewhat balanced media response and relying upon Don to provide it. However, within a few hours, he would be dead.

The next day, November 18, 1978, Ryan continued with his private interviews, and a very few people indicated that they wished to leave. After he had interviewed one family, they called me over for advice. The two parents were there with their daughter and her boyfriend. They found their stay at Jonestown to be interesting but the discipline far too rigid. They said that Jones told them that he did not mind if they left quietly, perhaps a few days after the delegation had gone. They asked me if I could guarantee that they would be able to leave then. I told them that I could not, since I would be gone before then, and even if I was present, I would not be able to influence any decision making.

They asked for my advice, and I said, "If you really want to leave, then leave now." I turned around and realized that Jones was standing behind me. He stared at me with such apparent hostility, I was not able to experience a comfortable moment in Jonestown after that.

Ryan had observed my conversation with the family, and he saw me leave with them and return with them and their suitcases. He asked what had happened, and I told him of our conversation.

He said, "Is Jim Jones sore at you?"

I said that I hoped not and that I believed that people should be free to come and go as they wished. I said that it would have been easier to accomplish if Stoen and the press had not encouraged Jones to believe that each person who left was a defector and had defied him personally. Ryan said that he tried to demonstrate that that was not his opinion.

I said, "It would have been better, Congressman, if you had come without the press."

He paused for a moment and said, "Maybe you're right."

Later that day, Ryan was in the pavilion and observed a man say he was leaving while his wife said she was staying. Ryan walked over to me and said, "The worst part of this whole thing is the pain of watching families split up." That was tragic. Soon matters got a great deal worse.

Not long after, Ryan and I were again standing in the pavilion when a tall white man with obvious physical strength came up behind Ryan and placed him in a choke hold. Clearly, the congressman thought the man was not serious, even when the man said, "You motherfucker, I'm going to kill you."

Ryan responded, "OK, that's enough fooling around. You can let go now."

I was several feet away, along with other onlookers. I was startled, but I thought that Ryan knew his assailant and certainly did not fear him.

Suddenly the man, using his other arm, spun Ryan around to face him. Ryan, apparently still unconcerned, said, "Do you think the joke is over now?" I thought that even if it was a charade, it was an irresponsible act since emotions had been stretched and the tension was obvious.

Ryan was driven into a crouch, and he looked toward me and said, "Help me." The assailant held a knife that he had pressed against Ryan's chest near his heart.

I grabbed the wrist of the hand that held the knife and tried to pull it away. There were many people witnessing the struggle, and I shouted, "Hit the son of a bitch. Stop him."

No one moved. For a period that no doubt seemed longer than it was, the struggle was limited to the three of us, and Ryan's power, added to mine, prevented the knife from being driven into his chest.

Finally, other hands behind the assailant pulled him away. Ryan fell onto his back, and I, still holding the attacker's wrist, stumbled and fell. At last, the knife was dropped, and the man who had brought it disappeared through a group of silent and inactive onlookers.[8]

Ryan was lying on his back. He wore a blue shirt with a button-down collar, and the top buttons of the shirt were undone. Part of the shirt was spotted with blood, another part drenched. I asked him if he had been stabbed, and he replied that he did not know. I asked him if the blood on his shirt was his, and, still in something approaching a condition of shock, he could only say, "Is it? I don't know."

I ripped open his shirt and discovered that he had not been wounded by the knife. Then I saw that my hand had received a minor wound, and while it was bleeding, it was just trickling blood. I knew that the blood on Ryan's shirt had come from neither one of us.

Jones had watched the entire event. He seemed calm for the first time during the last two days, which I took to be an important and fearful signal. He asked Ryan one question—"Does this change everything?"

Ryan answered immediately, "Yes. It changes everything."

Realizing that we were still surrounded by those who obeyed Jones, he then modified his answer, saying that muggings take place in American cities and that he would not judge Jonestown by one incident.

The news of struggle in the pavilion reached those who were ready to begin their journey to the Port Kaituma airport. Don Harris came running ahead and saw Ryan's bloody shirt. Ever the newsman, he turned around and called to the members of his television crew, stating, "Get the camera."

I said to Don, "Don't bring a camera here."

Don looked at me and then at Ryan, thought for a moment, and said to his crew, "Forget it. We don't need a camera."

I don't know where Dwyer was during the attempted murder; he did not help in the struggle to subdue the assailant, but he was certainly on the scene immediately afterward. Dwyer and I both agreed that Ryan should leave Jonestown. I thought that he had become a lightning rod and we had a better chance of avoiding further violence if he left. Whatever Dwyer thought, he told Ryan that if he left, he would be safe at the airport and able to get to Georgetown.

I was with Ryan, in fact never more than a few feet from him, from minutes before the attack until he boarded the truck to the local airport. I walked with him from the pavilion to the truck, and when it was suggested that he climb into the open truck bed along with others, I suggested that he sit in the passenger seat and helped him into the cab.[9]

Ryan was reluctant to leave, since he had not met with all of the families he had intended to interview. He asked if I would stay to complete his work if he agreed to depart. We all believed that those taking the truck ride at once to the airport would likely be safely on their way home, and we were less certain about the future of those who remained where the sanctioned attempted murder had taken place. I agreed to stay and told Garry, who was planning to leave, that since he was the attorney for Jones and his organization he was obligated to stay as well. It was clear that if we did not remain, Ryan would not leave.

We had little choice. I continued with the interviewing process Ryan had initiated until Jones instructed one of his lieutenants to order Garry and me to appear before him. He told me that I had thwarted the will of the people of Jonestown by preventing the murder. He ordered that we be placed under arrest in a wooden shack not far from the pavilion. The man assigned to make sure we did not escape was the person who had tried to kill Ryan. One of his hands was heavily bandaged, thus solving the mystery of where the blood on Ryan's shirt came from, which provided very little comfort at the time.

A group of young men came running toward and then past the building where we were and soon ran back to the pavilion carrying numerous automatic weapons. The wounded guard, apparently needed elsewhere, was replaced by two young black men, each carrying a weapon. They demanded that Garry and I come out of the building, stating that we were all going to die and that this was revolutionary suicide.

At that time, over the loudspeaker from the pavilion, we heard Jones making similar statements to the community that had been gathered there. We heard cries of protest while Jones sought to explain that it was best that they all die.

Garry refused to leave the little building and walk toward the two armed men. I told him that the bamboo walls hardly offered adequate protection, and, since we were lawyers, our only chance for survival was to make a very persuasive closing argument. I walked out and saw that the two men were standing several feet from each other, so that if we tried to rush and disarm them we would be unsuccessful. Although later a feature film about the event actually showed an actor playing me doing just that, it was an imaginative and fictional episode and the furthest idea from my mind at the time.

I tried to convince our captors that killing little children, an event that was taking place in the pavilion, was not revolutionary and was not suicide. I said it came closer to the excesses of fascism. They brushed aside everything I said by repeating that it was revolutionary suicide and that we were all going to die.

I sighed and said that at least they would know that Garry and I would tell the truth to the world about what had happened that day. That prediction was obviously based upon the premise that we were going to survive. One of the men, who had not only heard my talk to the community about Dr. King two months earlier but who had subsequently read a book that I had written with Dick Gregory about the subject, said that I had told the truth about Dr. King and that he trusted me to tell the truth about Jonestown. They agreed we could leave.

I knew that the road out to Port Kaituma ran through the area adjacent to the pavilion and that we could not utilize that route. I asked for different directions, and one of the men pointed to a spectacularly large tree hundreds of yards away on the other side of a river. I went back into the cabin and took my small shoulder bag while Garry carried a much larger suitcase and a hair dryer. As we approached the river, we heard screaming, protests, and shots being fired from the direction of the pavilion. Garry said that there were piranha in the river and it was too dangerous to cross. I plunged in as I said, "They're killing people right there, and you're afraid of a fucking fish." I, too, had heard the piranha story and never knew if it was true or if it had been manufactured by Jones and his aides in an effort to create an impassable border for those residents who were thinking of leaving. In any event, we saw no fish and climbed up the opposite bank, walking toward the one tall tree. In time, we found the road to Kaituma and for the first time felt that we might survive.

That feeling was short lived when we heard and then saw a group of armed men coming toward us from Jonestown. It was nearly dusk as we ran into the jungle, where it was almost entirely dark due to the impenetrable canopy above. Running for our lives, at least in our minds, we covered about one hundred or two hundred yards in near total darkness. Shortly, it was so dark that I could not see my hand in front of my face. Two city lawyers in an unexplored, uninhabited jungle were trying to figure a way out and back to the road.

Garry said that he had an excellent sense of direction and knew exactly how to reach the road. Foolishly, I followed him, and after a relatively short period of time, he decided that we were lost. We sat on a fallen log, and Garry, clearly in a state of denial, wanted to talk about my views of the Kennedy assassination. I told him I wanted to concentrate on finding a way to the road and that I knew that many people who were lost tended to exacerbate the situation by going in the wrong direction.

He said, "I thought you were interested in the Kennedy assassination," and I answered that at the moment, I was more interested in survival.

Before my flight left from the New York airport to Georgetown, Guyana, since I was quite early, I had visited a Hammacher Schlemmer store, which sold numerous interesting gadgets. I had purchased a small folding pair of scissors and tossed it in my pack. As I was able to make the trip to Guyana only at the last minute, I was ill equipped for the journey, so I also purchased a package of three white undershorts at another store.

As I rummaged through my shoulder pack, I found the scissors and the still unopened plastic-wrapped package of undershorts. I cut the shorts into strips. I thought that we could not be much more than a couple of hundred yards from the road. I suggested that Charles and I each take the strips and walk slowly in any direction, marking our path by placing the strips on branches every few feet. The first effort failed in that we did not reach the road. As we returned to our original starting point, we picked up the strips, which by then had become somewhat darkened by the atmosphere. We then set out in another direction. We repeated the sequence until we found the road.

As we walked toward Port Kaituma, we were finally met by the local military and received a ride into Georgetown and to the American embassy. Our hosts were surprised to see me since the press had reported that I probably had died. I called my law partner, April Ferguson, who told me that Dick Gregory had called her from his lecture tour to tell her that he had opened a page of the Bible in his hotel room to a passage making reference to someone's deliverance, and he was therefore confident I was still alive. He also told her that he had chartered a plane, and he would pick her up in Washington and fly to Georgetown and once there do whatever was required to make sure that I was found.

Almost one thousand Americans had been killed at Jonestown, the majority of them children and women. The American government proposed to the Guyanese that a large hole be dug and all the American bodies dumped in there. The government of Guyana rejected that crude suggestion, and its medical examiner began the inspection of the bodies. While the American government stated that a mass suicide had taken place and that the deceased had voluntarily consumed poisoned Kool-Aid, the Guyanese medical examiner concluded that many had been injected with cyanide and that the assertions by the officials of the United States that a mass suicide had taken place were not sustainable, since it was clear that there had been a mass murder.

My Day with Bill Buckley: The Trial of the *National Review* and *Buckley v. Carto*

19

IIIIIIIIIIIIIIIIIIIIIIIIIIIIIIIIIIIIIIIIIIIIIIIIIIIIIIIIIIIIIIIIIIIIIII

I have examined numerous witnesses, each of whom brought his or her own values and life experiences to the witness stand. I expected that crossing verbal swords with so celebrated a pundit as William F. Buckley Jr.—historian, secret CIA officer, writer, publisher, widely respected conservative activist, and host of the long-running *Firing Line*—would be most challenging. Would Bill have critiqued that sentence with "'Crossing verbal swords'? Mr. Lane, your metaphor is paltry trumpery"? Prepared as I thought I was for the confrontation with Buckley in the courtroom, I was nevertheless astonished by the unprecedented and ethereal adventure in the daunting world of Bill Buckley's mind.

My involvement began one otherwise pleasant autumn day in Washington during 1985. Willis Carto (the director of Liberty Lobby, a Washington-based group that published a weekly newspaper, the *Spotlight*) had arrived at my door with surprising news. The general counsel for his organization had disappeared. There had been no foul play; he had not been kidnapped. He had decided quite literally to sail off into the Florida sunset. The lawyer, a pleasant fellow, a gourmet, wine aficionado, and reputable sailor of small ships, had, to my knowledge, but one phobia. For most of the population

315

that disability would be of little or no consequence. It was, however, unpropitious for a trial lawyer. He was afraid to try cases.

This was a matter of genuine concern for Carto and his organization. They were defendants in a defamation case about to be tried in the US District Court, the case of *National Review v. Willis Carto, et al.* Buckley was the founder, editor, and sole owner of all of the stock in his *National Review*. He was also the most important prospective witness in the case. The circumstances did not favor Carto. Buckley was demanding $16 million for the slight against his good name. Even a small fraction of that sum would have forced Carto, Liberty Lobby, Inc., and the *Spotlight* into a bankruptcy from which none of them could have recovered. Eliminating a competitor was clearly Buckley's objective. Liberty Lobby was an outspoken conservative think tank advocating, it said, populist concepts. Its detractors said it was anti-Semitic. It clearly opposed the political philosophy of Zionism, and it considered Buckley to be a voice of the establishment.

Buckley and his publication were represented by J. Daniel Mahoney, a member of a politically connected New York law firm. Dan Mahoney was also the leader and founder of the Conservative Party in New York, a party that had supported Buckley when he ran unsuccessfully for mayor of the city. Buckley's brother had been appointed to the US Court of Appeals for the District of Columbia; the case was to be tried in the district. The case was long standing, contentious to the point of being well beyond uncivil, and complicated by claims and counterclaims. Buckley had filed four charges of defamation against Carto, who had filed two charges of defamation against Buckley. Long ago, as the case made its treacherous journey through the system, the judge, June Hens Green, had dismissed both of Carto's claims, meaning that the jury would never hear them. She was also asked by Buckley's lawyers to grant two of their defamation claims. In an unprecedented decision she did so, meaning that the jurors did not have to listen to the evidence to decide if Buckley was right because the judge had done that for them. All they had to decide was how much money they should award to Buckley for each count of defamation. In an oversight, Buckley's attorneys had failed to ask for a directed verdict regarding the other two counts. The jury would have to make those decisions.

The little that I knew about the matter led me to the conclusion that I was not interested in becoming part of it. Yet there was Carto, knocking at my door and asking for help. I agreed to appear conditionally before the court, explain the circumstances, and ask for a continuance so that Carto and Liberty Lobby, Inc., could seek new counsel. That was the totality of my simple approach. I should have heeded Bobby Burns about the value of a best-laid plan.

While counsel had fled the defendants, Liberty Lobby and Carto were not without assistance. A bright young woman, Brent Whitmore, had served as a paralegal for them. We discussed the motion for a continuance that I was preparing, primarily based not upon the absence of counsel, a voluntary act and therefore less compelling, but rather upon the fact that the case, not just counsel, was not ready for trial.

Judge Green had, during pretrial conferences, status calls, and argument, convinced both Carto and Whitmore that she was both hostile to Carto and his causes and favorably inclined toward the celebrity of the famous plaintiff. I knew that Judge Green had the reputation of being essentially a fair person, somewhat liberal, acquainted with the law, and generally kind and considerate. I thought Willis was exaggerating when he told me that his greatest fear was that the judge would, with the jury present, jump off the bench to shake hands with Buckley and ask for his autograph.

When we met in the judge's chambers, she said that the case would begin in a few days as scheduled and that it would conclude in two weeks, since she had an irrevocable commitment. She was going to China to study the judicial system. I told her that I was not prepared to try the case. She ordered me to proceed. I told her that there were ethical considerations and that, although I had never disobeyed a direct order from a court, I did not believe that I could participate. Although I was living in Washington, DC, at the time,

I was only a member of the New York bar and not yet admitted to practice in the District of Columbia. I advised the court that without local counsel—a lawyer admitted to practice in the District of Columbia—the rules precluded my appearance. She said she would waive that requirement, a ruling for which I believe she had no authority. When I declined to proceed, she said that Carto would represent the defendant, Liberty Lobby, Inc. I suggested that in the District of Columbia, and probably everywhere else in the nation, a corporation could appear only through counsel. She said that she would waive that provision as well, a decision that I knew she could not lawfully make and one that would have rendered any subsequent verdict against the corporation to be void *ab initio*, or invalid from the beginning.

I conferred with Carto briefly and surrendered. I would try the case and would do so in violation of the rules requiring that local counsel be present, since the court had so ordered.

I spent the remaining hours before trial in a dash toward preparation, knowing that it was a goal I could not fully achieve. Buckley and his team of lawyers had made it abundantly clear that they had no respect for Carto and his publications and that they considered him a racist. A young woman agreed to work with me in our jaunt to the imminent legal disaster that loomed. She was a recent graduate of Harvard Law School and obviously very intelligent and quick and was looking for temporary employment while she awaited the results of her bar examination. She was also an African American.

Together we discussed trial strategy. Without doubt, rumors about Carto's racism had abounded for years, and it was equally clear that he would not likely be nominated as the man of the year by the NAACP. Buckley and his counsel smelled blood in the water and had prepared for a scathing cross-examination when Carto took the stand.

It became clear from questions Mahoney posed to the potential jurors and from his selection process that he wanted an all–African American jury, not an impossible feat in the nation's capital at that time but not easily achieved without one-dimensional predetermination.

Mahoney succeeded. He got the all-black jury he so ardently sought, but so did we.

Before Mahoney began, Judge Green called us into chambers to negotiate a settlement or, as she so optimistically put it, an amicable agreement. Carto had reason to fear the trial. He offered $80,000 to settle the case. In chambers, the judge took an active part in settlement talks. She said, "Mr. Lane, this case will settle for $350,000. That is what I think is fair, and that is my decision." I was speechless for a moment and then found a few words and thanked her for her generosity and for offering $270,000, apparently from her own resources, to add to Carto's $80,000. She grasped but did not approve of the sardonic reply. She said, "Very well, Mr. Lane, we will proceed to trial, and you may determine that you have made a major mistake." I knew that Carto might later agree with her, and I wondered if I, too, might.

Mahoney's opening statement was impressive. It even impressed Carto, who talked with me about settling the case. I knew that Mahoney was a practiced speaker. I suspected that he was not an accomplished lawyer. Relying upon cross-examination to make your case may be a tactical error of substantial importance, since events precedent may preclude that strategy. Selecting a black jury when your client's undeniable record of arrogant racism may be easily located and exposed may be a more serious mistake. In short, Buckley was going to testify; Carto might not.

I stood to make my opening statement to the jurors. Most were women, and all were African Americans. Mahoney had spoken about his clients, his associate and hero, Bill Buckley, and the *National Review*. I decided to devote my opening to the same subject: not my client but his. I believed that I had learned a great deal about Buckley and that it might be useful to share that extraordinary information with the jurors. I had hoped to set our case on a course toward victory even before the first witness took the stand.

Documents to be offered in evidence have differing routes before counsel is permitted to present them to a jury. It is not an episode of a televised crime show where evidence, often in a plastic bag, emerges from thin air and surprises the witness. All parties see the documents to be offered, often well in advance, and only after both parties have been heard will the court rule on its admissibility. Often there is nothing in evidence until the first witness begins to testify; therefore, opening statements require counsel to paraphrase what he believes the evidence will show.

I approached the lectern without any documents or notes. On the counsel table, within reach, were stacks of copies of the *National Review*. Everybody at the counsel tables, including Mahoney and his assistant and Buckley, had access to the issues. I had identified each one by date and marked each one as an exhibit, and Mahoney had consented to their acceptance by the court as exhibits in the case.[1] However, apparently neither Mahoney or his staff had researched Buckley's now-inconvenient statements. Had they done so, they might have opted for a different jury.

Since the corporation had suffered no financial loss, and a corporation may not claim loss of reputation as a measure of damages, the case centered upon the owner of all the stock in the *National Review* and its publisher and its editor, each of whom could claim that their good name had been damaged. In this case, Buckley was all three. Therefore, I could only evaluate Buckley's good name and the reputation he had created for himself and his publication.

I said that "in a demonstration of chutzpah," Buckley and his publication came to our city, to Washington, DC, asking us to "please protect our good name." What good name was that? I asked. Simply put, Buckley was a rabid racist.

Was Buckley a racist, and did he use his publication to advance those views? Let me count the ways. I told the jury that on April 24, 1957, Buckley argued that African Americans should be denied the right to vote in the southern states of the United States. He explained why in an editorial that he wrote and signed: "The central question that emerges is whether the White community in the south is entitled to take such measures as are necessary to prevail politically and culturally in areas where it does not predominate numerically. The sobering answer is yes. The White community is so entitled because for the time being it is the advanced race."

I reminded the jury about Buckley's racist campaign to remove from office and indict Reverend Adam Clayton Powell, who had been the most influential African American political figure of the decade as the chairman of the Education and Labor Committee of the House of Representatives. Powell was responsible for increasing the minimum wage, reducing hours of work, and aiding public education. He steered into law proposals making lynching a federal crime and was responsible for bills desegregating the military and public schools. While Powell opposed the practice in the South of charging African Americans a poll tax in order to vote, Buckley was urging that blacks not be allowed to vote even if they paid the tax.

Buckley had used his enormous political influence to have Powell indicted in New York. Buckley later bragged about his role and wrote about it in the *National Review* in blatantly racist terms.

I told the jury that, years ago, Buckley wrote and published another attack on Powell under the headline "The Jig Is Up, Baby." I did not have to inform the jury that *jig* is a racist term and that *baby* is not generally part of the pseudo-sophisticated vocabulary affected by Buckley. Was this piece by Buckley an aberration?

No, it was more like a theme. Buckley entitled another of his racist assaults on Reverend Powell "The Jig Is Up for Adam Powell, Jr." After Powell was indicted, he retained Edward Bennett Williams, a leader of the bar in the district, to represent him. Buckley then began attacking Williams.

The good news, I told the jury, is that it is not required to be an African American to be defamed by Buckley. President Eisenhower had attended one of a series of conferences to control the proliferation of nuclear weapons. Of that effort Buckley wrote on January 18, 1958, in a piece entitled "The Tranquil World of Dwight D. Eisenhower": "What man who knows communism would have gone to Geneva to act as a sounding board for communist propaganda?"

I told the jury how, just after the death of Eleanor Roosevelt, Buckley wrote of a statement he had made earlier: "Following Mrs. Roosevelt in search of irrationality is like following a lighted fuse in search of an explosion; one never has to wait very long." It took me quite some time to explain this to the jury because throughout my opening statement Judge Green constantly interrupted me and questioned my statements. Again and again she summoned me to the bench, and my patience was wearing out. I finally said to her at the bench that I wished she would not speak to me in the tone she was utilizing in front of the jury. The judge replied that she had raised her voice so that I could hear her. She added that, while there was no time limit on the opening statement (there certainly had not been one for Mahoney), "it is going on a little long."

I pointed out that most of the time had been at the bench at her demand.

I closed by comparing the words of Adolf Hitler about advanced races and inferior races with Buckley's similar words on the same subject. Predictably, Mahoney was outraged, and the judge asked me to show her "something in the record" to demonstrate the similarity between what was published in the *National Review* and what Hitler said. I told the court that I did not "think I should be called upon to do this. I think I should be able to do this during cross-examination of Mr. Buckley." She responded that I should not say in my opening statement anything "which you do not believe you can prove." I responded, "I know I can prove it, Your Honor. Otherwise I wouldn't say it. But I should not have to prove it here at the bench every time I issue a statement." She said, "But you say you don't have it [the proof] right now." Patiently, I responded, "I did not say that, Your Honor, at all. I said I should not be compelled by you—" She interrupted my explanation to say, "I assume that means you don't have it here now." Hoping that we might soon get back to the jury I said, "Of course I have it here. I have documents for every single statement that I have made." The judge paused, looked at me, and asked, "You have documents for every statement you have made, sir?" Once again I said, "Yes."

Another pause, and then the final word from the judge. "All right. I will accept your word in that regard."

To the jury, at long last, I said, "You will have the opportunity, when Mr. Buckley testifies, to compare the words which appeared in the *National Review* with the words written by Adolf Hitler, and you can judge for yourselves whether Mr. Buckley has a right to unbridled passion, or does the *National Review*, when it is asserted that they are pro-fascist in their thinking."

When I returned to the counsel table, Carto said, "She may not be so eager to get his autograph now."

The first person to testify was Buckley. As he walked to the witness stand, all eyes were on Buckley. I looked at the jurors and thought that they were studying him with a degree of fascination mixed with at least a modicum of disgust. As he testified about his education and his honorary degrees, I was trying to take his measure as a witness.

I was surprised to learn that with all his pretense of scholarly erudition Buckley had obtained just an undergraduate degree. He later joined the CIA and worked with the future Watergate burglar and convict E. Howard Hunt as they contrived and published false propaganda from their base in Mexico City. Buckley left the CIA and then went to work for the *American Mercury*, a right-wing magazine. He testified that he then wrote a book. His next job was when "I went to work briefly for my father in the oil exploration business for about six months." Then he, with others, decided to launch the *National Review*. For an undisclosed reason Buckley "ended up owning all the voting stock," and then later "I ended up owning all the common stock."

Buckley testified that Charlton Heston, Tom Selleck, and Ronald Reagan all liked his magazine. Buckley listed the names of celebrities who had attended his lavish parties. The roster of the right-wing white elite was impressive. The jurors were undoubtedly interested, but I thought that perhaps they were even more alienated. Buckley paused, looked directly at the jurors, and stated triumphantly that present at one of the events was Lewis Strauss, paused again, and added with a flourish, "And he's Jewish." Emphasis was added by the tone the witness employed and by the fact that the word "Jewish" was stretched out to encompass many syllables. There may be some scientific method of testing the speaker's degree of innate anti-Semitism by meticulously calculating how long it takes to say "Jewish."

When I raised questions though a motion addressed to the court about the relevancy of those hearsay endorsements, Buckley spoke. "I am terribly constipated by these interruptions." Buckley continued to give long and rambling answers, sometimes to questions that had not been asked. I approached the bench and objected to these answers.

I told the court, "I was not permitted to raise any question about Mr. Buckley's association with the CIA, although he is permitted to do so when he testifies, first of all. Second, Mr. Buckley has even been permitted to say that Mr. Strauss is Jewish, and in response to no question anywhere related to whether Mr. Strauss existed, much less anything about his religion."

The judge said, "I would certainly go along with Mr. Lane that additions to the response may be unnecessary, but at the moment, I find no problem." The problem was that continuing violations of the rules governing our profession were taking place in front of her, and she both acknowledged and ignored that fact and even invited the Buckley Show to continue. I took the next step. "And it just seems to me, Your Honor is being very unfair in the proceeding at this time."

Judge Green seemed shocked by my statement. She said that she wanted my editorial comment deleted from the record. She added that I had a responsibility as an officer of the court to treat her with respect as a judge in this court.

"Your Honor, I have always treated this court with respect, and I will continue. But I am going to make a motion at the end of the day regarding the continuation of this case before this court." I said I was going to move that she recuse herself due to bias and partiality. I had rarely made such a motion in the past; in most of the few cases where I sought that extreme relief, it was granted. Many lawyers believe that the motion tends to outrage the judge and is, therefore, a dangerous step. My view is that if the motion is warranted it should be made, and, even if not granted, it may persuade the court to act more cautiously and in accordance with established procedure in hopes of not being overturned on appeal.

Buckley had not grasped the intricacies of race relations in America. He had the notion that if the black jurors heard that one Jewish person they had never heard of went to a *National Review* dinner they would know that Buckley was a friend of African Americans, even though he thought and wrote that they were too inferior to vote.

Mahoney was an affable man whom I grew to like and even assist more than once after the case ended. He was just not an experienced trial lawyer. He was in a difficult position representing a certified racist before an all–African American jury, but he was the person who deliberately chose that jury for reasons related to race.

The judge denied my motion to recuse her and stated that she could be fair and that she would be fair. In fact, her subsequent rulings for the most part after that exchange tended to comply with the rules of evidence and federal criminal procedure.

We were back in court on Thursday. Buckley was set to explain what he meant by *jig*, a reoccurring theme in his references to Adam Powell, and likely the jurors were interested in seeing by what means it might be explained away. Buckley said that the word *jig* was not "used in the South, for instance, where I grew up." He said that when he stated that "Negroes" were inferior, he meant it only in a good way, that is, since they had fewer advantages in the South than "those enjoyed by white people," it was natural that they were not as advanced. Buckley testified that he had never been informed that the word *jig* was a derogatory term for African Americans, yet he then admitted that he had been questioned on a national television program by Mike Wallace, who told him that it was a racist term. After that Buckley continued to use that word while referring to Powell. He blamed that on his sister, one of the innumerable family members working for his publication.

During cross-examination, I reminded Buckley that he had just testified that until he heard my opening remarks he had never heard of anyone comparing his words to those of fascists and that no one had ever said anything like that before. I asked if that was true. He responded, true to expectations, "Everything I say is true."

I then asked him if Gore Vidal had said to him on a network television program, "The only pro–crypto Nazi I know is you." Buckley admitted that Vidal had made that statement. I asked him if Vidal had written an article for *Esquire* in which he stated that Buckley's "views are very much those of the founders of the Third Reich who regarded blacks as inferiors, undeclared war as legitimate foreign policy and the Jews as sympathetic to International Communism." He admitted that Vidal had written those words but insisted that they were untrue and that he had won a defamation case against *Esquire*.[2] Of course, what was certified as being untrue was Buckley's previous testimony in which he denied that such words had ever been uttered.

We offered in evidence documents demonstrating that when Buckley ran for mayor of New York City the *New York Times* made reference to Buckley's "slurs on Negroes" and his "pandering to brutish instincts" in his campaign. Buckley recalled that when he asked the *Times* what instincts it was claimed he appealed to, the *Times* responded "fear, ignorance, racial superiority, religious antagonism, contempt for the weak and afflicted and hatred for those different from oneself."

Toward the end of the presentation by the plaintiffs, a number of jurists from China appeared as spectators. They were there to learn about the practice of law in the United States and then escort Judge Green on her trip to Beijing. Our days in her court were dwindling down to a precious few. Mahoney asked me how long my case would take to present since he was arranging for two rebuttal witnesses. One was a wide receiver for the New York Jets; I knew that he was an African American, as was the other, a teacher for some college in New York. They were no doubt being offered to show that some of Bill's best friends were black.

I met with Carto to discuss my proposed strategy. The future of his newspaper was at stake. He asked if I was sure that my approach would work. I said that I was not certain; it was my hope and my best guess. He agreed.

I asked Judge Green if we could meet in chambers. She smiled in anticipation of my next move. In chambers, all parties, counsel and the judge and her clerks, gathered around, and I asked that the matter become a matter of record, meaning that I wanted a court reporter to be present. Judge Green acquiesced.

I then asked the judge for an advance ruling. She nodded. "Theoretically, if a defendant in a civil case does not present any witnesses, can the plaintiff offer rebuttal testimony?" I asked.

She looked at me as if puzzled and said, "You are an experienced trial lawyer; you know that if you offer no witness there can be no rebuttal."

I thought, but did not say, that a number of rulings at this trial were novel and had no relationship to what I believed the law to be. To put a fine point on the issue I asked, "If I now state that the defense rests, there is no possibility that the plaintiffs can offer any additional testimony. Is that going to be your ruling, one I can rely upon in making a decision now?" She said that of course that would be her ruling, since that was well-settled law. I then said, "The defense rests." I believed that Buckley's blatant racism would likely cause the jurors to believe that he had no good name to sully. I knew that Mahoney expected Carto to testify and that he would try to do to him what I had already done to Buckley. I also knew that the two "rebuttal" witnesses would try, probably in vain, to resurrect Buckley's shattered reputation.

Judge Green smiled and said to me that she thought that might be what I was planning when I asked for the on-record chambers conference. She was pleased that she could return home and complete her preparations for the long and interesting trip ahead.

Mahoney was conferring with his clients and assistants in a corner of the room. He did not grasp the ramifications of recent developments. He said to the judge that he would call his two witnesses the next morning. She said that he had rested his case and that rebuttal witnesses could not be called. Mahoney said that their testimony would be relatively brief. She explained that brevity was not the issue. He protested. She patiently explained the rules of evidence. Mahoney then said, "Lane called my client a racist, and he has the right to answer." Judge Green said that the plaintiffs could not rebut questions and could not rebut answers given by his own client. She added that opening and closing statements, not being evidence, also cannot be rebutted.

Mahoney was furious. He claimed that I had unconscionably "pulled a dirty trick." Judge Green said, "Mr. Mahoney, in this building all assistant United States attorneys each day consider that the defendant may do what Mr. Lane has just done and adjust their tactics accordingly."

The jury considered four verdicts and four awards in a case in which Buckley and his magazine had demanded millions of dollars, including legal costs and expenses. They reached a unanimous decision in a very short time and then filled out the verdict form that the court had given to them.

It read regarding Count One, "The Court has already determined that the statement is libelous," and asked the jurors to determine the damages, both nominal and punitive, that should be awarded to Buckley. The jurors responded that no damages should be awarded.

Regarding Count Two, the jurors were told that the court "has already determined that the statements were libelous" and asked the jurors again to award damages to Buckley. The jurors responded that no damages should be awarded.

Regarding Count Three, the jurors found for Buckley and ordered that the corporation owning the newspaper pay the sum of one dollar in damages and that Carto pay nothing.

Regarding Count Four, the jurors found for Buckley and ordered that the corporation owning the newspaper pay one thousand dollars and that Carto pay nothing.

Buckley's well-documented racism, exacerbated by his unexcelled arrogance, had been costly. He did receive $1,001, which paid for but a small fraction of his costs for pursuing the action.

When Buckley died, a few reporters who knew I had been a guest on *Firing Line* and that I had opposed him at a trial called to ask for a comment. When I was a child my mother said that we should never speak ill of the dead. She was not superstitious; she thought it was unfair to make an accusation to which there could be no reply. When I confronted Buckley it was to his face; it was in a courtroom where a judge decided the rules, and it was while he was accompanied by two lawyers. I told the journalists that I was sad to hear that he had passed and that I had no other comment.

A Supreme Case
and Others in the District

20

||||||||||||||||||||||||||||||||||||||||||||||||||||||||||||||||||||||||||||||||||

During the last sixty years, I have appeared before courts in many states in both civil and criminal cases. I have appeared before many judges. Some have been less than fair and some have allowed politics, prejudice, or the power of a litigant to play a part in decision making. Others have met the obligations imposed by their office and are governed by commitment to ethics, justice, and the law. All cases are important to the parties, but some cases help establish precedent that reaches far beyond the narrow confines of the ordinary case. Here are a select few of my cases that I believe had an impact upon our country's jurisprudence.

In 1983 Jack Anderson was a widely read syndicated columnist. I had known Jack for some time and had worked with him on a couple of matters. He had hosted a television program for a short period, and I had cooperated with him for one presentation. Willis Carto was again my client, and for a hotly contested and nasty libel case the parties remained relatively civil.

The circumstances leading to the libel case began long before with a false and damaging article about Carto and his work with Liberty Lobby, Inc., published in *True* magazine. The authors of the defamation, including a writer, Joseph Spear, and the owner of the magazine, Fawcett Publications, Inc., admitted that the published statements were false. They paid Carto for his suffering and printed an abject apology as well as a four-page panegyrical article that referred to Carto as "a great American patriot" and concluded that his organization was "The People's Lobby." And thus the case was concluded.

A decade later Jack Anderson launched his own magazine and became the publisher of the *Investigator*. He hired Spear as the periodical's managing editor. Spear was a reporter with an unresolved mission against Carto, and that ancient loss apparently continued to plague him. He decided to publish the same allegations again, even after having admitted that they were false. Anderson compounded that error by encouraging the vendetta. Spear provided cover to distance himself from the two articles by assigning the task of writing them to an inexperienced writer who had been employed for just a few weeks. Spear gave him the *True* magazine article, which the recent hire primarily relied upon for the facts. The writer testified that neither Spear nor Anderson had ever told him that the *True* article was the subject of a lawsuit settled in favor of Carto. Since the writer, who had merely assembled the information given to him, was more a victim than a villain, he was not named as a defendant in the ensuing legal action, and it would be inappropriate for me to name him here.

The editor of the *Investigator*, William McGaw, testified that he had strongly objected to the publication of the articles, stating that they were "ridiculous" and "terrible" and likely "libelous" and that he had told that to Anderson before publication. In a sworn statement he said that Anderson then explained to him his motive for condemning Carto and Liberty Lobby as anti-Semites. McGaw said that Anderson approached him and the following colloquy took place.

Anderson said, "I want to explain that story, why we are running that."

McGaw said, "Please do."

Anderson said, "You know, when I addressed a meeting of magazine distributors in New York, I noticed they were virtually all Jewish. Anderson said that the reason he was running articles about Carto was "so that they'll be favorable toward us and give us prominent display on newsstands and supermarkets."

The judge was Barrington D. Parker, a conservative African American appointed to the US District Court by President Nixon. He had a reputation for being a cantankerous as well as compassionate man who ruled aggressively. I never saw the cantankerous aspect of his personality, and I appreciated his no-nonsense approach to the courtroom. Judge Parker was the reason that civility reigned in our case.

The defendants moved for summary judgment to dismiss the case, arguing there were no legal grounds upon which the plaintiffs could prevail, and Judge Parker granted the motion. The decision to dismiss the case was in accordance with the judicial march to eliminate defamation as an actionable tort. Most libel cases are dismissed by the court without a trial, citing the First Amendment as the basis. That amendment guarantees us the right to a free press and free speech. It tends to argue against prior restraint, and I know of no attorney who appreciates its reach and power more than I do. It does not, however, state or imply that once the defamation is uttered, the victim of that tort should be powerless to seek redress. Confusing First Amendment rights with the absolute right of the injured party to act is to make a leap so draconian that it imperils the rule of law.

On occasion, a new and refreshing voice is heard from an appellate court. We hoped for that when we drafted the appeal to the US Court of Appeals for the District of Columbia. In the statement of issues presented for review, I began with the issue of whether the District Court had applied the proper standard. I argued that the appropriate standard should have been a decision based upon "convincing clarity," not just the judge's own belief about the evidence. Having made that legal argument, I devoted most of the brief to the unfairness of the determination.

The unanimous court in a strongly worded opinion reversed the trial judge's decision and sent the case back for trial. Judge Antonin Scalia wrote the decision. In a ringing declaration for the rights of a person defamed by the media, he wrote:

> We are not yet ready to adopt for the law of libel the principle that 10,000 repetitions are as good as the truth. We see nothing to be said for the rule that a conscious, malicious libel is not actionable so long as it has been preceded by earlier assertions of the same untruth. To begin with, we cannot envision how a court would go about determining that someone's reputation had already been "irreparable damaged"—i.e., that no new reader could be reached by the freshest libel. More important, however, no significant First Amendment values would be furthered by the rule appellees suggest, since, where a person has been widely libeled by reputable sources, the defendant's good faith reliance upon those sources provides, as we shall later discuss, a complete defense. Proving such good faith reliance (or actually, even less than that, merely preventing the plaintiff from proving the opposite by "clear and convincing evidence") is not such a burden that a prophylactic rule need be adopted sanctioning willful character-assassination so long as it is conducted on a massive scale.

Anderson asked the Supreme Court to review the case. While a party in the US District Court has the right to appeal to the Court of Appeals, no party has the right to appeal to the Supreme Court. The losing party may file a writ of certiorari asking the Supreme Court to take the case; of approximately many thousands of requests each year, the court agrees to consider about seventy-five or eighty. The Supreme Court agreed to hear the case since it was interested solely in the standard that should be applied when a trial judge considers granting a motion for summary judgment. It was a narrow but important area of law that I had raised from the outset. I was to argue my first case before the Supreme Court, an experience that relatively few lawyers share.

The setting was grand, the rules explicit. My three adversaries seemed far more nervous than I, a fact from which I drew no small measure of comfort. Yet when it began, it was for me just another argument before a court. There were nine of them, all to be treated with the utmost courtesy, a standard that I regularly adhered to in the least prestigious of circumstances. I discussed the standard they had made clear they were interested in, but I also addressed fairness, the due process rights of a man who had been repeatedly defamed to the point where the court had said that the offensive conduct, when engaged in long enough, denied a litigant the right to defend his good name. I said that such a ruling, if upheld, would cast a chill over the meaning and efficacy of the First Amendment, the pillar of our Constitution that had made us a free people. Chief Justice Rehnquist intensely disliked Carto and harbored similar views about Anderson, whom he considered to be a muckraker. I considered that to be Jack's most endearing quality. Suddenly Rehnquist stopped doodling or taking notes, looked up from his pad, and said, "I say a chill on both of their houses."

The argument took place on December 3, 1985. On June 25, 1986, the Supremes published their decision. The decision of six justices—White, who wrote the opinion, and Marshall, Blackmun, Powell, Stevens, and O'Connor, who joined in—said that "clear and convincing evidence" was required before a court could dismiss a defamation case in which actual malice was an issue. As of that date, it became the law of the land and remains as one of the most oft cited and quoted cases in the area.

Justices Brennan, Burger, and Rehnquist ruled against us and for the trial court, seeking to reverse the Scalia ruling and to end the case. The Rehnquist dissent, in which Burger joined, demonstrated their careless handling of the issue. It was astonishing, suggesting that perhaps one could not distinguish between the evidence which should satisfy reasonable men and the evidence which should satisfy reasonable men beyond a reasonable doubt since "the line between them is too thin for day-to-day use," they wrote, as they borrowed from another jurist in a totally unrelated matter. It may be that the distinction is difficult to locate, but that is what the judges and justices are selected for, honored for, and paid for.

Brennan wrote a thoughtful dissent. He observed that the court had adopted new law, as if that is always a tragedy. "This conclusion, which is at the heart of the case, has been reached without the benefit of any support in case law." In short, he was lamenting the fact that a modicum of fairness had found its way through the forbidding stone wall of precedent.

As to Anderson and Carto, the matter had not as yet been finally resolved. The triumphant court of appeals called upon me for a suggestion about the next step. I replied, "Send it to the District Court for a new trial." When it was returned for trial, Anderson's counsel called me and asked what I would take to settle the case. It was a defamation case, and a demand had been made for reimbursement; it is difficult to sue for an apology. However, the case was decidedly not about money. We had long ago offered to settle the case if Anderson would state he had been wrong and apologized. He was adamant, stating that he had never lost a defamation case, never settled one, and never apologized. I suggested that just because he was out of practice it did not mean that he was permanently barred.

I told Anderson that the stakes were now higher. We wanted a withdrawal of the false statements and a token payment. I suggested some small sum. He agreed with the figure but did not want Carto to get the money. I suggested that he donate it to a nonprofit group working toward journalistic integrity. He agreed and issued the withdrawal of his remarks, and the case was settled.

||||||

During 1984 I was counsel for a woman who had been discharged by a television network because she had made a complaint that a national vice president of the organization had been sexually harassing her for many months. Her firing, done upon the advice of the network's lawyers, was a major error since although sexual advances generally take place in private and each participant offers differing views at trial, the retaliation here had many witnesses. As we were in the process of choosing the jury the network settled the case, one of the first lasting victories in the United States for a woman who had brought a sexual harassment action. The network insisted upon a "nondisclosure agreement" as a condition for settlement so that I may not now ethically comment except to report that the network issued a public statement that the plaintiff's work had been praiseworthy and that the network "does not condone sexual harassment or unlawful discrimination in any form." It also stated that the network made a payment to the plaintiff to settle the case.

I was also an attorney for an African American woman who had been employed by a major television network at its Washington news bureau. Our complaint stated that she had been the subject of discrimination by a defendant that created a hostile and intimidating work environment for women and minorities. We had the option of proceeding under the federal statute, Title VII of the Civil Rights Act of 1964, or the local Human Rights Act. The federal statute addressed only race, color, religion, sex, or national origin. The law of the District of Columbia was broader in scope, including those standards as well as the right to be free from discrimination due to sexual orientation, family status, personal appearance, or disability. The Human Rights Act, however, did not specify that there could be a jury trial or that the plaintiff might seek punitive damages. We brought the action in the US District Court under the local law with the hope that a fair-minded judge might establish the rule permitting those broader rights. When the case was assigned to Judge Charles R. Richey, who had been appointed by President Nixon due to his close relationship with Vice President Spiro Agnew, our guarded optimism began to fade.

On November 8, 1986, in a carefully reasoned opinion Judge Richey established the right of those seeking redress from discrimination in the nation's capital to choose a jury to try the case and to seek punitive damages. The law was enhanced by a judge who became a consistent advocate for enforcing the civil rights of all who came before him and who frequently expressed his skepticism of the government and its assertions.

In another case I represented two African American graphic artists, a man and a woman, in an action against a major television network based upon a complaint of racial and gender discrimination. During the discovery period we learned that the network at a high level and its law firm had presented vital documents that had been altered and offered testimony that was not true. The federal judge, Royce C. Lamberth, was not pleased. He halted the proceedings and asked each side to make a motion about how to resolve the matter. I asked, given the outrageous conduct uncovered, that we were entitled to the extreme sanction of striking the defendant's pleading and entering a default judgment on behalf of each plaintiff. I did not expect the court to direct that relief, but I thought it was appropriate since each party was required to rely upon valid, not altered or fabricated documents. The judicial system depended upon counsel and parties meeting that obligation to each other and to the court. In this matter the court ruled that both the plaintiffs and the court had been deceived. Judge Lamberth struck the answer and entered a default judgment against the network. The network immediately appealed to the US Court of Appeals for the District of Columbia, likely the most important court in the nation other than the Supreme Court. And then politics interfered with justice.

The most prestigious law firm representing the network was headed by a lawyer who had served as counsel to two US presidents, both Democrats. He had personally chosen numerous candidates for appointment to the courts, including the district courts, the appellate courts, and, most significant, the members of the court of appeals about to decide this case. As I entered the well-appointed and impressive courtroom, generally almost devoid of spectators, I saw that every seat was filled, every bench was packed, and any space where anyone could stand was occupied. Almost all of them were white men, and all were well dressed in expensive suits, even the few women present. All were members of the network's law firm, many from the district and many more who had apparently flown in from New York. Many, I suspected, were future judges. They were en masse giving up many thousands of dollars of billing hours. They were not there, I thought, as spectators, but rather to judge the judges. Before I could be heard the members of the court of appeals ruled for the network and overturned the dismissal, asked what else they could do to help, and offered to remove Judge Lamberth from the case although that had never been requested. The elite audience seemed pleased as they smiled at the judges and shook hands and congratulated one another.

Counsel for the network, knowing that their misconduct had been overlooked and seeking to avoid further embarrassment, approached me and offered a deal to settle the case that my two clients found satisfactory.

Years later, when I had no case pending before Judge Lamberth, I told him about the appellate court fiasco. He had not heard the details before, and he laughed. He was surprised but not astonished. He is now the chief judge for the US District Court for the District of Columbia. The three court of appeals judges who heard the case are probably still hopefully waiting for another vacancy on the Supreme Court to occur.

||||||

Defending against an indictment in the criminal courts is another matter. The playing field is often level in a civil case, but, as we have seen, not always. It is never level in a criminal case. The prosecutors decide which cases should be brought through an indictment after they examine the evidence. The defense lawyer is often at a disadvantage during the proceedings. If the prosecutors are corrupt, the rules governing mandatory discovery before trial are neglected or ignored and exculpatory evidence, uncovered by their team of investigators, agents, detectives, and experts, does not surface. There are almost unlimited funds available to the state or federal government to prosecute a case, and that is rarely true of a defendant. I recall one case where we were unable to hire a photographer for pictures of the crime scene for lack of funds until finally a volunteer with an inexpensive camera traveled to the scene by subway. The state was able to assemble an array of useful evidence by employing expert motion picture and still photographers who took aerial shots from a helicopter. While legal aid efforts are crucial for the system of justice to function and lawyers there are often skillful and experienced, they are also overworked. And in times of financial crisis their budgets are vulnerable to substantial reductions even as those in the highest tax brackets pay lower taxes. A fair trial is apparently not viewed as an obligation by all politicians.

Demonstration of prosecutorial misconduct may provide the best defense in a criminal trial, as the Richardson case and the Wounded Knee trial demonstrate. That approach is not viable when there is an ethical prosecution, and every so often there *is* an honest office of prosecutors. The best, and almost solitary, example of that phenomenon in my experience was the district attorney's office in New York County beginning in the 1940s and led by Frank Hogan. He was supplemented by Mel Glass and then Robert K. Tanenbaum. I had spent some time trying to prevail for my clients in the felony court in Manhattan, often with very limited success. Years after Hogan had died and after Glass too had passed, I spent time with Tanenbaum, whom I met when he was appointed by the US Congress to investigate the assassination of President Kennedy. Of course, I knew he was regarded by his peers as the most effective and ethical living former prosecutor. I asked about his standards. He told me that when he joined the office, Mel Glass was his mentor. Glass took Tanenbaum to the Tombs, a disgraceful jail at the criminal court building meant to be a temporary holding facility. I had visited my clients there many times. It smelled of urine and was crowded with many suspects, most of whom were very young black or Puerto Rican men awaiting their first court appearance or a trial. Some were doomed to remain there for months before trial. All were, according to legal theory, presumed to be innocent.

Glass told Tanenbaum that before Tanenbaum decided that a person should be arrested or high bail requested, he should think about the consequences and the conditions at the jail. He said that Tanenbaum must be one thousand percent certain of the person's guilt and in addition one thousand percent certain that he had admissible evidence to prove it. Later Tanenbaum ran the felony court for Frank Hogan's office, tried cases, and trained young attorneys. The evidence discloses that he never had forgotten the words of his mentor.

Radio Days

IIIIIIIIIIIIIIIIIIIIIIIIIIIIIIIIIIII

21

Jonathan P. Casey, an icon at WSNJ, New Jersey's first and oldest radio station where he served as a host on news programs, invited me to be a guest. I later discovered that he was a nationally respected musicologist as well. The station was located in Bridgeton, just seven miles from my wife's and my former home. The show featured conservative preachers and commentators. We talked for an hour one day in August 2004 about the assassination of President Kennedy. The response to the interview was noticeable. Calls came from many listeners still eager to learn about the case, knowing both its significance and its unsettled disposition. The calls continued for days after the program, and Jonathan asked me to return for a second program, for which there was an even greater response, and after that came more requests.

The management then offered me my own program. The proposal was for five afternoons each week at a salary we could negotiate. I was practicing law and starting to work on this book, and I knew I could not spare that much time. I suggested that I would do a one-hour show once a week for no salary, that Jonathan, whom I much admired, would sit in with me, and that there would never be management interference with my broadcasts. I did volunteer that I

344 | CITIZEN LANE

knew and would abide by the rules about obscenity. They agreed, and on the first Thursday in September at 5:00 PM, *Lane's Law* was born.

I began by announcing that all guests would be treated with respect, no one would ever be insulted, no one would ever be cut off for expressing ideas I did not agree with, all views were welcome, and all ridicule would be reserved exclusively for the leaders of our nation who had led us into a war in which they traded blood for oil. I read the First Amendment, to remind us of who we are, and the names of those Americans who had died that week in Iraq, to remind us of what we were doing. The callers were surprised and interested, some very supportive, and not one was hostile.

As Jonathan and I were about to leave the studio, the station's manager drove up to the door at some speed and then charged into the building. He was outraged; he said he disagreed with everything I had said. I suggested that he should have called so that we could have had that discussion on air. He was furious. He couldn't reduce my salary, but he could fire me. Jonathan and I went out for dinner.

The show became a major hit. Calls came in all week. The only protest was from a woman who said that her husband generally took the laundry to the cleaners each Thursday at five thirty but that he had announced that he would not leave the radio until six from then on. In three weeks Jonathan, the station's institutional memory, said that it had become the most popular program in the history of the station. From the manager's perspective it did not improve and probably became more unacceptable, with interviews of veterans who opposed the war, news stories that juxtaposed the fact that families had to buy bulletproof vests for their loved ones in Iraq while war profits made by Cheney's Halliburton increased, and always the names of those who had died. Although the station's traditional reach was limited, it streamed live over the Internet, and soon listeners from throughout the country were calling.

One day I noticed a car outside of the station that had been there the previous week as well. The only occupant was a distinguished-looking man. I said hello and introduced myself. I met Ed Churchill, a retired civil engineer and teacher. He had driven from Ocean City to Bridgeton, more than one hour each way, to listen to the program. He joined Jonathan and me for dinner and regularly made that trip week after week.

The program was devoted to action, often with a light touch and humorous manner to the delight of our audience, if not to various arrogant politicians.

||||||

On February 25, 1990, Terri Schiavo suffered respiratory and cardiac arrest resulting in extensive brain damage and a diagnosis of persistent vegetative state. She was placed in an institution in Florida and fed with a tube for fifteen years. Her husband and court-appointed guardian, Michael Schiavo, based upon expert medical opinion that his wife was brain-dead, asked the county circuit court with jurisdiction to remove the tube. One political party saw this tragic episode as an opportunity for political exploitation. The governor of the state of Florida, Jeb Bush, demanded that his state legislature pass special legislation to overrule the court's decision. They acquiesced, and he signed the bill. The president, George W. Bush, made the same demand of Congress, and he broke with his established precedent by returning from one of his vacations to sign the bill. Thus, the Republicans, the party that demands that the government halt its intrusion into the private lives of Americans, that says it opposes judicial activism, that states that it supports state and local constitutions, demonstrated through actions that it was duplicitous.

Most citizens recognized that the matter was medical, not political. Enter Dr. Bill Frist from stage right. He was the Republican's majority leader in the Senate.[1]

He took a look at the television monitor in his office. Terri seemed fine to him. He rushed onto the floor of the Senate to proclaim "as a physician" that Terri Schiavo "responds to her parents and to [her brother]." He challenged the findings of her physicians, those who had actually examined her and run all relevant tests, that she was in a persistent vegetative state.

There were immediate responses of outrage. A medical ethicist at Northwestern University was critical, stating that Frist had made a diagnosis without examining the patient and had questioned the diagnosis when he was not a neurologist. I took a more optimistic approach. Here we had a doctor so gifted that he could make an immediate diagnosis by looking at a picture. He did not require that expensive tests be conducted. Patients need not travel to his office as a medical examination was superfluous.

We were then the only industrial nation on earth that did not provide universal health care for its citizens, and here was a solution. Dr. Frist would be our national comprehensive medical health program. Surely he would share his talent with the American people. He was a patriot; after all, he was the leader of the Senate. With his ability to reject traditional medical concepts and the advice of doctors who had needlessly actually looked at their patients, he could solve nagging problems in a moment, with a mere glance. I broadcast the good news, accompanied with Christmas-like trumpet blasts. Our medical savior had arrived. I encouraged all those with physical problems to send a picture to Dr. Frist, along with a self-addressed envelope for the return of the diagnosis. I suggested that pictures of ailing cats, dogs, birds, or fish could also be submitted. In the event of a pesky or chronic illness that might benefit from a word of counsel, I broadcast his contact information as well.

Senator Frist's office called to warn me to cease and desist, as hundreds of letters were innundating his office. Frist did not make another pronouncement until after Terri Schiavo's death, which was followed by an autopsy. At that time, Frist agreed with all of the pathologists that Terri Schiavo had suffered "total irreversible brain damage" and had been medically dead for a very long time. He added that he had never said on the floor of the Senate those things that he had said on the floor of the Senate. Sadly, I reported to my audience that our country still would have no health program for our people.

||||||

While at the radio station one afternoon I checked the AP wire. There was a two-sentence item that said a woman in Provo, Utah, had sought to adopt a cat from a public animal shelter but was turned away because she had a puppy at home and a law in that city prohibited anyone from having both a cat and a dog in their home. I called the mayor and the council president who confirmed that such a law existed and was enforced.

I discussed the matter on my program. Our German shepherd's best friend was a feral cat who became part of our family when she was deserted at the age of three weeks. In Provo, we all would have been criminals. I urged people to call or write to the mayor and council members, whose contact information I supplied. We notified the press of our animal companionship effort to have the local law removed.

The issue was somewhat whimsical, except for its serious implications. The family seeking to adopt had two small children, and since their application was rejected it is possible that the kitten was no longer alive. More than five million dogs and cats are euthanized each year in the United States, most by animal shelters.

The reaction was immediate. The Provo officials asked me to call off the campaign, since hundreds of messages had been received and "the press has called from places like Boston and Los Angeles, and we are being made a national laughingstock."

"Really, you?" I suggested that they change the law, assuring them that as soon as they did I would broadcast the good news.

They said that the next scheduled council meeting was three weeks away. It was a Wednesday, and *Lane's Law* was scheduled for the next afternoon. They called the next morning from a hastily arranged special meeting to read the proposed new law to me. Within an hour the puppy/kitten antimiscegenation law became a thing of the past. The family adopted another kitten. For our audience the message was clear. Working together we can accomplish almost anything in a good cause. It started with a few people in south New Jersey who had neither influence nor power in Utah and ended up reforming the city code of faraway Provo to make it more humane.

||||||

One morning as I read the local newspaper I learned about the death of a very young man who had recently graduated from a local high school. The day after the September 11 attack, he had enlisted in the Marine Corps. There was no war in Iraq; he just knew our country faced danger. A year later, his younger brother also enlisted in the corps.

The newspaper said that Lance Corporal Harry Swain had been killed in combat in Iraq and that his parents prayed for the immediate return of their sole surviving son, James, a marine sniper serving in Fallujah who was then obviously in harm's way. The government, short of forces, had not agreed to send him home.

I called the two New Jersey senators and the local congressman. I sent messages to all of our contacts; I sent a press release by e-mail to all of the area's newspapers. And then I went to the radio station and urged the listeners to call their representatives at once. We devoted the program to the immediate return of our neighbor. When the program concluded, Jonathan and I were putting our files away and preparing to leave for dinner. As we reached the door, the host of the next program called us back. He was waving an AP wire story that he had just torn from the machine. The US government had announced that the young man had been pulled out of his combat division and was on his way home to his family in New Jersey.

||||||

By the first anniversary of *Lane's Law*, circumstances had changed, and I felt obligated to move to Charlottesville, Virginia, where my sister, then ill, was a professor at the University of Virginia. But the radio days and its lessons remain with me, and perhaps one day there will be an encore.

Epilogue: My Life Goes On
||||||||||||||||||||||||||||||||||||||||||||||||||||||||||||||||||||||||||||||

I am proud of the many friends and readers who have supported my work during the past half century. I am equally proud of the enemies I have attracted. I have earned them as well.

I love this country, my America, not for its waves of grain and purple mountains, as such magnificent scenery may be seen in many other places, but for its varied people, its First Amendment, and more for what it may be than for what it is. I have devoted my life to attempting to help this nation realize its shining promise. Often my efforts have been in vain or ill advised, but some things were accomplished and some changes made. I believe that there is no more constructive way to manifest patriotic ardor.

I practice law more actively than ever—sometimes even prevailing in challenging matters—write books, give lectures, raise hot peppers, and try to remind those in authority who have forgotten that we have a Constitution and that its First Amendment is the most important sentence in our remarkable history.

In my spare time I read a lot of biographies and autobiographies, many by or about our founders, and I remain in awe of a period when so many great men came together in a great cause to establish not just the nation but some enduring principles that remain in constant need of tending and sacrifice by each generation. Franklin and Jefferson, Madison and Tom Paine, Samuel Adams, Washington, and many others—what a time to have lived and, for those who missed that, what a time to remember. They were, of course, the greatest generation.

Yet no history of those remarkable days is adequate without understanding the role of women and people of color who risked their lives for the creation of a new world to be governed in some measure by those who had placed them in inferior positions all of their lives. The full history has not yet been written. Just bits and pieces, rarely mentioned, seem to have survived. So here we remain as long as we may, still representing those in need of counsel, trying to create the perfect mushroom-and-aged-cheddar-cheese omelet (still experimenting) and the perfect martini (getting very close), still searching for the perfect red wine (very much enjoying the chase), and still scouring the horizon for oppressive windmills in need of challenge.

Acknowledgments

||||||||||||||||||||||||||||||||||||||||||||||||||||

F or assistance with this book there are too many to include. My wife, Trish, has been my best friend, a constant inspiration, and an excellent editor. Sue Herndon's research and editorial suggestions have also been indispensable.

Some of my efforts have been in the Deep South and I am grateful to Professor Emeritus Paul Gaston at the History Department of the University of Virginia, a foremost authority on southern history, for his encouragement and continuing support. Much of my life has taken place in the courtrooms of our nation. I am indebted to Robert K. Tanenbaum, former bureau chief of the criminal courts and chief of homicide at the New York City district attorney's office, for reading the manuscript and offering good advice as well as inspiration. When America's most important living former prosecutor says such kind words about a defense trial lawyer, it makes me think that I must have done something right.

I herald those judges and justices who are governed by a commitment to ethics, justice, and the law, most faithfully exemplified by Royce C. Lamberth, chief judge of US District Court for the District of Columbia, and the late Fred J. Nichol, the US district court judge for South Dakota.

I am grateful to Martin Sheen for his introduction. The thought that my work has encouraged him to make such enormous contributions to America is more than comforting. I have long respected his commitment to his craft and his lifelong efforts on behalf of causes and people in need of support. He continues to question unwise decisions by authorities even when it results in his arrest.

And Pauley Perrette, whose contributions are unforgettable. She produced and directed a documentary about my life, visited my elementary school in Brooklyn with me (built long before she was born) and the lot where my law office had been in East Harlem, and helped me to remember and visit many forgotten places. But I am most grateful to her for her persevering work on behalf of the homeless, the families that go to sleep each night hungry, those who suffered due to Hurricane Katrina, and for her work so that any two people in our country who love each other have the opportunity to be married to each other.

Steve Jaffe, Dick Gregory, and Carolyn Mugar have been with me stride for stride when we sought to accomplish the impossible over the decades.

After considerable research, Trish and I decided that we wanted this book to be published by the Chicago Review Press. The folks there, led by Sue Betz, the editor for Lawrence Hill Books, and all of my other new friends including Mary Kravenas and Michelle Schoob and their associates at Independent Publishers Group, including Jen Wisnowski, have been remarkable.

The book covers numerous years and an effort to name all those who have participated in many of our skirmishes is a task far too daunting. Many of them are identified in the pages of this work and without their encouragement, sacrifices, and leadership my life's work would have been far less useful and I am forever in their debt.

But it all began with Elizabeth Brown Lane of Rochester, New York, and Harry A. Lane of Buffalo, New York, who taught their children about the American way of justice for all and fair treatment for all, although they never spoke those words; they just lived them.

Notes
||||||||||||||

Chapter 1: Brooklyn Days

1. On February 9, 1950, McCarthy's reign began with a speech in Wheeling, West Virginia, in which he stated, "I have in my hand a list of two hundred five—list of names that were known to the Secretary of State as being members of the Communist Party and who nevertheless are still working and shaping policy in the State Department." His assertions were untrue. In 1954 the Senate voted to censure McCarthy, and he died in 1957 at the age of forty-eight of acute hepatitis.

Chapter 3: Storefront Lawyer

1. *New York Times*, June 9, 1955. In that front page story the headline read "BOY KILLER WINS 2D-DEGREE TERM." The article began, "Frank Santana, 17 years old, was permitted to plead guilty yesterday to second-degree murder in the slaying April 30 of William Blankenship, Jr., 15.

"In a dramatic scene in Bronx County Court, William Blankenship Sr., the victim's father, asked Judge William Lyman for clemency for Santana. Later, an assistant district attorney attacked the 'model boy' reputation of young William."

2. The history of that period has been recorded in a long article on the Internet: "Tenant Power in the Liberal City 1943–1971" by Joel Schwartz, www.tenant.net/Community/History/hist04c.html.

3. Irwin D. Davidson and Richard Gehman, *The Jury Is Still Out* (Peter Davies Ltd., London and New York: 1959).

4. *Miranda v. Arizona*, 384 US 436 (1966).

5. I was having breakfast at a small café in the French Quarter with Mary Howell, a civil rights attorney with whom I was working. A man approached us, gave his name, and invited us to dinner that evening. He inquired as to which hotel I was staying at and said that a limousine would pick us up at 7:00 PM and take us to the Commander's Palace, an excellent upscale restaurant where both Paul Prudhomme and Emeril Lagasse, two of the country's finest chefs, were later among its most famous alumni. He said he would explain his motivation after dinner. The dinner was extravagant and the champagne extraordinary. Over coffee he explained.

He had been a court reporter in New York. They are independent contractors who work with, but not for, the court system.

"You," he said to me, "filed a motion and demanded a hearing challenging the jury system for the deliberate and systematic exclusion of minorities. You called witnesses, and the hearing lasted a week. Newspaper reporters and radio and television crews from all over the country, and a few from Europe, were there listening to you examine the jury commissioner who had made the selections. It was high drama, front-page stuff, and it went on for days. I was the court reporter for that courtroom. The press wanted immediate copies of the proceedings each day. The judge allowed me to set up an operation to meet the demand with mimeograph machines and secretaries in a room off his chambers where we cranked out expensive contemporaneous transcripts as quickly as we could and sold them to the waiting media representatives. I made so much money from that one enterprise in a week that I opened my own court reporting service. It now is now one of the most successful around."

He raised his glass filled with an after-dinner cordial, saluted me, and said. "Thank you. It was mind-blowing cross-examination." I was speechless; Mary was not. In a friendly southern drawl she asked, "Where is Mark's cut?" He smiled and said, "You just ate it."

Chapter 4: Wassaic

1. *New York Times*, November 18, 1955, and December 3, 1955. In rewriting the history of the institution, the state inaccurately asserted that it had been called the "Wassaic State School for the Mentally Retarded," not a great leap forward.

2. Sue Herndon, who works for our firm as a paralegal, discovered that fact; Peter Tomasino found the section where the articles are stored, and Anna Tomasino spent two days meticulously examining the microfiche files and sending the copies to me.

3. *New York Times*, October 28, 1955.

Chapter 7: The Campaign in East Harlem

1. In 1970, literacy requirements were banned for five years by the renewal of the Voting Rights Act, and in 1975 they were permanently banned by the US Supreme Court.

2. I never ran for local office again. In 1968 I ran for vice president of the United States in the Dick Gregory/Mark Lane campaign to raise questions in opposition to the war in Vietnam.

Chapter 8: The Assembly Line

1. *Time*, February 16, 1962.

Chapter 10: Rush to Judgment

1. Powell, as chairman of the Richmond, Virginia, school board, opposed the Supreme Court's historic decision *Brown v. Board of Education* ending public school segregation. His law firm represented one of the defendant school districts.

2. Bertrand Russell was awarded the Nobel Prize in Literature in 1950; the Russell family had taken part in almost every great political event in Britain for centuries. Bertrand Russell's grandfather had been prime minister, and his godfather, who influenced him greatly, was John Stuart Mill.

Principia Mathematica, written by Russell and Alfred North Whitehead, and Russell's essay "On Denoting" had a substantial influence upon mathematics and logic as well as analytic philosophy and linguistics.

3. Our paths crossed again in a most dramatic and unpredictable manner. On July 2, 1966, while in New York, I read a story in the *New York Times* that said an American woman, who had been arrested in East Germany, had been given a long prison sentence at hard labor. The arrest took place on November 24, 1965, but the US government had kept it secret for more than seven months. Her crime was attempting to help people escape from Communist East Germany. Her name was Hellen Battle. The harsh sentence indicated that the authorities were convinced that she had been associated with American intelligence agencies. I felt certain that such an assumption was not true.

I checked the time difference between the continents, decided that it was too late to call Bertie, and placed a call to Ralph who, I rationalized, never slept anyway. Soon the three of us were talking and the London connection was in play.

The US government had made no efforts on her behalf, possibly because it knew through its embassy that she had cooperated in an effort to discuss the assassination of President Kennedy. Bertie and his associates began to communicate with the officials in East Germany. The communication began with a letter from Russell to Walter Ulbricht, the president of the country. Eventually, I received a communication from the minister of justice from the DDR, the East German government, inviting me to meet with his office so that I could be interviewed. Of course, I accepted and soon was on my way to Europe.

I was questioned extensively about the matter by the office of the minister of justice. The interrogation was thorough and, while not friendly or overly polite, remained respectful for the most part. I assured them that they could rely upon my assessment of the facts, my judgment, and my truthful answers. I expected that Hellen would be asked, or had been asked, similar questions and our answers would be compared. I just did not know what her responses would be, and I knew that any hope we had would rest upon the similarity of our responses. They offered me coffee, another official entered the room, thanked me, and shook my hand, and I left.

Soon after my interview, Hellen was questioned by an official who asked her if she knew me and then informed her that I had contacted Lord Russell on her behalf and that he had asked for clemency for her. When Hellen asked if a clemency request had been made by her own government, she was told that no such application had been made. An attorney based in London and retained by Bertie visited Hellen and presented a formal request for clemency to the government of East Germany. Later, a message was sent by the government of East Germany to the attorney in London assigned to represent the interests of the Bertrand Russell Peace Foundation in the matter of the state versus Hellen Battle. It was a six-page document entitled "Amnesty and Clemency for Hellen Battle, prisoner of the German Democratic Republic" and stated, "This report is not for transmittal to anyone except Lord Russell and Ralph Schoenman." The report concluded, "Hellen was released."

Hellen Battle wrote a book about that episode in her life, *Every Wall Shall Fall* (Ada, MI: Hewitt House, 1969).

4. Benjamin Sonnenberg, *Lost Property: Memoirs and Confessions of a Bad Boy* (New York: Simon and Schuster, 1991).

5. Arthur Cohen was a remarkable man. When the intelligence agencies told the controlling forces at Holt, Rinehart, and Winston that the book should not be published, Arthur stated that the firm should either double the advertising budget for the book or, if it yielded to the demands of the government, dissolve itself and state that the protection of our First Amendment rights having been obliterated, publishing was no longer an honorable pursuit. He also said that he would quite publicly resign as would all the editors working with him. The book was published, and we became good friends. Later Arthur left publishing to become a leading American Jewish theologian writer, and editor.

6. I left England shortly after that and never found time to thank Vanessa. I did meet her again, about forty years later, at a film festival in Charlottesville at the University of Virginia where we both were speakers. She asked how the meeting with Tony had gone. I thanked her belatedly and profusely and offered to buy her a drink; it was a cocktail party and they were free, but I did fetch it for her from the bar.

7. This matter is discussed in detail in *A Citizen's Dissent* by Mark Lane (New York: Holt, Rinehart, and Winston, 1968).

8. June 3, 1967. Crowther was an author and journalist and the film critic for the *Times* for twenty-seven years. Numerous directors, screenwriters, and actors said that his reviews helped direct their careers.

Chapter 11: Chicago, August 1968

1. Mark Lane, *Chicago Eyewitness* (New York: Astor-Honor, 1968).

2. The pictures were published in sequence in *Chicago Eyewitness*, pages 123–27. Almost all were taken by Carolyn Mugar; those slightly out of focus were taken by me.

Chapter 12: James Joseph Richardson

1. Mark Lane, *Arcadia* (New York: Holt, Rinehart, and Winston, 1970).

2. James N. Baker with Howard Manly, "From Tragedy to Travesty," *Newsweek*, April 24, 1989.

Chapter 13: The Winter Soldier Investigation

1. William F. Crandell, *What Did America Learn from the Winter Soldier Investigation: The Sixties Project*. www2.iath.virginia.edu/sixties/HTML_docs/Texts/Narrative/Crandell_Winter.html.

This text, made available by the Sixties Project, is copyright (c) 1996 by Viet Nam Generation, Inc., or the author, all rights reserved. This text may be used, printed, and archived in accordance with the Fair Use provisions of U.S. Copyright law. This text may not be archived, printed, or redistributed in any form for a fee, without the consent of the copyright holder. This notice must accompany any redistribution of the text. The Sixties Project, sponsored by Viet Nam Generation, Inc., and the Institute of Advanced Technology in the Humanities at the University of Virginia at Charlottesville, is a collective of humanities scholars working together on the Internet to use electronic resources to provide routes of collaboration and make available primary and secondary sources for researchers, students, teachers, writers, and librarians interested in the 1960s.

2. The GIs, and soon all of us, referred to the statements as *testimony*. In the biblical sense it was testimony. Since no sworn officer had administered an oath and the oral statements were not subject to the penalty of perjury, it was not testimony as defined by law.

3. Colson served as Nixon's special counsel. He conspired to firebomb the Brookings Institute, worked out a program to hire enforcers from the Teamsters to physically attack antiwar demonstrators, and pleaded guilty in a plot to defame Daniel Ellsberg and obstruct justice in his case. He is a convicted Watergate felon.

4. While I was interviewing former US servicemen who had moved to Sweden, I arranged a press conference in Stockholm so that they could discuss their experiences in Vietnam. The numerous reporters present examined their documents and fully reported their words. A Swedish publisher asked me to draft a manuscript about the men and their revelations. It was published as a book, *And Not Just Song My*, and caused serious questions to be raised about the justification for the war.

5. Gerald Nicosia, *Home to War: A History of the Vietnam Veteran's Movement* (New York: Carroll & Graff, 2004).

Chapter 14: Mountain Home

1. John O'Connor, the first to publish his name in opposition to the war, the first to demand that the governor of Idaho speak out, was also discharged for his effectiveness. His discharge, as were all of the others, was honorable.

Sergeant Patrick Ward, an early activist, was deployed to Vietnam. I have not heard from him since then.

Airman First Class Bob Sytsma, among the first to join, was deployed to Vietnam. I have not heard from him since.

Captain Steve Miller, an active member of the Wagon, was encouraged by the air force to resign. He declined.

Lieutenant Bill Etnyre, a courageous and active member, was encouraged by the air force to resign. He declined.

Captain Knudsen was asked to resign. He refused the request.

Tom Mason was granted honorable discharge and has been involved in community and veterans' work ever since.

Jimmy Schaffer was granted an honorable discharge, continued on with counseling GIs, and continued with his musical career as well as becoming a first-class carpenter.

Captain Gary Aker was granted an honorable discharge and later worked as an executive assistant to a member of the US Congress.

Carolyn Mugar invented Farm Aid and, with Willie Nelson, is still its principal organizer.

Chapter 15: Wounded Knee

1. Eda Gordon, a young woman, was among hundreds of non-lawyers who helped and learned. She studied the advanced and intricate methods counsel engaged in while selecting a jury for the first trial of the Wounded Knee leadership, *US v. Dennis Banks and Russell Means*, and helped defend numerous others in the non-leadership cases tried in Lincoln, Nebraska. I last saw Roger and Eda during 1974 or 1975 until I arrived in Albuquerque, New Mexico, thirty-five years later, to try an unrelated case in the US District Court there. Roger had become a seasoned and respected federal public defender in that court, and Eda, then living in Santa Fe, was a nationally known professional expert in jury trial selection and trial preparation. Our reunion was filled with joy as we celebrated the events that had changed and enriched the lives of our clients and those who assisted them during the time of great trouble.

2. Much later, during 1975, Williams and another FBI agent, Jack R. Coler, were killed in a shoot-out on the Pine Ridge reservation. They had charged into the area in two separate unmarked automobiles, armed with shotguns and pistols, allegedly looking for a person to question about having stolen cowboy boots.

Subsequently, Leonard Peltier, an active member of AIM, was arrested, convicted, and sentenced to two consecutive life terms for the two murders. I was not counsel in that case, but I had informed Peltier's attorney of my experience with Williams. The conviction was, and remains, the basis of substantial controversy. Numerous people, including Nelson Mandela, the Dalai Lama, Archbishop Desmond Tutu, and the influential David Geffen, a film producer, record executive, and philanthropist, as well as organizations including Amnesty International, the European Parliament, the parliaments of Italy and Belgium, and the UN High Commissioner for Human Rights have supported Peltier's claims of innocence or have expressed concerns regarding the unfairness of his trial. Many have called him a political prisoner.

As Clinton's presidency was ending in 2000, many called upon him to grant clemency to Peltier. It appeared that Clinton was considering that petition when hundreds of FBI agents protested outside of the White House, FBI Director Louis Freeh wrote to Clinton opposing clemency, and the FBI Association placed advertisements in newspapers stating that its more than "15,000 active duty and former FBI agents" demanded that Clinton reject clemency for Peltier. Clinton yielded to the emotionally charged demands of the FBI. Peltier remains in prison.

3. *Newsweek*, September 30, 1974.

Chapter 17: Memphis, America

1. In Skokie, Illinois, in 1977, one of every six Jewish residents of the Chicago suburb was a survivor of the Holocaust or was directly related to a survivor. A group of American Nazis decided to march there. The village officials, knowing that the event was an effort to intimidate victims of terror who had moved there expecting to escape from further persecution, won an injunction to prevent the demonstration. The ACLU decided that this was a worthy First Amendment case and represented the Nazis.

2. Jim was born in Pennsylvania and later lived in Ohio. He went to Nagpur, India, to study *satyagraha*, the teachings of Mahatma Gandhi, setting forth the principles of nonviolent resistance. Later, while attending the Graduate School of Theology at Oberlin College in Ohio, he met Dr. King, who urged him to move to a southern state where he was needed. "We don't have anyone like you down there."

Jim moved to Nashville, enrolled at the Divinity School of Vanderbilt University, and organized and led nonviolent training sessions for many, if not most, of those who later led the civil rights movement. These activists participated in forming the Student Nonviolent Coordinating Committee; they led sit-ins in Nashville to challenge segregation; and they were active in the March on Washington in 1963, the Mississippi Freedom Summer, the Selma Voting Rights Movement, the Chicago Housing Movement, and the Freedom Rides to Jackson. In response, Vanderbilt expelled Jim from the university. The response created a surge in the civil rights movement and so embarrassed the school that during its 2006 graduation ceremony Vanderbilt apologized for its treatment of Jim, who now serves as a member of the Vanderbilt faculty.

3. Jasper Newton "Jack" Daniels founded the company in 1875. He was not married, and he had no children. He gave the distillery to his nephew, Lem Motlow, in 1907. Apparently, there was no Charlene Daniels.

Chapter 18: Jonestown

1. Two years later my book about my experience in Jonestown was published. (Mark Lane, *The Strongest Poison* [New York: Hawthorn Books, 1980].)

2. For example, he performed "miracles" by curing multiple members of a cancer that they never had. They had been induced to believe that they faced almost immediate death before his intervention.

3. When I revealed those facts some lawyers were harshly critical of me, including William Kunstler and other progressive attorneys. They stated that I owed some special, but unspecified, responsibility to Garry since we all shared similar political perspectives. My view was less obtuse. I believed my duty was to protect the innocent, even if they were being abused by a friendly lawyer. Some of those children and adults, held captive by unethical means, later died in Jonestown.

4. *Press Democrat*, June 22, 1978.

5. In fact, it appears that John Stoen was not the biological son of Timothy Stoen. I have mentioned that some elements of the drama were bizarre, none more so than the arrangement that resulted in John's birth. When they were in the United States, Jones told Stoen that Stoen was under a great deal of pressure and that he needed relaxation to relieve his stress. He

suggested that Stoen have intercourse with a number of the young women in the group and directed that the women comply. Stoen's wife, Grace, learned of the activity when Jones provided details to her while condemning Tim's philandering activity. He neglected to mention that he had suggested it. Grace was also a member of the temple and compliant.

At a meeting with Jones, Timothy Stoen and Grace Stoen agreed that Grace should have intercourse with Jones so that she could become the mother of his child and so that Jones could have a young child to take care of. Grace gave birth to John Stoen on February 1, 1972. On February 6, 1972, Timothy Stoen, a lawyer and a prosecutor, signed a document under penalty of perjury, stating that Jones had fathered the child with Grace at Tim's suggestion, because he had been unable to "sire one myself." Stoen has acknowledged signing the sworn statement but later stated that it was not accurate, an assertion that he would be required to make if he brought legal action to gain control of the child. While admitting that he signed the document, he has refused to say why he did so.

The relationship between Grace and Tim dissolved when she left the Peoples Temple together with a man whom she had met. Tim, the chief adviser to Jones, said that he had conducted research and that Guyana was a place that did not have arrangements with the United States in custody contests. Stoen assured Jones that the local government would always support his efforts to raise his son. Stoen strongly advised that Jones leave immediately for Jonestown and live there with his son, John. Jones acted upon that advice.

Shortly thereafter, Tim and Grace Stoen began a joint custody battle for John against Jones. In September 1977, the court in Guyana issued an Order to Show Cause why Jones should not be compelled to return John to Tim and Grace. Jones was informed that the defense forces of Guyana would enter Jonestown, with force if necessary, and take the child. By then, of course, Jones was convinced that Stoen had misled him about Jonestown being beyond the reach of the courts. He also knew that Stoen was belatedly and falsely claiming to be the father of his child. Jones, outraged that his son might be taken from him, publicly stated in radio broadcasts, "We will die unless we are granted freedom from harassment and [granted] asylum."

The government of Guyana took that death threat seriously, and the deputy minister, Ptolemy Reid, after a period of time and negotiations, assured the Jones family that the defense forces would not invade Jonestown. At that time, Jones had reached the conclusion that he could no longer rely upon the government of Guyana for sanctuary, and he began to make inquiries about the possibility of moving the commune elsewhere.

6. The 1974 Hughes-Ryan Act amended the Foreign Assistance Act of 1961. That act was specifically critical of the CIA and required that the president of the United States report all covert operations of the CIA to various congressional committees within a set time limit. Further, it prohibited the use of appropriated funds for CIA covert actions unless the president issued an official "finding" that each proposed operation was important to the national security.

7. Harris's interview of me had been objective and fair. However, I felt that his questions directed to an elderly woman were not appropriate. I told him so at the time. Later, he was assigned by NBC to present the defense view on the television case of *People v. James Earl Ray*. Harris told me it was an unprecedented role for him. He did an excellent job. I told him I thought so, and we shared a drink or two in Memphis, and our friendship continued over a dinner some time later in Washington, DC.

8. In an FBI report dated November 30, 1978, the special agent stated that while Congressman Ryan was at the Port Kaituma airport awaiting the arrival of a plane on which he was to depart, "he sat down in a little shed" and told those present "what happened to him back at Jonestown." The FBI reported that Ryan said "a young white male had lunged at him with a knife, that he had fallen back and that Mark Lane . . . had saved his life, as he had wrestled the knife wielder to the ground."

9. Later, Dwyer testified to a congressional investigating committee that after the attack he had ordered Ryan to leave the area upon his authority as the senior federal officer present. Dwyer testified that he had also told Ryan that his conduct had been provocative and had created the conflict. The congressional committee sealed the evidence it had uncovered and refused to even make it available to members of Congress.

Dwyer had never ordered Ryan to leave and had never been contemporaneously critical of his conduct. Ryan had been low-key and friendly and had found reasons to praise the accomplishments of the people of

Jonestown publicly when he was there and privately when he spoke with me. The attempt to revise history by the government and place any blame on Ryan for the massacre was an effort to extricate itself from the mischief it had wrought by having misled the congressman.

Chapter 19: My Day with Bill Buckley

1. Judge Green, in what she apparently conceived to be an effort to limit the scope of my opening statement, insisted that I offer in evidence, even before a witness was called, every issue of the *National Review* I was going to rely upon. I was pleased to do that, although I had no choice in the matter since she ordered that procedure. Now, after sixty years of practice, I still have never encountered any case where any other judge has ever adopted such an approach.

2. The "victory" in the defamation case was less than clear. The war of words in *Esquire* was initiated by Buckley. He wrote that Vidal was "afflicted" by homosexuality and was, therefore, an "addict" and that he should "bear his sorrow quietly" rather than write pornography. Vidal responded with an article in the same publication stating that Buckley was a racist, "anti-Semitic," and a "warmonger." The judge ruled that Vidal's conclusions were fair comment and in view of Buckley's editorial statements could not be said to be completely unreasonable. However, the court also ruled that the assertion that Buckley had vandalized a church was without foundation. Instead of trying the case on that narrow question, the parties agreed that Buckley's legal bill would be paid, but nothing was offered for damages to his reputation.

Chapter 21: Radio Days

1. Frist is a multimillionaire, his income derived from his family-owned for-profit hospital chain that was found guilty of massive Medicare fraud and required to pay $1.7 billion dollars in criminal penalties. Frist supported the use of torture at secret CIA prisons and said that the interrogation techniques employed at Guantanamo were safe and humane.

Index

||||||||||||||

WITHDRAWN